Identity, Islam and the Twilight of Liberal Values

Identity, Islam and the Twilight of Liberal Values

By

Terri Murray

**Cambridge
Scholars**
Publishing

Identity, Islam and the Twilight of Liberal Values

By Terri Murray

This book first published 2018

Cambridge Scholars Publishing

Lady Stephenson Library, Newcastle upon Tyne, NE6 2PA, UK

British Library Cataloguing in Publication Data
A catalogue record for this book is available from the British Library

ISBN (10): 1-5275-1652-0
ISBN (13): 978-1-5275-1652-6

CONTENTS

ACKNOWLEDGEMENTS

I owe a huge debt of gratitude to a small but sterling set of liberal academics who have also become friends as well as allies over the past several years. Foremost among them are Swedish sociologist Goran Adamson, without whose support and encouragement I may never have found a publisher, and Rumy Hasan, who has been a constant collaborator and trusted friend. Heather Brunskell-Evans has also been a vital sounding board and mentor. Her wisdom and courage are an inspiration. As founder and former Editor-in-Chief at *Conatus News*, Benjamin David has provided an invaluable platform not only for my writing but also for Muslim liberals, Muslim apostates, Muslim reformers and Muslim feminists, as well as for many ex-religious people of all faiths. I would also like to thank Craig Winchcombe and Karen Staples at Fine Arts College, who provided generous assistance with formatting and endured my grumbling with saintly patience.

INTRODUCTION

At the eve of the last millennium Francis Fukuyama published what became perhaps the most seminal book of the latter half of the twentieth century. In *The End of History and the Last Man* (1992), Fukuyama expounded his thesis that, following the French Revolution, Western liberal democracy has proven to be a better system (ethically, politically and economically) than its competitors – the one political model with sufficient moral and practical resilience to endure through the vicissitudes of future historical events. As the Cold War was coming to an end, he was able to predict that we may be witnessing not just the passing of a particular historical impasse, but

> "...the end of history as such: that is, the end point of mankind's ideological evolution and the universalization of Western liberal democracy as the final form of human government."[1]

Since its publication in 1992, an array of commentators has criticised Fukuyama's arguments for giving insufficient weight to liberal democracy's ethno-religious rivals. They claimed that religious fundamentalism, and radical Islam in particular, pose a powerfully resistant bulwark against the spread of liberal democracy and an influential counter-force against it. If ever there were reason to doubt Fukuyama's optimism about the continuation of Western liberal democracy, now is the time to do so.

There have been a few perceptive attempts to diagnose the cause of the West's "moral-cultural deficit". In October 2016, George Weigel speculated in *The National Review* that the secular liberal-democratic state rests on a fund of cultural capital that it cannot itself generate. Referencing the so-called Böckenförde Dilemma, Weigel surmised that liberal secular political culture paradoxically cannot sustain liberal freedom from within its own system and went on to claim that the resulting cultural malaise is more pronounced in Europe.

In a somewhat similar vein, Douglas Murray has argued that the retreat of Judeo-Christian religion in Europe left a gap at the core of European culture that modern post-Enlightenment European culture has failed to fill. Murray concurs with German philosopher Jürgen Habermas in believing we have lost a sense of purpose in our "post-secular age" and says that an existential nihilism underlies our society.[2]

But Murray also says that instead of defending our own cultural traditions, Europeans have been persuaded to see our cultural inheritance as the enemy, and to assail it. Those who took for granted that a system of "rights" would protect women, homosexuals, and religious minorities are finding out that a growing number of people believe not only that these "rights" are not self-evident, but that they are fundamentally wrong.[3]

While these broad, historically contextualised psycho-social diagnoses of European anaemia and self-loathing have some resonance, and probably explain why religion might hold some appeal, I suspect that the failure of liberals to address Islamists' civilisation-jihadist process (their term[4]) owes less to Europeans' unfulfilled or latent affinity with religious morality than to the clever ways in which Islamists have sold their ideological product.

Islamists' ultimate aim is a global caliphate. Theocracy is a top-down form of government. While democracy is a "bottom-up" form of government designed to take absolute power out of politics, theocracy does the opposite: it takes the politics out of power. Once established, theocracies rule supreme, and there is very little that can be done to redress citizens' grievances. It is useful to remember that religion has been a politically useful tool in maintaining the stability of empire, just as empires can use and spread religion. Therefore, the notion that religion is distinct and separate from political culture is rather naïve.

In addition, the West's millennials and generation x, thanks to the hard-won civil liberties and human rights victories of previous generations, have not had any urgent need to familiarise themselves with the key tenets of liberal political philosophy. For the most part, they could assume (along with Francis Fukuyama) that the significant debates had been won and that human history had at last reached a golden age of reason, freedom and human rights. There was no need to unpack what these abstract concepts actually meant or how they function practically, whether at the local, national or international levels. Again, Douglas Murray's diagnosis captured this political disengagement when he noted that Europe's cultural sickness is due in part to the utter shallowness of consumer culture, where even the most educated among us is content to say, as his best intellectual offering, that the world is complex.[5]

We've moved from a politics of fear to a fear of politics and worse, a fear of democracy. Fear has been the main product of American media for decades, but now we are being urged to fear the president himself (and/or the very means by which he presumably got into office) and to embrace the proffered solutions to this fear as absolute necessities. It is enough that we know what Trump stands for: Trump (as symbol) is a proxy for Nazis, fascists, bigots, sexists, racists and (in a nutshell) everything that liberals hate. This makes him the ideal political "bait" for steering and manipulating liberals' sensibilities, which are basically good.

Liberals remain painfully ignorant of how easily political strategists exploit their decent moral instincts. While the political left is merrily playing shuffleboard on deck or railing against "Trump and Brexit" with people who thoroughly agree with them, the liberal ship of Theseus is being dismantled and re-built plank-by-plank into a neoliberal (and socially conservative) Titanic, with the liberal establishment's passive support. Instead of scanning the horizon for approaching enemy ships, the liberal crew should realise that the enemies are already on board and they are very busy. By the time it arrives back at port, this vessel will no longer be recognisable as the one that set sail in the second half of the eighteenth century.

Politics as Branding

There can be no doubt that, where liberalism has espoused unfettered capitalism, it can do great harm to individuals and can lead to serious social inequalities. However, liberalism is fragmented from within, most notably in the economic sphere, where there is a gulf between classic liberalism and welfare liberalism. The former seems to have morphed into a neo-conservative hybrid creature that hates state intrusion into private wealth but loves inserting its tentacles into every other private crevice (quite literally!) of individuals' lives.

Furthermore, it is no secret that, in modern democratic societies, the mass media is effectively in the hands of an oligopoly. This means that the voices of the elites who own the media set the cultural agenda and drown out alternative voices. In today's liberal democracies, who pays the piper calls the tunes and so the free market and freedom of thought are often opposed. The "freedom" of capitalist liberal democracies is arguably the freedom to make profit – not the freedom of individuals.[6]

American society is infused with marketing culture, which creeps into almost every non-corporate space, including politics. As Canadian *No Logo* author and political analyst Naomi Klein has observed, today it is routine to see the absorption of radical political movements and ideas into the latest marketing campaigns for *Coca-Cola*, Starbucks or Benetton. But the infusion also goes in the opposite direction. Klein has observed how the seemingly disparate worlds of marketing and politics are unified by a single idea: that corporations should produce brands, not products.

Nowadays it is routine for governments to use public relations firms to sell their policies to the public. Here's what the firm 5W Public Relations, Public Affairs has to say about their services on their own website:

5W Knows How to Influence Public Opinion

The 5W Public Relations (5W) Public Affairs and Government Relations team confidently solves tough problems. Our team has done it all, from managing high-profile local issues, to handling major public affairs projects in the U.S. and abroad, to hosting foreign dignitaries on U.S. visits.

5WPR helps you manage your reputation and monitor the regulatory and legislative environments in which you operate. We work with your organization to identify the top issues and legislative battles that impact your business. From there, we identify stakeholder groups that can have an impact on your organization and then we establish and cultivate positive relationships with your key audiences.

From elected officials and news media to industry experts and academic voices, 5W engages opinion leaders who will champion your cause and serve as an ambassador to your audience.[7]

Klein points out that while President Barack Obama paraded the anti-war, anti-Wall Street image to his grassroots base, he simultaneously took more money from Wall Street than any other presidential candidate and pursued "bipartisanship" with conservative Republicans once in the White House. He sent more than 300,000 additional troops to Afghanistan, bailed out Wall Street banks and endorsed a ballooning military "security" budget that drained the national economy.[8]

Two months prior to Obama's election, world markets were limping into financial crisis and blame was being directed towards the economic deregulation and privatisation long preached from the pulpits of the US-dominated IMF and WTO. Obama didn't just re-brand America; he revived the neoliberal economic project just when it was on the verge of facing the music. As his senior advisor and political strategist David Axelrod said, Obama ensured that "Anti-Americanism isn't cool anymore."[9] Expensive market research had found a genuine appetite in people for ideals – equality, inclusivity and civil liberties that reminded them of the former 1960s image of America. This was an image of which they could be proud. It was the opposite of torture, war, corporate politics, crony capitalism and global warming – the things that the Dubya Bush's presidency had come to symbolise. They wanted justice for all and the noble sense of self-love and communion with others that comes from knowing you're on the right side of history.

Of course, it is not surprising that Obama used the same hope-inspiring emotional appeals that any politician uses nowadays. But the lofty ideals his brand was peddling did not come close to realisation. Naomi Klein has cited how Obama nominated the first Latina to the Supreme Court while enforcing Bush-era measures in a new immigration crackdown, or how he sang the praises of "clean coal" while refusing to tax emissions (which would have actually reduced the burning of fossil fuels).[10]

Liberals were gullible in responding positively to symbolic (but ultimately empty) gestures under Obama's presidency. Now they are falling for the same emotionally driven "Trump-bashing" brand of moral righteousness. Both presidencies manipulate public perception through "personality". Obama, even when he didn't follow through with promised changes, was perceived as personally innocent of any disingenuousness: he was simply "powerless" against the will of Congress. On the other hand, Trump's persona is the epitome of evil, whatever the content of his actual policies may be (and often they are not very different to Obama's or those of previous administrations).

These criticisms of liberalism provide good arguments for regulating markets, raising taxes for the super-rich, revising international trade agreements, and enforcing tough laws on multinational corporations. Applying the harm principle[11] to giant corporations decades ago, before they grew onto enormous tails that today wag the dog, could have prevented many of the economic inequities that now exist. But there is no need to throw out the 'baby' of social liberalism along with the neoliberal economic bathwater. While selective liberal reforms may sound incredibly idealistic at this late stage of the game, the alternative is a cynical abandonment of politics, and resignation to the fact that we now live in a post-political world where only might ever makes right.

This book attempts to diagnose the ways in which European and American social liberalism has been eroded in the post-9/11 era, not due to its intrinsic flaws but because Westerners have been reluctant to defend its strengths and to apply its principles internally. Had they done so, then we might not have seen tolerance and genuine diversity replaced by a paternalistic orthodoxy that demands positive "respect" or deference towards those who oppose liberalism, secularism and democracy. The primacy and liberty of the individual (including the Muslim individual) might not have been supplanted by communitarianism and collectivism (re-branded as "culture" and "race"). Reason and anti-clericalism may never have been steamrolled by superstition and tradition (marching under the banner of "diversity" and "religious freedom"). Universal human rights, reciprocity and principled politics would perhaps not have given way to moral relativism and total subjectivism ("feelings" and "lived experience"). None of this was inevitable.

The fact that some have failed (either by accident or by design) to adhere to the principles of political liberalism in practice is not a reason to abandon those principles. It is a reason to work harder to make sure they are more effectively applied, enforced and preserved in the future.

Notes

[1] Fukuyama, Francis (1989). 'The End of History?' *The National Interest* (16): 3–18.
[2] See Murray, Douglas, *The Strange Death of Europe: Immigration, Identity, Islam* (London: Bloomsbury, 2017), pp. 258–260.
[3] Murray, 2017, p. 269.
[4] According to a May 1991 memorandum written by Mohamed Akram, a.k.a. Mohamed Adlouni, for the Shura Council of the Muslim Brotherhood on the general strategic goal for the Muslim Brotherhood in North America, *the process of settlement is a "Civilization-Jihadist Process" with all the word means. The Ikhwan must understand that their work in America is a kind of grand Jihad in eliminating and **destroying the Western civilisation from within and "sabotaging" its miserable house by their hands and the hands** of the believers so that it is eliminated and God's religion is made victorious over all other religions.* [emphasis mine]
[5] Op. Cit, p. 263.
[6] Grant Bartley, 'Knowledge & History' in *Philosophy Now* magazine, November/December 2009, Issue 76, p. 21.
[7] Accessed at http://www.5wpr.com/practice/publicaffairspragency.cfm on 3 August, 2017.

[8] Stone, Oliver and Kuznick, Peter, 'Don't Betray Us Barak, End the Empire' at *Alternet*, April, 15, 2011. Accessed on 2 Feb., 2017 at http://www.alternet.org/story/150630/oliver_stone:_don't_betray_us,_barack_--_end_the_empire

[9] Ward, Jon, Axelrod: Anti-Americanism now 'not cool', *The Washington Times*, April 20, 2009. http://www.washingtontimes.com/news/2009/apr/20/axelrod-anti-americanism-now-not-cool/

[10] Klein, Naomi, 'Rebranding America', *The Guardian* Review, Saturday 16 January, 2010.

[11] John Stuart Mill's 'harm principle' states: "The only purpose for which power can be rightfully exercised over any member of a civilised community, against his will, is to prevent harm to others." I see no reason why the same principle that applies between individual members of society, or between citizens and the state, could not also pertain between corporate 'agents' (which are vastly more powerful than individuals) and individual citizens, or between different corporate entities.

CHAPTER ONE

BIOLOGISM, BIGOTRY AND THE
BACKWARD MARCH OF HISTORY

From Free Individuals to Neo-Conformism

The liberal model of man that dominated the forty-year period from the end of WWII until the eighties pictured human nature as essentially adaptable and plastic – or free. Whereas naturalistic explanations for human institutions and social arrangements had de-politicised the entire realm of socio-political relationships, the revolutionary liberals of the 1960's maintained that unjust social arrangements were institutionally erected and sustained by powerful individuals and human choices.

As the dust cleared in Post-War France, Jean-Paul Sartre emphatically argued that humans are responsible for themselves, for what they do and what they become. As such, they are responsible for the future of humanity itself. He contrasted his existentialist view of man to the characters in the novels of Emile Zola, for whom, "the behaviour of [his] characters was caused by their heredity, or by the action of their environment upon them, or by determining factors, psychic or organic." Sartre claimed that most people would be greatly comforted if these excuses were accepted as explanations of their behaviour. They would say, "You see, that is what we are like, no one can do anything about it."[1]

Sartre thought we are in bad faith when we portray ourselves as passive creations of our gender, our race, our class, job, history, nation, family, heredity, childhood influences, or subconscious drives. Existentialists did not deny that cultural factors are important or suggest that we should have no compassion for victims of systemic injustice. Rather, certain conditions "situate" each of us and form the background against which we must act in the world. They define the conditions, political and personal, within which we exercise our freedom and define ourselves.

Feminist existentialist Simone de Beauvoir gave more weight than her male peers to the difficulty of breaking out of constraints like social status and cultural influences. She knew very well how an alienated sense of "self" can come from the outside – from community expectations and roles – and then become so internalised as to seem inevitable. Despite this, she maintained her belief that we remain existentially free. Her own response to sexism was not to resign herself to the status of a passive "victim" of environmental patriarchy. Rather, she chose an unconventional lifestyle, neither marrying nor raising children, and instead had many lovers and wrote philosophy. She conversed with men as their equal, authored books and actively became the change she wanted to see in the world. She left a legacy to future generations and became a role model for aspiring female (or male) philosophers.

The existentialist revaluation of identity also played out in the exchanges between Sartre and Jean Genet, who was an "out" homosexual. Genet had been an object of Sartre's admiration and was even "canonised" by Sartre in his novel *Saint Genet* (1952), a biographical work in which Sartre praised the way in which a person can take other people's labels and decide what to do with them, transforming persecution or oppression into art or freedom. Sartre especially admired how Genet, through a series of reversals and creative manoeuvres, came to *own* his alienation and his outsider status as thief, vagrant, homosexual, and prostitute. While Genet always regarded his homosexuality as more like left-handedness or hair colour than as a voluntary response to his social environment, Sartre's main point about Genet's sexuality was that the man had never let others define the *significance* of his sexuality *for him*: he was his own man, not a "type".

In the 1970's Michel Foucault critiqued the Freudian form of cultural determinism. He was ambivalent about gay essentialism, and therefore never commented explicitly on the causes of same-sex desires. He was more concerned with the generation and proliferation of social and medical knowledge *about* homosexual *behaviour*, and the interpretative role that theoretical models and language play in the generation of "knowledge" about people whose behaviour deviates from social norms.

Even Martin Luther King, Jr.'s philosophy of non-violent resistance was fed by his reading of Sartre, Heidegger and the German–American existentialist theologian Paul Tillich. King's most lasting legacy is perhaps to be found in his understanding that the litmus test of human character is not to be found in the static facts of biology but in the dynamic acts undertaken by the individual in the project of living. We can respond to the circumstances and facts of our lives in myriad ways, and these choices become the measure of our manhood.

Bayard Rustin, one of King's key political strategists and a chief organiser of the March on Washington (mostly unknown because of his homosexuality), argued that the African-American community was threatened by the appeal of identity politics, particularly the rise of "black power". He thought this position repeated the political and moral errors of previous black nationalists, while alienating the white allies needed by the African-American community. Rustin argued that the relevant question was

> "... not whether a politician is black or white, but what forces he represents. Manhattan has had a succession of Negro borough presidents, and yet the schools are increasingly segregated...
>
> What I am saying is that if a black politician is elected because he is black and is deemed to be entitled to a "slice of the pie," he will behave in one way; if he is elected by a constituency pressing for social reform, he will, whether he is white or black, behave in another way."[2]

Rustin thought that proponents of "black power" imagined themselves to be leading the Negro people along the same path that past immigrant groups (Irish, Italians, Jews) had travelled to achieve political power, by sticking together along the lines of group identity. But, says Rustin, the reality was that it was through alliances with other groups, whether in party politics or unions, that these groups acquired sufficient power to have a voice in American society. "They certainly did not make isolation their primary tactic." What united these allies was not biological similarity but shared values and ideals, or a common goal that transcended superficial differences in the interest of more important affinities.

Since the mid-nineties, the broad liberal consensus on the primacy of the individual has been eroded both by the deterministic assumptions of sociobiology[3] and a therapeutic culture of "victimhood" in which all human behaviour is read through the lenses of childhood trauma or social victimisation.

Dr. Ruth Hubbard of Harvard University forewarned in 1993 that the incipient shift from nurture to nature was part of a conservative backlash against the gains of the civil rights and women's movements. The nurture model had shown that the inferior social status of women and African Americans was a product of institutionalised racism and sexism, not of "natural" inferiority or "innate differences". She urged her readers to go beyond "defining [women as a whole] as victims of male power and dominance," and pushed for women everywhere to show independence and individuality while learning to accept and embrace the biology that is continuously used by male chauvinists to undermine them. While it was important to recognise that "inferiority" was a product of socialisation and not nature, the cultural determinism implicit in perpetual "victimhood" was also too reductionist and implied cultural determinism.

Veteran British anti-racist broadcaster and politician Trevor Phillips OBE has also disparaged the idea that under-achievement or failure amongst people of colour must stem solely from unequal treatment by the dominant society. He claims that this "patronising guff" implies that all those who come from minority groups "have no agency other than that allowed by whites. People of colour, for example, become puppets of others' prejudices, with no capability of managing or improving their own lives."[4]

Identity politics has severed identity from agency, turning back the clock on the progressive gains made in the twentieth century's post-war period. In a February 2017 British television documentary titled "Has Political Correctness Gone Mad?", Phillips argued that left-wing political activists need to re-think their approach to identity politics. Attempts to muzzle – rather than engage with – the arguments of outsider parties may have been responsible for the popularity of leaders like Nigel Farage and Donald Trump, he suggested.

It is time for liberal Londoners and their clique of jet-setting university-educated friends to contemplate whether the failure of the liberal left to engage with the concerns and complaints of allegedly xenophobic groups or individuals (many of whom are minorities themselves) has left a vacuum that the far right has filled. Phillips argued that the left would do well to learn to live with offense and to stop mistaking symbols for substance. He suggested that liberalism and the peculiar fear of offending minorities had stifled legitimate debate in a way that had backfired.

Yet the liberal left has never taken any responsibility for the apparent recent rebirth of nationalist sentiments in the UK. This, they presume, is the doing of those backwards bigots – white British brutes who lurk in the midlands and the north, far removed from London's international intelligentsia.

Phillips is probably correct. In refusing to confront the complexities of immigrant cultures and the ultra-conservative religious ideologies some immigrants bring with them, liberals left a vacuum that was bound to be filled by less nuanced thinkers from the far-right. Not only have London's smug elite failed to comprehend the complex make-up of "immigrant cultures", they have also been remarkably snobbish in their refusal to listen to what their own compatriots have to say. Urbane Londoners have failed to notice that the complaints raised by these "rednecks" and "backwards yobs" have often been more closely aligned with traditional liberal values (including minority rights) than the accommodations and exceptions flogged by mainstream British policymakers and media. The latter have used the *rhetoric* of "diversity" to peddle policies that have substantially curtailed any genuine liberal dissent from the establishment's orthodoxies and politically correct posturing. This has resulted in a decrease in intellectual diversity and the fetishisation of tokenism and taboo.

Millennials' Erosion of the Post-War Liberal Consensus

The merging of biology and character so beloved of twenty-first century identity politicians is what the post-war liberal social justice movements *opposed* and sought liberation *from*. The reduction of a person's character to a general or abstract "type" to which they belonged (an identity group) is what every progressive left social critic – from Simone de Beauvoir and Martin Luther King Jr. to Michel Foucault – rejected or critiqued. Minorities were, to be sure, victims of injustice. But they were most harmed by the assumption that their group identity *mattered*, while their individual moral or intellectual merits did not. Group identity was the prison that chained individuals forever to skin colour, biological sex or sexual orientation. Group identity was at the very root of their victimhood, not the thing that would liberate them. Sexists, racists and homophobes had disempowered members of these ostensible "groups" on the basis of the reductionist biologism that claims nature is destiny, or culture and social arrangements are fate – the inevitable outcome of natural selection.

Often it was not so much even a *natural* feature of minority groups that was fixated upon so much as a reified[5] theological or cultural belief *about the natures* of these peoples that had been foisted onto them by the dominant culture's propaganda. Against group slurs, positive identity slogans like "Black is beautiful" or "Gay and proud" or "Born that way" were positive rejoinders to the reductionist biologism that had assigned unflattering personality or character traits to biology or physiology. "Naturalising" the inferiority of some social classes absolved the human agents who kept minorities "where they belonged" (whether in the kitchen, the closet or the prison) of accountability and blame.

The liberating solution to reductionist biologism was not simply to use *the same logic* of naturalistic generalisations but to flip them in the other direction, by saying that *all* women are superior, or that *all* black people are inherently "civilised" (whatever that means), or that *all* gay people are morally virtuous. Inversion only retains the dominant culture's binary and its generalisations. Instead, progressive social movements *subverted* naturalistic group generalisations: they stressed common *human* abilities like reasoning and reflection and demanded to be seen primarily as individuals who could choose to "make something of themselves" by means of their choices. Minorities did not expect their "groups" to be idealised instead of demonised. They wanted individuals to be released from abstract "group identity" and treated as free moral agents who could take responsibility for their behaviour and whatever praise or blame their choices merited.

Indian economist and philosopher Amartya Sen has observed that staunch communitarians take community identity to be paramount and predetermined, which implies that identities exist without any need for human volition or supporting institutions, just "recognition".[6] By contrast, he argues that reasoning and scrutiny play a major role in identity formation. Identities are not merely *discovered* so much as they are selected and prioritised by human agents. This is not denial of our situated selves, but an acknowledgement of the need to decide, when conflicting loyalties arise, on the relative importance of the different identities we have inherited.

Identities are not merely discovered and then passively "recognised" but also actively reinforced and/or maintained by customs and traditions, which in turn are upheld by community leaders. The social legitimisation and reinforcement of group "identity" (uniformity) or community standards by religious and cultural institutions (like social custom, modes of dress, and cinema and television) implies active human agency, not just the inevitable workings of nature.

Political Ideologies 101

Classic social liberalism holds an "atomistic" view of society as an aggregation of individuals. The Enlightenment championed a vision of human flourishing linked to personal autonomy and the belief in universal reason. The natural rights theories that emerged in the seventeenth and eighteenth centuries treated individuals as "ends in themselves", each worthy of respect and dignity, and not merely "means" to the ends of others. Consistent with that outlook, twentieth century liberals strived to establish conditions in which people could be free to pursue their own vision of the "good life" (as each defines it) without state authorities or majority groups prescribing to the individual how he must live. Although the individual is sovereign over her own body and mind, each must respect the fact that every other individual enjoys an equal right to liberty, such that everyone is entitled to the widest possible liberty consistent with reciprocal liberty for all.

A belief in the primacy of the individual is *the* characteristic theme of liberal political ideology, even if it has developed in a variety of ways. Liberals advocate individuality not just for its own sake, but as a condition of social progress and human flourishing. In his 1859 essay *On Liberty*, John Stuart Mill wrote:

> "Where, not the person's own character, but the traditions or customs of other people are the rule of conduct, there is wanting one of the principal ingredients of human happiness, and quite the chief ingredient of individual and social progress."

Liberal democracy is above all concerned with protecting the freedom of individuals from the tyranny of the majority in society and preventing coercion in spheres of activity and thought that many view as private.

By contrast, traditional conservatives have rejected the "atomistic" view of society as an aggregation of autonomous individuals in favour of a more communitarian perspective. Conservatives tend to give less emphasis to the private sphere and do not recognise a sharp division (if any at all) between the private and public spheres. Conservatives do not primarily stress the individual's rights but the bonds of duty and obligation that hold the "social fabric" together. Conservatives have traditionally held a view of society known as "organicism", stressing that societies are not human constructs based on reason and innovation, but are more like living organisms, in which the whole is more than the individual parts. An organic society is formed not by human ingenuity or abstract principles, but by natural necessity.

The organic metaphor has profound implications. If natural forces beyond human comprehension or control have shaped society's arrangements and institutions, then its delicate "fabric" should be conserved and adhered to by the individuals who live within its structures. Religious conservatives have seen social arrangements and hierarchies as God's creations. To flaunt the 'natural' arrangements is to reject God, and this has variously been construed as a form of moral disobedience, "sin" or corruption.

Traditional conservatives tend to believe that society is naturally hierarchical. They perceive various classes and groups in society as having specific roles. There are natural leaders and followers, and those who go out to work and get paid for it and those who stay home and raise children (without pay). Natural inequality of wealth and social position is justified because there is a corresponding inequality of social responsibility: those who have more liberty also have the responsibility to "protect" the less autonomous. Paternalism is thus deeply implicit in conservatism. Authority is beneficial because it gives individual human beings the security of knowing "where they stand" and what is expected of them. In British conservatism, organicism is exemplified in the traditionalist mantra of "faith, family and nation" as vital elements in the moral fabric of society.[7]

The Guilt-Shame Dynamic

Today's young social justice warriors virtue-signal their bans on offensive words in the belief that they are noble defenders of minorities even as they subject them to new horrors. We are witnessing a full-scale re-branding of conservatism that has bent and twisted the political spectrum beyond all recognition. The result is a political culture in which the religious right's ultra-conservative spokespersons enjoy exclusive immunity from criticism, socially constructed ideas and concepts are again being reified as biology, and would-be liberal critics of these regressive cultural shifts are shut down. We should not be surprised if far right voices and parties have filled the void produced by this situation.

Like conservative communitarianism, identity politics pictures individuals as "embedded" in a particular cultural, social or ideological context. Multiculturalism emphasises how culture shapes the values, norms and assumptions through which the individual forms his identity and his worldview, as though all members of a culture were both passive receptacles and identical in their needs, values or interests. Encouraged by these new cultural models, many individuals nowadays tend to see themselves primarily as products of biological bigotry who have inherited "baggage" from others (whether family or cultural forces) that will eternally define their place in society as victims, and therefore entitle them to special consideration without any need to prove the merits of their views. Guilt-tripping those who disagree with them will suffice in place of mustering a better argument: all whites are guilty of racism until proven innocent, all men are "privileged" and all transgender sceptics are bigots or "transphobes".

What political commentators today refer to as "liberalism" tends to be a politics that has been transformed into little more than conservative (and often deeply religious) social politics re-branded with liberal labels, images and semantics. Counter-Enlightenment ultra-conservatism has hijacked the moral prestige of liberal terminology and transferred it to an ultra-conservative social politics while retaining the libertarian economic policy of free markets. As Pakistani-American broadcaster, journalist and author Tashbih Sayyed has argued,

> "By casting its fascist agenda in terms of human rights and civil libertarian terms, political Islam has successfully been able to use the American liberal and progressive groups to project itself as an American phenomenon and win American intellectual elites, liberals and the media with left leanings on its side. Islamist organizations like CAIR and MPAC have transformed our democratic institutions of free speech and academic freedoms into a weapon of mass destruction to defend their jihad by creating an environment of doubt about the U.S. policies among the masses, with tragic results."[8]

While much of U.S. foreign policy deserves to be "doubted", Sayyed's basic point about how political Islam has projected a false image that has captured the sympathies of liberals and transformed democratic institutions is perceptive.

Like Sayyed, Ayaan Hirsi Ali has explained how the ideological infrastructure of political Islam has continued to grow, largely by means of the organisational infrastructure known as *dawa* that political Islamists use to inspire, indoctrinate, recruit, finance, and mobilise those Muslims and non-Muslims whom they win over to their cause.[9] She warns that the refusal to engage in a battle of ideas against political Islamism is a grave error.

On this point Hirsi Ali is in good company with Maajid Nawaz, co-founder of *Quilliam* (a counter-extremism organisation) who has been at the vanguard of the battle of ideas between genuine and faux liberalism (as the latter has been deployed by Islamists). Nawaz is a former member of Hizb ut-Tahrir, the first Islamist group to popularise the idea of creating an "Islamic State". He has a broad understanding of the machinations of political Islamism as well as militant Islamism, noting that violence is not the primary means by which the former seeks to impose its views, but rather gradualism and the ballot box are used to infiltrate the West's non-Islamic social institutions from within.

In their objective to dismantle the political institutions of a free society and erect strict Sharia in their stead, Islamists deploy both violent and nonviolent means. One such non-violent means is to misrepresent themselves as "moderate Muslims" and to gain official sponsorship by Western states. A variety of Islamist groups enjoy the status of "moderate Muslims". They include The Council on Islamic-American Relations (CAIR), The Muslim Public Affairs Council (MPAC), the Islamic Society of North America (ISNA), the International Institute of Islamic Thought (IIIT) and The Islamic Society of Boston.

Violent acts of terror have the effect of misleading people into thinking that anything short of terrorism is "moderate". But the ideology of an organisation may be extremist and deeply illiberal even if the group does not utilise direct violence to promote its views. Indeed, it may not need to if people are sufficiently afraid. It is more and more common to find people afraid not only of physical violence but of transgressing the politically correct ideologies that permeate social media and college campuses.

As Institute of Ideas director Claire Fox says at the end of her book *I Find That Offensive* (Provocations Series, London: BiteBack, 2016), university students complaining about safe spaces and "respect" for their fragile identities are simply reciting from an orchestrated script prepared for them by cultural authorities. These self-styled "rebels" are kicking an open door, singing from the cultural relativists' PC hymn sheet, not saying anything new. Their unpaid youthful zeal lends credibility to existing policies that leave *real* progressive leftist causes floundering. Authentic rebels need the kind of moral autonomy and independence that is achieved through genuine intellectual argument, not just smearing the opponent or appealing to infantilizing authoritarian "protection" from his superior reasoning. Today's zeitgeist, says Fox, venerates the vulnerable victim form of personality such that strength is demonised as arrogance or misrepresented as violence.

Many would-be liberals have erred in believing that Leftist liberation movements of the past were based on biological or cultural identity. As Mitchell Blatt argued in *The National Review*, "The problem is social-justice liberals view the world entirely through a prism of identity. To them, no one is an individual, but rather an amalgamation of stereotypes associated with their race, gender, or group."[10]

The latest fashionable neologism, "intersectionality", is yet another instance of pseudo-intellectual semantics being introduced to the political terrain without critical scrutiny. Intersectionality adds nothing new to identity politics, other than multiplying its force by encouraging individuals to see themselves (yet again) as possessors not of a single, but multiple, stereotypical group identities, seemingly to facilitate score-keeping on the victimhood charts.

So potent is the guilt-shame dynamic for securing political privilege that it invites the invention of new biological minorities. Race (identity) and religion (ideology) are routinely conflated, making valid criticisms of religious doctrines or symbols a crime tantamount to "hate speech".

Gender too has been re-biologised and reified, despite the fact that liberal feminists and queer activists of the twentieth century made their social gains by exposing gender as a flimsy social construct. Today gender is re-defined variably as an intrinsic, heritable or deeply significant part of the human "psyche" (sometimes understood biologically) such that "Trans kids" have either male or female "minds" (or brains) and what distinguishes one from the other is somehow *not* a product of cultural conditioning. Apparently, gender-bending social progressives were just wrong: men really *are* from Mars and women from Venus. Consequently, valid criticisms of the clinical "transgender" model (that arguably pathologises homosexual children) are unanimously dismissed as "Transphobic" (more on this in chapter 10).

The Enlightenment ideals embodied in documents like the US Constitution, even if the U.S. State Department has not always acted in harmony with them, have been seriously eroded in the past decade by academics and the mass media. At universities, the liberal value of tolerance for *all* views (irrespective of content) has been ditched in favour of PC gate-keeping. The young social justice warriors responsible for this

U-Turn have been duped into thinking they will be on the right side of history. In reality, they are on the right side of the political spectrum.

Notes

[1] Sartre, Jean-Paul, *Existentialism and Humanism*. Based on a Lecture given in Paris at *Club Maintenant* in 1945. In Kaufman, W. (ed), *Existentialism from Dostoyevsky to Sartre*. Trans. Mairet, P. Meridian Publishing Company, 1989; World Publishing Company in 1956.

[2] Rustin, Bayard, *'Black Power' and Coalition Politics* (Commentary, 02 – '65), accessed online on 19 June, 2017 at:
http://cf.linnbenton.edu/artcom/social_science/clarkd/upload/BLACK%20POWER %20and%20Coalition%20Politics-Rustin.pdf

[3] The term "sociobiology" was introduced in E. O. Wilson's *Sociobiology: The New Synthesis* (1975) as the "systematic study of the biological basis of all social behavior" (Wilson, 1975, 4).

[4] See Phillips, Trevor, *Race and Faith: The Deafening Silence*, London: Civitas, 2016.

[5] Reification is when an abstraction (an abstract belief or hypothetical construct) is treated as if it were a concrete, real event or physical entity -- when an **idea** is treated as though it were a material substance.

[6] Sen, Amartya, *Identity and Violence: The Illusion of Destiny*, New York: W.W. Norton & Company, 2007.

[7] These three values can be gleaned from the *Generation Conservative* website, in an October 20, 2016 piece by David Sergeant titled "Can We Please Stop Pretending There's Anything Remotely Conservative About Free Markets?", accessed online on 19 June, 2017 at: https://www.genconservative.co.uk/single-post/2016/10/20/Can-we-please-stop-pretending-there's-anything-remotely-conservative-about-free-markets

[8] Sayyed, Tashbih, "Are Islamist Leaders Winning Over American Muslims?", 21 March, 2007, *Islam Watch*, accessed on 21 June, 2017 at http://www.islam-watch.org/TashbihSayyed/Islamist-Leaders-Winning-American-Muslims.htm

[9] Hirsi Ali, Ayaan, *The Challenge of Dawa: Political Islam as Ideology and Movement and How to Counter It* (Hoover Institution Press, Stanford University), 2017, p. 2.

[10] Blatt, Mitchell, "Why Social-Justice Warriors Think It's OK to be Racist Towards Asians" in *National Review*, Feb. 18, 2017, accessed on 17 June, 2017 at http://www.nationalreview.com/article/445044/asians-face-racism-social-justice-warriors-accuse-them-privilege

CHAPTER TWO

MULTICULTURALISM:
THE ILLUSION OF DIVERSITY

Many educated Europeans, when they hear the word "multiculturalism", assume it to be synonymous with diversity. This is not surprising, since the word seems to be a conjunction of "multi" (many) and "cultural" (cultures). So, the logical conclusion is that multiculturalism is simply a doctrine that says mixing lots of cultures together is good. Cosmopolitan Europeans are accustomed to living among a wide variety of people from a vast array of cultural and ethnic backgrounds who speak different languages and pray to different Gods. This is an enriching experience. It allows us to see our own background beliefs and perspectives as less than obvious. Beliefs or assumptions we may have taken for granted are relativised, their universality or absolute "truth" called into doubt by the encounter with others who do not share our worldview. Thus, cultural mixing improves our education and expands our critical faculties. It makes us better able to empathise with others and to see their human experiences as valuable.

However, "multiculturalism" is not the same as cultural diversity. In political theory it refers to an approach that states adopt in order to negotiate the relationship between specific cultures and other members of society. Multiculturalism as a political ideology grew out of a rejection of modern Enlightenment values, which historically extended civil rights and liberties to blacks, Jews, gays and women. Multiculturalism is rooted in the belief that universal citizenship, equality before the law, and equality of opportunity are insufficient and that citizens in liberal states must be obligated to recognise and positively respect members of a cultural minority, should not be permitted to offend them, and must actively support the protection of their cultural beliefs from insult or criticism.

In practice, what this policy has meant is that only Western Europeans can benefit from seeing their own background beliefs and perspectives as less than absolutely True. Only Westerners' beliefs can benefit from the perspective that comes from exposure to other cultures. Non-Westerners' beliefs and assumptions are sacred and absolute. If non-Western citizens cannot respect other people's beliefs, then they alone are permitted to assert their own cultural identities and to take offense to Western host cultures and demand deferential respect for their practices and customs. Their intolerance towards other ways of life is "culture". Western principled tolerance, (and the expectation that others in Western states will reciprocate it) is "cultural imperialism" or "xenophobia".

In order to understand how illiberal multiculturalism is, and what kinds of demands it places on citizens, it is important to understand its paternalistic concept of "respect". It does not require that respect be earned through robust debate and argument. Rather, "respect" is enforced under threat of legal sanction or penalty. In his book, *Why Tolerate Religion?*, Brian Leiter distinguishes between "recognition respect" and "appraisal respect". The latter involves the notion that religious convictions *per se* have a special kind of value that others (including the non-religious) should appraise highly.

British philosopher Simon Blackburn has noted that "respect" is an ambiguous term. He describes the phenomenon by which the request for principled toleration "turns into a demand for more substantial respect, such as fellow-feeling, or esteem, and finally deference and reverence."[1] This "respect creep" (Blackburn's term) goes beyond liberty to practice religion without interference. It imposes a claim right that requires *all* to bow down to other peoples' sacred cows.

As British political columnist Nick Cohen has pointed out, this is the kind of "respect" that Tony Soprano might demand. One must perform a silent, polite deference towards doctrines that one disbelieves and/or disrespects, even to the extent of repressing one's own opposing views. The demand is not merely that citizens refrain from harming or legally discriminating against others with whom they disagree. It is that they must behave as though they have positive regard or esteem for others' views or practices. This entails that they may not express objections to, say, ideologies or religions, even if they are deeply offensive or arguably harmful to others. This demand goes far beyond merely tolerating (putting up with) other people's beliefs while at the same time finding them unpersuasive or downright distasteful or immoral. It is a demand that everyone in society behave as though they are silent or vocal followers of the "other's" belief system, effectively turning the concept of tolerance into a demand for deference.

To truly understand the extent of the demand this type of "respect" makes upon us, imagine telling a conservative Muslim that he has to have positive respect for the homosexual lifestyle, or for Western feminism's doctrines or dress codes. This would mean that he could not preach (whether in his mosque or in written pamphlets or on social media platforms) the immorality of homosexuality without risk of prosecution under "hate speech" legislation. Nor could he criticise the "immodest" way that Western women, or liberal Muslim women, behave or dress. Effectively it would mean that an imam could not express his own religious beliefs but would have to silently conform to Western liberalism's beliefs. Multiculturalists understand that a Muslim should not have to positively "respect" non-Muslims, but they do not seem to recognise the reverse. In a liberal society, non-Muslims should not have a duty to act or to speak as though Islam were good or even morally acceptable. Like the religious fundamentalist, non-religious citizens too should be permitted to voice their objections to lifestyles and practices, without being caught in the "hate speech" net.

Liberal tolerance (which entails voicing disagreement, satire, and active engagement with opposing ideas) shows respect for the other by treating him or her as an adult capable of resilience in the face of disagreement. Instead of granting a minority culture's ideas special immunity, and treating its adherents as fragile infants, it treats them as adults capable of submitting their beliefs to public scrutiny and of defending them in response to critical examination or of coping with defeat if they cannot do so. Former *Quillliam* spokesman Haydar Zaki has referred to this patronising attitude towards Muslims as the "racism of low expectations", whereby Western Europeans assume that minorities cannot be expected to have the same sort of resilience to opposing views and arguments as everyone else does. They cannot be expected to defend their values or ideas on the same rigorous grounds as *we* do. This "lowering" is just a form of insult, but one that wears the face of a kindly patron.

Nowhere is subjecting viewpoints to critical public scrutiny and debate more important than when religious or political ideologies are concerned, since neither are private matters and both involve (sometimes huge) claims about how others should live, what they should value or honour, and what they may or may not say, wear, eat, drink or do with their own bodies.

Multiculturalism has been influenced by an assertive identity politics. Because it is closely related to communitarianism, identity politics is conservative and reactionary. It is grounded in the belief that individuals' identities are constituted primarily in relation to the social institutions of the communities to which they belong, including the family and the church.

A core multiculturalist assumption is that personal identity is embedded in group or social identity. Therefore, like nationalism and even racialism, it is a form of collectivism. Because individuals are formed by the social bonds into which they have been born, they owe a debt of obedience and respect to their society's traditional institutions. Consequently, individuality is relatively unimportant. Communitarianism views individuals as thoroughly "enmeshed" in their traditional social roles. On this model, I am assigned my identity by my family and my culture. I am first a woman, a daughter, a wife, a sister or a Christian, before I am an individual.

As an ideology, multiculturalism encompasses a variety of approaches, not all of them inconsistent with Enlightenment, liberalism or modernity. Liberal multiculturalism celebrates diversity within a liberal framework, rejecting intolerant or authoritarian practices that are inherently incompatible with individual liberty. Pluralist multiculturalism, however, places greater emphasis on diversity than on equal rights and equal opportunities for all. Its advocates push for value pluralism and moral relativism: the idea that different moral outlooks (both those that respect individual liberty and self-determination, and theocratic or fundamentalist ideologies that do not) are equally legitimate. One problem with this is the assumption that someone who is coerced to conform to an ideological worldview can accurately be described as holding "values". Holding values involves a choice. Submission to someone else's ideology under threat of punishment or death does not. Arguably, pluralist multiculturalism does not lead to value pluralism and actively prevents it.

Cultures are not homogeneous but complex. Pluralist multiculturalism describes loose groupings of individuals with similar backgrounds, religions or language as a "culture" and then assumes that the diverse individuals within that culture belong to the same "community". Far from protecting, say, "all Jews" or "all Muslims" from generalisations, it reinforces the political fiction of cultural or religious unity. Whether any such cohesive community exists is doubtful. To suppose that there is a broad consensus among, say, all Muslims, about every aspect of their religion or their culture is a myth. In their report *Living Apart Together* (2007), Policy Exchange authors Mirza, Senthikumaran and Ja'far note that privileging cultural difference has led to multicultural policies ignoring the needs of less powerful sections of ethnic communities:

> "Organisations like the Muslim Women's Network have argued that community leaders silence their own women and prevent the criminal justice system from tackling problems such as domestic violence, honour killings and forced marriages." (p. 24)

Even as staunch defenders of pluralistic multiculturalism constantly remind us that there are "many Islams" and that "not all Muslims are the same", they simultaneously defend (even patronisingly protect) "the Muslim culture" from criticism and satire, as though they know that "Muslims" (as a group) will feel uniformly offended by any criticism or ridicule of their religion or its prophets. It could be that a majority of Muslims are tolerant and moderate, and so, like any other tolerant religious believers, enjoy send-ups of their religious orthodoxies or its dogmatic spokespeople or the attitudes they personify.

Amartya Sen (2006) has developed a substantial attack on what he calls the "solitaristic" theory underpinning multiculturalism, according to which human identities are assumed to be moulded by membership to a single group or monoculture. If people identify only with their own monoculture, this diminishes cross-cultural understanding and creates "ghettoisation" and insularity. Those who stress "intersectionality" have distorted Sen's concept by prioritising the individual's membership in multiple sub-cultures of oppression, domination, or discrimination to the exclusion of membership in groups of privilege and power. A Muslim man from Pakistan may share both the oppressed status of an ethnic minority in a European host culture, while also enjoying huge male privilege both in his own culture and in his Western European host culture. Therefore, a Western European Christian woman may identify more strongly with a Pakistani woman than with a Western European man. Intersectionality seems to overlook this. As AREO magazine editor Helen Pluckrose has noted, the concept of intersectionality was first introduced into the academic landscape by UCLA and Columbia Law professor Kimberlé Crenshaw. Pluckrose explains:

> Crenshaw opposed the mainstream liberalism of the time for its aim to look past categories of race, gender and sexuality, thereby levelling the playing field and enabling all people to succeed by their own abilities. She felt this neglected identity and identity politics which she argued to be personally and politically empowering.[2]

On issues of race, gender and sexual orientation, the recent trend in academia and online discourse is to force individuals back into "group identities" whether they like those identities or not, and to categorise individuals as oppressed members of those groups if the group is itself perceived as "oppressed" by a white Western culture, i.e. if it is a minority group or has been one at sometime in the past. The fallacy here is that if you are, say, Muslim (a religious identity group) then you are oppressed, even if male Muslims receive social or legal privileges that white men, white women and black women are denied, such as the right to marry multiple wives, or to inherit more wealth than female siblings.

As Pluckrose has astutely observed, "Intersectionality, by undervaluing shared human experience and rights — universality — and personal autonomy and distinctiveness — individuality — and focusing intensely on group identity and intersectional ideology, places individuals in a very restricted "collectivist" position previously only found in very conservative cultures."[3]

As any homosexual or gender-queer person born in the West before the mid-nineteen eighties or in a Muslim-majority country today knows, culture can be a form of oppression or captivity. A large part of what culture involves is socialisation. Even as multiculturalism's Western European or American defenders rage against patriarchal constructions of gender in their own cultures, they simultaneously defend very similar religious constructions of gender in minority cultures. Unless socialisation is grounded in free, informed choice (rarely the case in religious indoctrination), then it amounts to an assault on personal autonomy, and becomes what traditional liberals have called "a tyranny of the majority".

As nineteenth century political philosopher John Stuart Mill perceived, cultural or social tyranny can become as formidable as any oppressive state apparatus, because it inserts its tentacles into the minutiae of personal life and leaves no part of it untouched. Liberals have always maintained a robust defense of the private sphere in order to protect individuals from the pressures exerted by majorities.

Another problem with pluralist multiculturalism is that adherents of cultures that exist within host nation states and alongside its other citizens sometimes view their cultural identity as primary and separate from their political citizenship within the state. They may feel a stronger sense of loyalty to norms, authorities or Gods of their own culture than to the laws of the host nation. Consequently, pluralist multiculturalism presents a problem for social cohesion because it can conflict with the laws of nation states.

A clear example of how multiculturalism impacts the rule of law in nation states came into focus in Germany in 2017. In an interview with the German magazine *Focus*, Ralph Ghadban, a Lebanese-German political scientist and an expert on Middle Eastern clans in Germany, explained a trend that he had been observing for years, stating how very large clans of thousands of Middle Eastern men have seized de facto control over large swathes of German cities and towns where police feel powerless to enforce the law. As Ghadban says,

> "The clans now feel so strong that they are attacking the authority of the state and the police. They have nothing but contempt for the judiciary.... The main problem in dealing with clans: state institutions give no resistance. This makes the families more and more aggressive — they simply have no respect for the authorities....
>
> "The clans adhere to a religious group, a kind of sect with an Islamic orientation. The Islamic understanding of their spiritual leader, Sheikh al-Habashi, who died a few years ago, justifies violence against unbelievers. He taught that there is only the house of war [Dar al-Harb], which justifies plundering unbelievers and possessing their wives...."[4]

Finally, and most crucially, the politics of cultural recognition and assertion undermines the idea of a common humanity. This limits peoples' sense of moral responsibility to members of their own cultural community. The constant demand by some cultures that others acknowledge them, their culture or their belief system is not, even by their own accounts, one that can be reciprocated. This is where liberalism (and liberal multiculturalism) has a distinct advantage over pluralist multiculturalism's moral relativism. Liberal multiculturalism allows diverse ideologies to co-exist on equal terms.

Despite false claims to the contrary, liberalism does not hypocritically impose "its own ideology" on other sub-cultures within liberal states. Liberalism is a political framework or set of rules which function as a "container" for multiple ideologies, while not being an ideology in itself. Ideologies involve the identification of a social problem, a proposed solution, and an ideal goal or state of affairs that serve as an ultimate goal for all. Often ideologies involve the veneration and adulation of charismatic figures who occupy a mythological status within society.

Liberalism is expressly anti-ideological because it requires state neutrality with respect to ideological, theological or moral visions of "the good life". Its demands on citizens are very minimal. The aim of the liberal state is not to make people good (according to some form of "Western ideology") but to create the conditions within which the free pursuit of moral virtue ("the good life", as each individual defines it) is conceptually coherent. Liberal states secure the individual's negative liberty (freedom *from* coercion by others) so that she may, without harming others, pursue goals that are genuinely her own. Those who disagree with self-determination of this kind nevertheless want it for themselves, or agree with the principle at least selectively (when it protects *them* from coercion by others, but not when it is *reciprocal*).

Political liberalism has been more successful in protecting an expansion of rights to minorities than any other political framework in history. This is because of its underlying insight that, without liberty and self-determination, moral virtue (or vice) becomes incoherent. The very idea of "values" is meaningless in the absence of freedom of conscience and the political liberty to live one's own life according to personal convictions. No one can be made (coerced) to be a virtuous person or to live a morally good life. One can certainly be made a slave or a "performer" of other people's moral rules, but such a follower, acting from fear and self-preservation rather than from her own convictions, is no moral agent. She makes a mockery of moral agency and renders it hollow. This kind of conformity amounts to little more than ape-like imitation, as Mill described it. It does not allow the individual to develop his or her own discernment, reflection, and reason, and it discourages genuinely informed choices.

It is in order to avoid this kind of slavish obedience to others' fallible beliefs that liberalism provides a fair framework within which any ideology can be pursued, within limits that protect the equal and reciprocal pursuit (by others) of rival beliefs. By contrast, illiberal cultures will not tolerate rival ideologies and police dissent from their own. Liberal multiculturalism can, and does, protect and promote diversity, while pluralist multiculturalism threatens to erode it. Pluralist multiculturalism in its current form only promotes diversity *from* secular liberal democracy and European values. It is less about intellectual diversity, than about cultural opposition to the West.

In his book *The Trojan Horse: A Leftist Critique of Multiculturalism in the West,* Swedish sociologist Goran Adamson explained how states' adoption of the multiculturalist agenda seemed to overshadow everything else, including research findings about what might actually benefit immigrants themselves.

Adamson was commissioned by the European Union Agency for Fundamental Rights to determine the best methods for increasing political participation among immigrant groups in Europe. Having studied the empirical data, he discovered that the separate-but-equal model of a pluralist, multicultural society was less effective at encouraging political participation among immigrant groups than a more classically liberal approach, whereby immigrants are invited to participate in public life on equal terms, as citizens. Adamson's report, *Immigrants and Political Participation*, was quickly dismissed even by those who commissioned it.

This attempt by the EU to quash findings that disagree with a pre-determined multiculturalist agenda didn't surprise Adamson. Citing Wolfgang Kowalsky, a policy adviser at the European Trade Union Confederation (ETUC) and an expert in far-right demagoguery, Adamson concurs with his view that the methods and theories of multiculturalists are similar to those of right-wing extremists: both want to force reality to conform to their worldview, rather than respond to it as it is.

In her book *I Find That Offensive,* Claire Fox offered a similar example of how the erosion of leftist politics can be seen in multiculturalism's annexation of anti-racism. With British state support linked to identities, Fox cites a case where a group of mainly ethnic minority women artists was "encouraged" to self-identify as a Muslim group and subsequently focus their output on Islamophobia (none of them were religious) in order to merit consideration for future funding.

Then there was the feminist organisation that allied itself with a group of men from the Islamic Society who wanted to shut down ex-Muslim feminist and human rights campaigner Maryam Namazie, when she attempted to address the *Atheist, Secularist and Humanist Society* at Goldsmiths University of London. If the Muslim men really felt that their "safety" was threatened by Namazie's speech, it would have been easier simply not to attend a meeting that was intended for secular humanists anyway. By disrupting Namazie's speech, the group ensured that not even humanists (her intended audience) could listen to her impious discourse. The bigger picture, though Fox does not spell it out, is that multiculturalism trumps all other progressive left values when they conflict, as so often they have done ever since "diversity" became the normative ideology from which no one must diverge. In this context, diversity does not mean that a plethora of different ideas can be expressed and debated. That is what liberalism means by diversity. Rather, the new "diversity" that is imposed by state policymakers is one in which diversity *from* liberalism is valorised and trumps the liberal definition of tolerance at every turn.

There are other parallels between multiculturalism and old-fashioned racial thinking. Goran Adamson has argued that multicultural ideology makes a fetish, like other racial theories, of ethnic diversity. What matters is not, as Martin Luther King Jr. believed, the content of one's character, but the colour of one's skin. Common human traits, such as the capacity for abstract thinking, creativity and self-consciousness, are effaced in the name of what divides us. In this sense, multiculturalism is just as fixated on race as the racist thinking of the past, says Adamson.

Adamson further argues that the multicultural view of immigrants doesn't treat them as individuals who have a basic human need for self-determination. Instead, "the immigrant" is an abstract type, a species, a race. Racist implications loom large underneath pluralist multiculturalism's ostensible anti-racism. The "other" is presented in token fashion as either inherently fascinating or as a fragile victim. They are not like us. And in this separation of us from them, racism festers, claims Adamson. After all, the idea of diversity rests on the belief that immigrants are different to us, that their difference should be the object of celebration and adulation. Accordingly, the universalism and inclusivity of the civil-rights movement appears to the ardent multiculturalist as an embarrassing form of "cultural imperialism".

One might view this noble defence of the minority, and their critique of a potentially oppressive majority culture, as a matter of principle. But it isn't, claims Adamson. The annihilation of the other is regarded as an exclusively Western phenomenon. When it comes to ethnic groups themselves, the rights of dissenting minorities *within* these groups are rarely defended. That's because the multicultural agenda treats ethnic subcultures as homogeneous groups, as though individuals within them uniformly share a common identity defined solely by their common heritage or religion. Thus, annihilation of the other is acceptable, so long as the majority responsible for doing so is ethnic.

We have to protect "their" difference from us, it seems, but never the ethnic dissident's individuality or "difference" from their own cultural traditions. Adamson cites the example of Tasleem Begum from Bradford, who, after leaving her husband (from a forced marriage), was shot in the head by her brother-in-law. The brother-in-law's sentence was commuted from murder to manslaughter by a sympathetic British judge on the grounds of "provocation", stemming from the shame Begum had brought on her husband's family's "honour". Such light sentencing of the perpetrator shows little regard for the humanity of the victim, and a disproportionate degree of deference to the perpetrator's "culture". But would the victim appreciate this deference to a culture that stripped her of autonomy and supplanted it with the abstract idea of family "honour"?

Anti-racist liberals' concerns about far-right, xenophobic politics, with its inflammatory rhetoric of "us" and "them", are legitimate. As ever, we must take a principled, anti-racist approach to immigration. At the same time, the political and cultural impact of immigration and people's concerns about a lack of integration also need to be taken seriously. There must be a balancing of rights, not a diminution of them.

Notes

[1] Blackburn, Simon, "Religion and Respect", in *Philosophy without Gods: Meditations on Atheism and the Secular Life*, ed. Louise M. Anthony (Oxford: Oxford University Press, 2007), p. 180.
[2] Pluckrose, Helen, 'The Problem with Intersectional Feminism', AREO Magazine, February 15, 2017, accessed on 19 June, 2017 at https://areomagazine.com/2017/02/15/the-problem-with-intersectional-feminism/
[3] Ibid.
[4] Interview mit Ralph Ghadban, 'Experte: "Clans in Deutschland fühlen sich so stark, das sie zum Angriff übergehen", *Focus Online*, 26 April, 2017 accessed on 20 June, 2017 at: http://www.focus.de/politik/deutschland/interview-mit-ralph-ghadban-experte-clans-in-deutschland-fuehlen-sich-so-stark-dass-sie-zum-angriff-uebergehen_id_7034136.html

CHAPTER THREE

IDENTITY POLITICS:
RE-BRANDING INTOLERANCE

The culture of offense-taking and withdrawal into identity politics has had a serious impact on free speech and open debate. As *Sp!ked* editor Mick Hume argued so cogently in his book *Trigger Warning: Is the Fear of Being Offensive Killing Free Speech?*, a self-defined identity is seen as static; a self-enclosed state or sovereign territory immune to external laws or universal rules of engagement.[1] The members of an identity group assume the right to define the truth about themselves from within, and they insist on a moral monopoly over their story. This is especially odd given that morality only makes sense in relation to morally significant others who could be beneficiaries or victims of an agent's behaviour. Nevertheless, any outside attempt to challenge an identity group's claims about itself or its victimhood is likely to be condemned out of hand as offensive or bigoted. As Hume has noted, this has led to a privatised form of blasphemy; the criminalisation of criticism.

Unlike physical assault or institutional discrimination, where there are objective measurements of injury, it is solely up to the victim whether he has been offended or not.[2] Since the claim that you have been offended is un-testable and subjective, the victim is always right. Thus, there is a powerful incentive to *be* the victim, just because it provides a seemingly unassailable case for demanding redress in any situation.

Identity politics has become the sphere of competitive victimhood. Within this context, each individual is the only possible judge of whether he has been offended, regardless of the intentions of the "offender" or the context in which he speaks. The speech crimes from which such victimhood springs are potentially endless.

As a second year LSE philosophy student said in response to the banning of lectures and academic events there because of pressure groups, "they're so eager to get offended that they don't even listen."[3] The self-proclaimed victim's opponent will always be put immediately on the defensive, and the ostensible "victim" will have gained the upper hand and the moral high ground. This form of politicised offence-taking has become the fashionable alternative to reasoned argument. Columnist Julie Burchill took an appropriately snarky swipe at the tactic in a 2015 *Spectator* article, calling those who resort to its use "cry bullies", a hideous hybrid of victim and victor.[4] A quintessential example of this new phenomenon, said Burchill, is Islamism:

> "...on one hand stamping around murdering anyone who doesn't agree with you, on the other hand yelling 'Islamophobia' in lieu of having a real adult debate about the merits of your case."

When the LSE University Student Union decided (on behalf of all LSE students) to "no platform" Nick Lowles, the chief executive of *HOPE not Hate*, for his allegedly "Islamophobic" views, something has gone terribly wrong. Whether or not Lowles's views really *are* accurately described as "Islamophobic" is exactly what needs to be proved, and the only way to do that is to hear them. Even if they were Islamophobic, hearing them would only serve to "protect" the ostensibly marginalised and persecuted group against ideas. Ideas have never harmed people's permanent interests as progressive beings except in contexts where opponents were not allowed to challenge them, such as is presently the case in Muslim majority countries. A case in point was in February 2016 when forty state-run media outlets in Iran raised $600,000 (£420,000) to add as a bounty to Ayatollah Khomeini's death fatwa on the writer Salman Rushdie, because of his novel *The Satanic Verses*.

Double standards seem to be perfectly acceptable where Islam is concerned. Generalisations about "all Muslims" are rightly deemed ignorant. Yet generalisations about all critics of Islamic religious ideology have become the norm. We can laugh at *The Book of Mormon* or *The Jerry Springer Opera* when they lampoon other religions but try putting on a theatrical rendition of the "Book of Islam" and you may find yourself murdered.

Yet that probability somehow does not become the object of ridicule. In the past, liberals would have deemed as intolerant the religious fanatic who responds to ridicule of his religion with murderous violence. Today his refusal to countenance views that openly rebuke his religious worldview is no longer deemed intolerant. Rather *he* is a victim of speech crimes, while faux-liberals pour scorn on the satirist (of Islam) for his "irresponsible" use of free speech, reminding him that violent reprisals *should be expected*. After all, he will have "brought them on himself". Satirists, you see, are responsible moral agents who choose their actions. Religiously motivated murderers are not. And if they kill others to defend their faith, they are "mentally ill", or fringe extremists, but *not* intolerant religious authoritarians and certainly not representatives of any *real* religious system. The impunity with which "victim cultures" are treated is not a remedy for discrimination, but an egregious instance of it. Never mind that the satirist may herself be a minority and may be from the same religious background as the one being scrutinised and roasted over the hot coals of social satire. According to this Newspeak, Ayaan Hirsi Ali is somehow not a "liberal" Muslim feminist, but a "right-wing" critic of Islam.

Since the *Charlie Hebdo* massacre in January 2015, a chorus of commentators have promoted the notion that perpetrators of the heinous crime of giving offense are more responsible for their own murders than the offended "victims" who couldn't help but pull the trigger to shut them up. The year 2015 marked the first time in modern history that the Western liberal establishment defended the violent murder of journalists for the offensive content of their publication. In the wake of the *Charlie Hebdo* shootings, cultural commentators from Pope Francis to Will Self could not stop reminding us that our right to freedom of speech comes with responsibilities.[5] Implicitly they were referring to our responsibility *not* to offend religious sensibilities when exercising this vaunted "freedom". Opponents[6] of this shifting of "responsibility" to victims for the crimes of those who assault them, argue that such caveats merely shackle free speech to conditions that undermine the very principle.

'Incitement': the Abdication of Agency and Choice

One argument against free expression increasingly emphasises the paramount importance of law-enforcement, social order and security. In a geo-political landscape that has been re-defined by threat of "global terrorism" the value of security has sometimes been placed above individual liberties such as free expression. We need to ask, then, how exactly free speech threatens to undermine security. If it does not, then we need not accept a false dilemma that tells us it is impossible to have both free expression *and* security.

Some have argued that speech is more than "mere words" and must be censored when it is likely to "incite" dangerous actions. The American courts have agreed with this in cases where there is reasonable and compelling evidence that the speech in question was the direct cause of dangerous *behaviour*. The quintessential example is when someone yells "fire" in a crowded theatre. But the idea that any repugnant ideology, or even unpopular viewpoint, can "incite" violence or hatred is a distortion and abuse of the original legal concept.

What originally made "incitement" a unique category of criminal speech was the realistic perception that it would precipitate immediate harm. Even John Stuart Mill accepted that suppression of speech could be justified in those rare situations in which it constitutes a catalyst to harmful action. But crucially, Mill justified this prohibition on the ground that some speech acts constitute a harmful action, *not* because they constitute a harmful opinion. In Chapter 3 of *On Liberty* Mill drew a clear distinction between actions and opinions. His example is a situation where someone expresses the opinion that corn-dealers starve the poor because they keep prices high for their own benefit. However, Mill would only censor this speech in a situation where an angry mob is gathered with torches outside the corn-dealers home. Arguably, in this situation the speech would be likely to provoke immediate violence, and the only reason for censoring it was that the speech was so closely connected to a context in which it was reasonable to believe that mob violence would follow from it. Importantly, Mill did *not* think expressing the opinion on the corn dealers' practices and motives should be suppressed in other circumstances. It was not the expression of the opinion he rejected, but the context and manner in which it was expressed.

But it is questionable whether speech can really incite responsible adults to bad behaviour. In the case of the angry mob it is arguable that speech of this sort constitutes the first step towards an illegal act. But recent bans on hate speech assume that provocative speech can "incite" even future behaviour, where no immediate threat exists. This implies that someone can make you act against your will. To claim that someone can incite you to do anything in this context is to abdicate personal responsibility. Jean-Paul Sartre, writing after the horrors of the holocaust, aptly called this attempt to escape personal responsibility "bad faith" (by which he meant a kind of self-deception). If we cease to hold individuals accountable for their own behaviour, we can criminalise anyone we claim has 'influenced' the criminal's actions – parents, teachers, film or television personalities, musical artists he has listened to, authors of books or blogs he has read – all are fair game. But this, of course, turns the perpetrator himself into a victim. It presupposes a deterministic model of human nature in which human individuals are not responsible, free moral agents, but are more like automatons that hear words and blindly obey them like a dog obeys its master. If this were the case then, given all of the possible influences on a person, it would be virtually impossible to decide which of them "influenced" a particular act.

Human beings have competing desires and choose between them all the time. I may have a first order desire to go out with friends tonight, but I also have the second order desire to finish this book. I choose between these desires and only I am responsible for the decision to prioritise one over the other. In this sense, we are responsible even for choosing our desires. When someone influences me, it is because *I value* what he says or writes. I select these opinions or perceived truths as more important than other opinions or viewpoints to which I've been exposed. If I am led to accept falsehoods because I am ignorant of other, better, views then I am partly to blame for my passivity in accepting them without scrutiny.

Nevertheless, I am entitled to my ignorance within limits. The demand for certainty increases in direct proportion to the extent that my beliefs are the justification for causing harm *to others*. Since no one is infallible, it is rarely the case that one's viewpoint can justify harming another person. There is a substantial difference between defending beliefs that harm others and yet have no sound evidence to support them and holding beliefs that harm no one and do have sound evidence in their support. The burden of proof is always greater on one who would endanger another's well-being or interfere with his liberty in the pursuit of a righteous goal. One does not have an absolute right to be wrong when one is risking more than one's own safety on the basis of a belief.

Critics of the *Charlie Hebdo* journalists have been highly selective about which groups have to "take responsibility" for their behaviour. While responsibilities are indeed the concomitant of rights, most of the commentators who seized on this fact assigned disproportionate (or very little) responsibility to the criminals who shot the journalists. In civilised society, full rights and responsibilities are only granted to mature adult agents because it is assumed that children and mentally disabled persons are unfit to handle the sometimes strenuous burden of assuming responsibility for themselves and their actions. To deny this kind of responsibility to religious groups is to infantilise them. Along with the responsibilities with which adults are burdened go a raft of freedoms. The problem with the "irresponsible journalists" finger-wagging was the assumption that the terrorists who murdered them, by contrast, somehow were *not* to be held responsible in the same way. The problem is not in attaching responsibilities to rights but in applying a double standard. Either *all* of us are responsible for our behaviour, or none of us are.

The *Hebdo* journalists could have expected to take heated criticism or possibly even a defamation lawsuit for their editorial choices. But it is contradictory to admit that the killers deserve moral blame for shooting the *Hebdo* ten and then to say that the *Hebdo* ten were responsible for getting themselves shot. If the *Hebdo* journalists were really responsible for their own deaths, then it must be because either (1) certain words trigger uncontrollable responses such that they compel a violent response, (2) any author, filmmaker, artist, writer or speaker is potentially responsible for how others react to their expression, or (3) offensive speech about certain topics really ought to be a capital crime so that anyone who offends, say, a religious person or creed deserves the death penalty. If you accept the first of these options, and if you're consistent, you must find it utterly miraculous that *everyone* who had read *Hebdo* didn't descend on their editorial offices with guns, bombs and knives. If you prefer option (2) then it will be impossible to see exactly who is responsible for any violent crime. How could we ever determine exactly which of the many influences on the perpetrator of a violent crime was the decisive cause of his action? The potential list of guilty parties is seemingly endless: parents, teachers, religious leaders, siblings, television programs, music artists, authors, film directors, etc. If you accept option (3), then you really espouse blasphemy laws and should opt to live in a theocratic country or join a campaign to turn your own into one, if you aren't already doing so.

We are all responsible for our own actions or none of us is. If we renounce human agency and relinquish individual responsibility for our actions, then we do not deserve to be treated as adults with all of the rights and liberties this entails. We invite a form of paternalistic authoritarianism that is legitimised by the myth that human beings lack sufficient moral autonomy to govern themselves.

The "incitement" argument against free speech, in its current (distorted) usage, presupposes a direct link between the expression of extreme views and extremist or violent behaviours. So, for example, if a Muslim cleric is permitted to advocate violence, or to express offensive anti-American or anti-Western sentiments, then he is indirectly guilty of inciting illegal actions in his listeners. This view is incoherent and, worse, it undermines the very legal system that "law and order" policies are entrusted to enforce. If someone commits a criminal act of terrorism, we do not accept "outside influences" as a mitigating factor when determining their guilt. Although defence attorneys attempt to diminish the defendant's responsibility in various ways, if the forensic evidence points to their guilt, and they are adults of sound mind, we do not accept outside influences as somehow *causing* them to act. If we did, we would reduce their sentence accordingly – but we do not. The fact that adult citizens are responsible moral agents entitles them to basic rights and protections on the one hand and obligates them to accept full moral responsibility for their actions on the other. Civil liberties come with concomitant responsibilities. Personal accountability for criminal actions is one of them. "Incitement" cannot be a reason to prohibit extreme speech unless we are also willing to relinquish our cherished belief in personal accountability. As Benjamin Franklin said in 1759: *"They that can give up essential liberty to obtain a little temporary safety deserve neither liberty nor safety."*

Censoring 'Incitement to Hatred'

In October 2007 the British government proposed the introduction of new legislation into their already dubious "Criminal Justice and Immigration Bill" that would make it a crime to incite hatred because of a person's sexual orientation. Firstly, mere emotions (like hatred) against any group is not a crime, so inciting it shouldn't be either. If hatred is expressed in actual harmful acts, then it *is* a crime. But hatred itself is not something the state has any business legislating against, just as they have no business compelling love for their policies or politicians. No external authority can dictate to the citizens of a free society what they must value, love or hate, and any society that condones such coercion is not worthy of being called "free".

The government's "incitement" measure is anything but a defence of liberal democratic values...although superficially it may appear that way. Liberals defend freedom of speech, expression and assembly, as well as freedom of religion. The true test of that principle comes when we are asked to permit freedom of expression for views we detest. This bill was nothing more than an attempt to enforce the values status quo, a deeply illiberal move that presupposes the infallibility of our current "community values", or fashionable notions of political correctness. While our politically correct view *may* indeed be morally just in this instance, it isn't always so, and we give up the right to dissent from popular beliefs at our peril.

A society that is confident in its values and convictions is one that can tolerate dissenting views, and countenance the possible fallibility of its own. If we stifle controversial viewpoints today then we can just as easily do so tomorrow, when the religious right's homophobia or theocratic doctrines may be as politically correct as today's toleration for homosexuality. Once we relinquish the rights of "outsiders" to express unpopular viewpoints there will be no possibility of correcting popular and persuasive, but morally bankrupt, ideas. We will *all* lose our liberty if we give the government the power to exclude and silence the voices we (or it) dislike.

In an atmosphere where many shades of criticism (not all of them stemming from ignorance, bigotry or non-Muslim perspectives) are lumped together as "Islamophobia" tout court, question-begging becomes the norm. This peremptory, dogmatic tactic of silencing dissent from the pluralist multiculturalist status-quo has become a kind of universal gambit. It stigmatises legitimate critics (including Muslim critics) of religious authoritarianism and recognises no valid form of criticism of Islamism or religious fundamentalist ideology. It simultaneously insists that there is no universal truth, and then paradoxically treats *that claim* as the only universal and infallible Truth.

We need to welcome all faiths into the public square on equal terms. With the privileges and liberties of living in an open democratic society come the concomitant adult responsibilities and obligations. The price of living in a free country is that we all sometimes have to tolerate (not respect) ideas or speech that we find offensive or distasteful. Citizens cannot expect to reap the benefits of living in a free society without being willing to pay the costs. And the price of liberty is, at least for now, really quite cheap. However, as we continue to erode the principle of free and open critical debate, the price will increase accordingly.

Notes

[1] Hume, Mick, *Trigger Warning: Is the Fear of Being Offensive Killing Free Speech?*, (London: William Collins Books), 2015, p. 191.
[2] Ibid., p. 193
[3] 'Controversial Welfare Lecture Shelved Amid National Press Coverage', *The Beaver* (Newspaper of the LSE Students' Union), p. 1, Issue 849, 23 February, 2016.
[4] 'Burchill, Julie, 'Meet the Cry-Bully: A Hideous Hybrid of Victim and Victor', *The Spectator*, 21 April, 2015.

[5] See for example Greenslade, Roy, 'Charlie Hebdo Cartoons: Press Strives to Balance Freedom and Responsibility' at *The Guardian*, 11 January, 2015, accessed on 20 June, 2017 at http://www.theguardian.com/media/2015/jan/11/charlie-hebdo-cartoons-uk-press-publish, "Francis on Charlie Hebdo: with free speech comes responsibility", *Catholic Voices Comment*, 15 January, 2015, accessed on 20 June, 2017 at http://cvcomment.org/2015/01/15/francis-on-charlie-hebdo-with-free-speech-comes-responsibility/ and Self, Will "The Charlie Hebdo Attack and the Awkward Truths About Our Fetish For 'Free Speech'' at *Vice*, 9 January, 2015, accessed on 20 June, 2017 at http://www.vice.com/en_uk/read/will-self-charlie-hebdo-attack-the-west-satire-france-terror-105
[6] For example, *Sp!ked* editor Mick Hume, *Trigger Warning: Is the Fear of Being Offensive Killing Free Speech?* London: William Collins Books, 2015.

CHAPTER FOUR

FAULT LINES WITHIN ISLAM

While sparks fly between Islamist jihadists and their Western targets, with sporadic terror attacks on European and American citizens by religious extremists followed by inflammatory responses from right-wing nationalists grabbing the headlines, several intelligent commentators from within the Muslim community have urged us to shift our gaze to the deeper fault lines within Islam itself. In so doing, they have revealed how those dominating Islam's internal struggle are manipulating Westerners' perceptions of Islam, a religion and/or theocratic ideology whose final definition is yet to be determined.

In their 2007 report titled *Living Apart Together: British Muslims and the Paradox of Multiculturalism*, Policy Exchange authors Munira Mirza, Abi Senthikumaran and Zein Ja'far reported research findings that suggested a far more politicised interest in religion among younger Muslims aged 16 – 24 than in their parents' generation. Younger Muslims showed a stronger preference for Islamic schools and Sharia law. The research showed that 36% of the younger British Muslims believed that Muslims who convert to another religion should be punished, with 74% preferring that Muslim women should choose to wear the veil. "There is clearly a conflict," the report said, "within British Islam between a moderate majority that accepts the norms of Western democracy and a growing minority that does not." (p. 5)

As co-founder and director of the civil society group *Inspire*, a counter-extremism organisation that has cooperated with the Government's 'Prevent' strategy, Sara Khan has observed first-hand how a politicised Islamist ideology has torn families apart, seduced youngsters into violence, increased sectarian rifts and encouraged intolerance and dehumanisation of both non-Muslims and other Muslims. Like so many British Muslims, Khan has watched with trepidation both increasing sectarian hard-line interpretations of Islam within Muslim communities and growing anti-Muslim attitudes from outsiders. The former act as moral police, pouring scorn on the "filthy kuffar" (non-believer); the latter speak an ugly language of "us" and "them". As a reward for their work countering extremism, Khan and other liberal Muslims countering extremism have been labelled "apostates", "Islamophobes", "sell-outs" and "native informants" by Islamist extremists and their disciples.

Cemal Knudsen Yucel, a Norwegian ex-Muslim, has described how Muslims have smeared him with racial slurs like "coconut" – "brown on the outside and white on the inside". Turning to the Left for support and solidarity, many liberal Muslims have found only more rejection from well-meaning liberals who align themselves with Islamists in the mistaken belief that the latter represent "Muslims".

There is no consensus among Muslims about what the word "Islamic" means, who best represents its values, or which activities deserve the appellation. While many Muslims are at pains to stress that acts of terror or coercion have no foundation in the Islamic faith, others who engage in terrorist slaughter, jihad or "honour" killings describe their actions as "Islamic". The sheer brutality and scale of their violence, whether in Nigeria, Pakistan or France, impacts on Muslims and non-Muslims alike.

At the core of the battle within Islam is the question whether Muslims believe that Islam is reconcilable with secularism and universal human rights, or whether they adhere to religious supremacist ideas that transcend the rule of law in democratic nation states while reviling "man-made" concepts like gender equality and democracy. In her book *The Battle for British Islam* Sara Khan provided an up-to-date detailed account of how these tensions have played out in the British context since the new millennium.

Khan, who was appointed to head the UK government's Commission for Countering Extremism in January 2018, has explained how Western political naïveté about Salafi-Islamism and its rhetorical tactics had led to a de facto merger of segments of the Left with an ideological movement antithetical to classical liberal ideals and hostile to progressive egalitarian principles. Not only is the intra-Islamic conflict choking the lifeblood out of an arguably more authentic Islam, it is also distorting the political spectrum – altering the content and substance of "left" and "right" wing political positions beyond all recognition. One consequence is that, whereas in the past liberals were staunch opponents of the religious conservatives, now they make common cause with the religious right in opposing the nationalist right.

The backdrop against which secular Muslims find themselves marginalised (even in the West) is the fairly recent convergence of Salafists and Islamists, two ideological strands that previously competed for the loyalty of young British Muslims. Ideologues from the theologically puritanical and ultra-conservative Salafist movement and activists for a global political Islamist order exhibited a new willingness to collaborate in the post-9/11 pressure cooker that melded them together in a climate of defensiveness. In the past fifteen years, Salafi-Islamism has attracted an increasing number of youths attempting to define their identity, and has exerted a powerful influence within British Islam, according to Khan. The Islamists crowd out other Muslim voices and promote a compelling victimhood narrative that has won them many left-leaning allies among student unions, academics, the media and even politicians.

The movement has effectively hijacked key liberal terms and concepts, deploying them in new contexts in defence of an illiberal ideology, transferring the moral prestige of liberal political language into the service of an ultra-conservative theocratic movement. Using the semantics of civil rights, multiculturalism, diversity and equality, Islamists have won over audiences and neutralised the opposition. This, says Khan, is part of a multi-stage, long-term strategy to reach the goal of achieving Dar Al-Islam (state under Islamic rule) and to erect a global political order based on Islamic principles (a caliphate). Getting there might involve gradual Islamisation via the mechanisms of democracy or violent upheaval – or a mixture of both.

A tactical and sophisticated "soft Islamism" disseminated by organisations like the iERA (Islamic Education and Research Academy) and MEND, essentially the movement's public relations arms, promotes Islamist norms through the discourse of diversity, multiculturalism and inter-faith outreach, while always keeping the victimhood leitmotif spinning and misrepresenting its political aims as "combating Islamophobia". The outcome has been to marginalise secular Muslim voices within Islam.

Question Begging

While Islamism (a socio-political system which advocates an expansionist Islamic state governed by Sharia law) is not definitive of Islam (the faith), the pro-Islamist Left has been very gullible in accepting the mythical conflation of the two. Embracing multiculturalism and moral relativism, the regressive Left now regularly bolsters political movements and ideas it would have once opposed. The term "regressive left" was coined by anti-Islamism activist Maajid Nawaz, who used it in his 2012 book *Radical: My Journey Out of Islamist Extremism*. "Regressive left" or "regressive liberals" is a political term Nawaz used to describe a section of left-wing politics that paradoxically holds reactionary views because of their tolerance of illiberal principles and ideologies, particularly Islamism, for the sake of multiculturalism and moral relativism. Consequently, would-be liberals have contributed to the erosion of their own progressive political philosophy, not only by ignoring internal Muslim dissent from fundamentalist and ultra-conservative narratives, but also by actively assisting Islamists in stifling it. Aligning themselves with the guardians of "safe spaces" and "no platforming", Islamism's Western identity politicians silence liberal voices within Islam and shut down free expression.

While organisations such as 5Pillars, Islamic Education and Research Academy (iERA), the Muslim Research and Development Foundation (MRDF), Muslim Engagement and Development (MEND) and CAGE (initially CAGE Prisoners) claim representative status for "Muslims" in Britain, in so doing they persistently beg the central question at issue. The notion that their Islamist ideology is synonymous with normative Islam is treated as a foregone conclusion. Statements by leading Islamist pundits invariably assume without argument that their version of politicised Islam is normative rather than a selective or distorted rendering of Islam, which is exactly what needs to be proved.

An example of this followed the 1 May, 2014 SOAS University screening of *Ijtihad: Feminism and Reform*, a film by Nancy Graham Holm in which progressive Muslims including Reza Aslan (a vehement defender of Islam), Mona Eltahawy and Tehmina Kazi were interviewed. The film raised pressing questions about who speaks for Muslim communities and who has the authority to interpret religious texts. In a Facebook Letter of 9 May, 2014 titled *"To Reform or to Deform?"* leading British-Bangladeshi imam Ajmal Masroor voiced his disapproval of the film. Masroor is a member of the Muslim Council of Britain and a spokesman for the Islamic Society of Britain. He has been a Liberal Democrats parliamentary candidate for West Ham in 2010 but stood down after it was found that he had posted on the Muslim Public Affairs Committee UK (MPACUK) forum, an organisation that has several times been accused of anti-Semitism and/or racism. Masroor makes regular appearances on British television as a leading spokesman for British Muslims and has presented his own programs on Islam Channel and

Channel S. He was a panellist on the Channel 4 program *Sharia TV* and in 2009 presented a BBC One program titled *Celebrity Lives – Sharia Style.*

Masroor's response to this small independent film assumed that the version of Islam that he champions is the one that is free from "seriously distorted and disjointed ideas about Islam", which is exactly what needs to be proved.

It may well be that the Muslim community (if indeed any such homogeneous "community" exists) is accustomed to internal debates, led, as Masroor's letter claimed, "by scholars and experts". In his Facebook letter Masroor contrasted this category of "qualified leaders" to the *Ijtihad* nine who, by comparison, "possess very little knowledge of Islam". This characterisation of his Muslim opponents was not entirely fair, given their impressive credentials. But more importantly, it begged the central question, which is whether his chosen "scholars and experts" uniquely possess a correct interpretation of Islam, while the *Ijtihad* nine are mere "deformers". It appeared that the bludgeon of theological elitism was being wielded to silence those Muslims who were most critical of the "personal and social parameters" that his select cultural gatekeepers wished to defend. This suggests that the intellectual debates and discussions with which he claims to be familiar are *not* as "vital and dynamic" as he makes them out to be.

His claim that some from the mainstream media and the establishment love to be in bed with such people (i.e. the *Ijtihad* nine) and champion their agenda is rich coming from a man who only a day prior to writing his critique was interviewed by Radio 4's *Today* Programme, no doubt because he is seen by the establishment media as a chief spokesman for London's Muslim community. That being the case, his resentment towards the small publicity afforded to this group of Muslims whose message, as he himself admits, is "not even causing a small ripple" was somewhat excessive. It seems inexplicable, unless his true objective was to avert a genuine debate about Islam, i.e. one that isn't just among an exclusive group of "scholars and experts" who fundamentally agree with one another on Islam's personal and social parameters, and who apparently hold a monopoly in "the real Islamic intellectual arena".

Masroor accused the *Ijtihad* nine of corrupting the sacred features of Islam with values and practices antithetical to it. But the assumption that his version of Islam is sacred and that theirs represents "corruption" is precisely what the *Ijtihad* reformers wished to interrogate. Masroor's understanding of Islam conflates personal and social moral parameters as if there were no distinction between the two, again begging one of the central questions raised by the nine reformers depicted in the film. In his estimation, personal parameters are defined theologically and so all personal matters are subsumed under the social moral code.

In spelling out why individuals cannot exercise critical reasoning about Islam in the way suggested by the reformers, Masroor implied that a heart that is harmful to societies' collective interest, or neglects a set of "universal" [Islamic] values, is "selfish" and detrimental to harmonious existence or "peace". The universal values Masroor describes are not like the ones inscribed in the UN Declaration of Human Rights. What he means by "universal values" is Islam-friendly community standards. However, the question whether individual liberty and freedom of religion (including freedom within the religion of Islam, and from it) are socially destructive has yet to be answered.

Social conservatives say very similar things about the relationship between individuals and society, so we can draw some parallels. Social stability, security and order are prized over and above individual liberty, since the established institutions and traditions are supposed to represent what is best for everyone collectively. On this communitarian view, social hierarchies are not a means by which one group dominates the others and controls the public agenda so that it serves their own interests. Rather, nature has ordained that there are natural leaders, and the very fact that they are in charge proves that they *should be* in charge. A dash of social Darwinism is added to bolster the impression that all social hierarchies are inevitable outcomes of natural selection and survival of the fittest, never mind that the theological institutions and arguments (not nature) are the *real* firmament that supports the (heterosexual male) social pillars and holds people in their assigned "roles" ("God" being the alleged creator of these "natural" laws). As Masroor says in his letter, "These values cannot be whimsical or self-serving. They should emanate from a source that is unbiased and pure." This means that the theocratic values endorsed by the all-male elite are unbiased and infallible, and that obedience to them, in outward behaviour, is the best way of manifesting faith and a clean heart. This is little more than a recipe for theocracy, which is at odds with his somewhat equivocal invocation to "embrace modernity".

After listing how the Quran's instillation of values encompasses every aspect of human life (the "private sphere" of modern liberalism being utterly demolished), Masroor went on to the subject of punishment in

Islam. Its purpose, in the context of so-called "justice", is to deter crime and instil fear of the consequences. In addition, he says punishment is designed to counteract something harmful or undesirable from society.

Fear of harmful "consequences" does not appeal to purity of heart; it appeals to self-interested prudence. It is not based on persuasion or religious conviction but on coercion and intimidation. Furthermore, whether or not a particular form of behaviour is socially "undesirable" depends upon whether society (in the *inclusive* sense of that word) actually does not desire it. It does not depend upon what a paternalistic sub-set of self-appointed imams proclaim is "desirable" for society as a whole. As it stands, Islamic justice (with its hudud punishments) means that people who disagree about what is "desirable" are stigmatised or punished, as the *Ijtihad* nine were finding out. When Masroor explained the strict conditions under which the Islamic penal code must be implemented, he explicitly stated that society must be free and not ruled by illegitimate governments, dictators and despots. Would he also include the ulema? Or shall we assume that they can never be illegitimate, dictatorial or despotic? Why should we accept the belief that they alone are immune from corruption, fallibility, and despotism?

Masroor was advocating a religious authority that comes "from above" and as such cannot be questioned. As he says, "if you want to be a Muslim you must be prepared to submit to Quran and the teachings of the blessed Prophet." The only alternative is to leave Islam. By contrast, the *Ijtihad* nine seemed to believe that individual imams and believers *choose* whether or not to give the Quran its authority over their lives, and that the authority of the "scholars and experts" likewise comes from their own free decision to invest their fundamentalist reading of the Quran with special authority and political power. They have decided not only that Islam is the correct religion to follow, but which of its holy texts and teachings is to be used for guidance, and exactly how these are to be interpreted.

There is nothing about these human decisions that makes them infallible. All persons, unless they have been indoctrinated into a belief system, possess the freedom to give authority to books and teachings of their choice. There is no legitimate reason on earth why a particular minority should have the exclusive privilege of choosing on behalf of others the religious doctrines and teachings that govern how they must live. To assume otherwise is to lay claim to an infallible authority that no human being possesses. It is only relative to his own beliefs about what are the "right principles for living" that Masroor (or any other expert) can judge that fundamentalist Islam's moral code is right. As Akmal Safwat remarked in his response to Masroor:

> Early Muslim scholars did their best to interpret the Qur'an and Sunna through consensus, analogy and ijtihad. They presented their results to us as Islamic fikh and shari'a laws. But history matters. In a world that was and is continually changing, this process should have continued.[1]

Ultimately human reason is the test of whether anyone should follow divine directives, since human beings decide which ones are indeed "divine", "good", "just" or "holy". To abdicate responsibility for this, by pretending that a divine being appointed some sub-set of men to represent Him on earth, is a formula for autocracy, not faith.

A further example of how Islamists pretend to speak on behalf of Muslims (in general) came when FOSIS[2] proposed gender segregation at university events. Muslims who attempted to debate the issue were summarily accused of vilifying "Islamic" societies and "Muslim" students. The underlying assumption was that none of those opposed to gender apartheid were authentic Muslims, since apparently *all* Muslim students would agree on the practice of gender segregation. Another textbook example was the claim[3] by the Islamist organisation CAGE that Prevent was engaged in a Government-directed policy of attacking "Islam" (in its totality).

In reality, the Prevent Duty has to do with safeguarding children from terrorist indoctrination (of any kind, whether right-wing nationalist or Islamist radicalisation) and nothing to do with basic Muslim practices such as dress codes or beards, as a CAGE protest letter misleadingly suggested. We can also cite the situation in which the Council of Ex-Muslims of Britain were described as "Islamophobic" when they held signs in the 2017 London PRIDE march stating, "East London mosque incites murder of LGBT". This was intended as a form of protest against homophobic hate preaching at the mosque. These people are not "phobic" towards Islam; they have made a conscious choice to leave their religion of birth. If anyone else *except Muslims* were to reject their culture of origin and embrace, say, Islam, it would not make them "phobic". It would make them a shining example of the virtue of diversity.

A familiar line-up of Islamist activists (Ajmal Masroor, Dr. Abdul Wahid, Haitham Al-Haddad, Abdur Raheem Green, Sufyan Gulam Ismail, Mozzam Begg, et. al.) increasingly claim to speak for all British Muslims. Sara Kahn observed how, in January 2015, a group sent a letter to the

House of Lords complaining about the government's proposed Counter-Terrorism and Security Bill, condemning the new law (that many moderate Muslims welcomed) as "manufacturing a witch-hunt against Islam and Muslims". They then produced a piece on the Hizb ut-Tahrir website[4] with the misleading headline, "Muslim Community Writes to the House of Lords over the new CTS Bill". A more accurate headline would have read: "*Some Islamist Muslims* Write to the House of Lords…" but instead they chose to posture as representatives of a mythological monolithic "Muslim Community".

As in Britain, Islamist organisations have begun to claim representative status for Muslims in the United States (in the U.S. a good example is CAIR). A familiar line-up of Islamist activists (Linda Sarsour being a typical example) increasingly claim to speak for American Muslims or on behalf of the "Muslim community". Naïve liberals always manage to perceive the existence of a non-extremist strain of Islam when the far-right over-generalises, but then ignore Islam's internal diversity whenever Islamists generalise about what it means to be "a Muslim".

Double Standards

In pushing the idea that their own politicised Salafi-Islamism is synonymous with Islam (the faith), the Islamist religious right also supply the nationalist far-right with their most basic premise: that their extremist, intolerant version of "Islam" is definitive. The only difference is that Islamists are allowed to push that theory, while their non-Muslim detractors are not. Right-wing American ideologue Robert Spencer opined that there is no distinction between a true peaceful Islam and the hijacked Islam of terrorist groups. When Spencer or other right-wing non-Muslims erase the important distinctions within Islam, the left immediately perceive that such smears are not representative of "the vast majority of Muslims" and rush to the defence of Muslim moderates. Yet when an identical conflation of distinctions within "Islam" issues from the lips of a politicised Islamist who describes integration, human rights and gender equality as hostile to normative Islam, suddenly the left rushes to his cause, treating the views of Muslim moderates as negligible. The double standards are truly epic and have a distinct whiff of reverse racism. Exemplary of this is how student groups have barred right-wing speakers from universities while welcoming Islamist "civil rights" groups like CAGE (an Islamist organisation whose leading members have legitimate grievances against the West but whose representatives have made comments that, according to Amnesty International, are "at odds with human rights principles").[5]

Key Myth: Islamism is Grievance-Based and Ideology-Free

Drawing on a plethora of case studies from her eight years on the front-lines fighting radicalisation and extremism, Sara Khan quashes any remaining doubts about the extent to which Salafi-Islamists have shaped the defensive grievance narrative that has become the mainstream perspective on "British Muslims". It is commonplace for aggressive Islamist ideologues and their left-wing apologists to claim provocation by Western foreign policy, or even by mild religious satire. Every terrorist act is framed (even by Western journalists) as an inevitable by-product of US and UK intervention in Muslim countries, or of some deplorable form of "speech offense" against the faithful. All "Muslims" (not just Islamists) are depicted as uniformly opposed to religious satire and "The West" is caricatured as monolithic entity.

Importantly, Khan argues that Islamist terror cannot be explained away as merely a response to grievance over foreign policy, but also requires positive buy-in to an ideology that legitimises and necessitates violence. German-Egyptian author and political scientist Hamed Abdel-Samad has also written at length on the long history of the military theology of jihad within Islam and traces it back centuries, before the United States began its meddling in foreign affairs.

In 2017 I interviewed British former Deputy Mayor for Culture and Education in London, Dr. Munira Mirza for *Conatus News*. I asked about her past research on race, culture and identity. Dr. Mirza has written and broadcasted about race, culture and identity for over fifteen years. In 2005 she presented the BBC Radio 4 series, *The Business of Race*. I asked her whether grievances over Western foreign policy are a reasonable explanation of jihadists' motivations. Mirza said that this did not make sense because Islamism as a political philosophy predates many of the foreign conflicts being cited now. Furthermore, the patterns of terrorism do not correlate with the foreign policy actions of government (France was opposed to the war in Iraq but still suffered attacks by Jihadists). While she stated that foreign policy is not irrelevant, she also claimed that it had become an excuse for broader dissatisfaction and malaise. "In our research ten years ago," she said, "we found many young Muslims would cite foreign policy as concerns but were largely ignorant of the basic facts and were persuaded by a vague narrative of victimhood more than anything specific."

The Policy Exchange research showed that Muslim anger about foreign policy was more of a talking point than a grievance that could be backed up by specific historical facts, with the survey revealing a "surprising lack of knowledge about basic facts relating to international issues." (*Living Apart Together*, p. 56) Only a small minority of British Muslims could even name two influential figures in the Israel/Palestine situation, with young Muslims half as likely to know the answers to these basic questions compared to the 55+ age group. The report concluded from this that "pity can be a distorting lens, reducing complex political struggles to a simplistic morality play of good and evil." (p. 58)

But according to Sara Khan, the CAGE position is basically that grievance cancels out ideology. In a 2013 document, CAGE expounded the contradictory view that terrorists have an ideology but acts of terrorism are not caused by ideology. Instead, they imply, terror acts are always a response by Muslims to "unrepresentative regimes, often aided by Western policy and occupations". Parroting this narrative, *Guardian* journalist Seamus Milne, now a Labour Party executive director of strategy, wrote that the Woolwich butchery of British Soldier Lee Rigby was "backlash" for Western wars fought in Arab and Muslim countries, the predictable consequences ("blowback") of an avalanche of violence unleashed by the U.S., Britain and others.[6]

The defensive narrative of victimhood trades on the truth that Western agencies have waged overt and covert wars on democratically elected governments for decades (and not just in Muslim majority states). However, Islamists have shrewdly taken a leaf out of the propagandist's playbook in using parcels of truth to tell overarching lies, re-arranging true facts into a mosaic that will produce the overall impression they wish to convey. The mixing of falsehoods with truth or half-truths, and deploying them in the service of false conclusions and ideological ambitions, is textbook spin.

As Iona Italia argued at *Conatus News*:

"This isn't a battle between East and West, and this isn't a battle between brown people and white people, nor is it a battle between non-Muslims and Muslims. This is a struggle between, on the one hand, those fighting for human rights and humanitarian values, and on the other hand, those who favour regressive values and theocracy."[7]

A False Dilemma

Western apologists for the Islamists' "victimhood" narrative subscribe to the false belief that a vigorous critique of Western foreign policy must necessarily exclude castigation of its violently regressive Salafi-Islamist counterpart. This is a false dilemma. Those who oppose Islamism can, and often do, skewer Western hypocrisy and its bellicose interventionist activities in Muslim majority countries and elsewhere. The demand is not to choose sides, but to defend principles.

As Kenan Malik has observed, the Haitian revolutionary struggle of the 1790's was partly a struggle against identity politics. "The French Revolution of 1789 provided both the material and the moral grounds for the Haitian Revolution. It upset the delicate balance between the classes that had held colonial society together. And in the Declaration of the Rights of Man, Haitian revolutionaries found the intellectual argument for change."[8]

Self-determination, equality and human rights – values that were formerly a litmus test against which Western hypocrisy could be measured – are now seen as hopelessly slanted. The left's acolytes of Islamism have embraced such a thoroughgoing moral relativism that they have no firm grounds from which to launch any moral critique of human rights abuses, whether perpetrated by the West or anyone else. In their embrace of the Islamist version of anti-colonialism, they have jettisoned the values that gave the 1960's revolutionary movements the moral high ground vis-à-vis imperialist rulers.

Having thrown out the Enlightenment baby with the colonialist bathwater, their righteous criticism of "the West" *simpliciter* has been hoisted on its own petard. Hypocritical and covertly criminal agencies of Western governments have held hands with the repressive Wahhabist Saudi regime for decades, with both Western and Arab leaders demonstrating equal contempt for human rights and civil liberties. In the past left-wing liberals would have condemned both on the same broadly liberal grounds, and with reference to the same humanitarian principles. Islamist demagogues and their Western "fellow travellers", as Maajid Nawaz aptly calls them, have caused such a deep crisis of liberal values and confidence that this is apparently no longer possible.

Alignment with Leftist Movements

Islamist strategists have also successfully exploited various European leftists' existing grievances against the West or capitalism. Frustration at the lack of success in opposing Western military interventionism and/or the West's hypocrisy has thrown both leftist anti-War activists and Marxists into sympathy with Islamists because of shared opposition to the West. The Stop The War Coalition (STwC), whose officers span the Labour Party, Green Party, Respect, National Union of Students, trade unions and far-Left groups, have a cordial relationship with the Islamist group CAGE. STwC and CAGE share the view that there is a clear linkage between Wars in the Middle East, the rise of Islamophobia and the UK Government's Prevent counter-terrorism strategy, says Sara Khan.

STwC's affinity with Islamists is most alarming in light of the 2001 defection of two Left-wing Iraqi activists from STwC on the grounds that it refused to condemn Islamist-inspired terrorism. The defectors, both members of the Worker-communist Party of Iraq, resigned from the STwC steering committee claiming it had abandoned the "ongoing struggle for freedom, equality and well-being by the working-class, the communists, the women, the radical and secular people and freedom lovers in those countries" and had instead fallen into step with "the savage Talibans and the likes of Political Islam."

Other Marxists, such as Chris Harman, editor of *Socialist Worker*, urged a careful course through the contradictions of Islamism, deploring its clericalism and discrimination against women, while appreciating its powerful potential to destabilise capitalism's hold over the Muslim world. In cooperating with Islamists, Marxists maintained an underlying assumption that they (Marxists) would ultimately be sufficiently intellectually and politically dominant to steer Muslims gradually away from Islamism towards socialism. In fact, says Khan, it seems that the steering has gone the other way round.

The Assault on Prevent

A large part of Sara Khan's work has dealt with Islamists' coordinated attempts to derail and discredit the government's Prevent strategy, apparently from a need for self-preservation. Islamists' widely disseminated persecution discourse has made the government's initiative a soft target for all kinds of unrelated issues and a dumping ground for

Muslim grudges about "the media" or other policies not within the Prevent remit. This is despite the fact that Islamists are the UK's media darlings and spokespeople on all things "Muslim". While Khan does acknowledge Prevent's imperfections, and admits several unfortunate referrals, her book details how these have been given an exaggerated high-profile in the press through misleading vividness: lots of sensational misinformation has been circulated about a very small number of misreferrals.

As an insider, Khan has furnished some perspective on the hysteria that Islamists have circulated and amplified in their attempts to hamstring the only mechanism in place to intervene between terrorist radicalisers and their vulnerable targets. She points out that the freedom of religious expression and worship could not be compromised by Prevent even if that were its aim (which it is not). Both UK law and Article 9 of the European Convention on Human Rights robustly protect religious freedoms.

In their attacks on Prevent, Salafi-Islamism's apologists have stuck to the trope of treating Islamism as representative of "the Muslim population". Their suggestive rhetoric failed to account for the significant part of "the Muslim population" which supports Prevent's aims and has no affinity whatsoever with Salafi-Islamist ideology. Many British Muslims do not wish to dismantle Prevent, or other tenets of liberal democracy. Only Islamist Muslims do. Khan cites a recent Demos survey which revealed that British Muslims are generally more patriotic than the average British citizen, as well as a parallel trend over the past twenty-five years showing that British Muslims have grown more conservative on social and equality issues. But again, this does not account for the entire "Muslim" population.

How Islamists Use Terrorist Attacks

Following each new terrorist attack on European soil the same script is recited from with mind-numbing predictability. The 3 June, 2017 London Bridge terror attack was no exception. It was the third terrorist attack on British soil that year. Each attack is framed in the same way: terror is just the inevitable repercussions of legitimate grievances over Western foreign policy, or for current "racism" towards Muslims (never mind that Muslims are not a race). Furthermore, "Muslims" are the only *real* victims of Islamist violence since *they* will all be tarred with the same brush by bigoted, ignorant Europeans. Therefore, we must not fear Islamism, but the far-right, a product of *our own* European chauvinism and ignorance.

With military precision, Western European targets are hit with a combination of hard and soft Islamism. The hard Islamism comes in the form of bombs, knives, and vehicular homicide. The soft (and more insidious) Islamism comes in the follow-up reporting and commentary *about* these massacres, which essentially function as apologia for Islamism and shaming of the West.

The hard Islamism is carefully calibrated. It is not so hard that people actually start to worry that something like this is likely to happen to *them* or their loved ones. The scale of each attack is small, and the frequency regular but not sufficiently accelerated to cause genuine alarm. Britons can rest assured that the statistical likelihood of a terrorist incident actually harming them or someone they know is miniscule. In these circumstances hysteria is inappropriate, but the message is clear: if the pressure applied by soft Islamism doesn't work, there will be other methods available to enforce conformity.

The soft Islamism is equally well devised. By now the rhetoric has become familiar. The all-important subtext in this narrative is that Western Europeans, not Islamist terrorists, are intolerant and bigoted. The British far-right, not murderous jihadis, are too ignorant to use intelligent debate to defend their values. Islamists are not comparable to fascists but *we* are (*if* we protest violent religious intolerance). "Religious intolerance" isn't what jihadis do, it is what *Westerners* say in response to jihad. And so, to avoid repeating history (our own evil history), we must remain passively docile and "tolerant" of authoritarian conservative religious ideology as it becomes increasingly normalised in our midst.

This two-pronged approach has facilitated one of the most effective cultural "conversions" in human history. It has warped the political spectrum so completely that the ostensibly "left-wing" acolytes of Islamism resemble the religious right politicians they opposed only thirty years ago in every substantial respect (other than semantic labelling). So shallow has political analysis become that liberals have bought into an ultra-conservative religious ideology merely because its shiny new "anti-racist" re-branding looks so appealing. The actual substance of this allegedly "anti-colonialist" and "anti-racist" politics is itself theocratic, colonising, intolerant, misogynist, and homophobic – ideas that historically the political left would never have willingly endorsed.

But today would-be liberals rush to embrace the Islamist's innocent "Muslim victim" figurine with zealous enthusiasm, perhaps because they regard it as a noble cause. In doing so they trample secular Muslims, tolerance, free expression, feminism and LGBQ rights underfoot. This may be less their fault than a symptom of the fantastic success of *dawa*.

Dawa is the organisational infrastructure and rhetoric by means of which Islamists inspire, propagate, indoctrinate, recruit, finance and mobilise those whom they win over to their cause. To fully understand the depth and breadth of *dawa* and the means by which it succeeds, one must understand that the obscure status of its most ardent critics (e.g. Ayaan Hirsi Ali and Maajid Nawaz) is itself an effect of its success. The branding of these two secular liberal activists - both quintessential examples of moderate, tolerant Islam - as "right wing" is a clear example of *dawa*'s triumphant spin and infiltration of traditionally left-wing organisations. The relative publicity, priority and representative status given to Islamist propagandists like Linda Sarsour speaks volumes about the power of *dawa*.

As the Saudi Grand Mufti Ibn Baz stated in 1998,

"The truth has been spread through the correct Islamic da'wah, which in turn has been aided and supported by jihad whenever anyone stood in its way. It was jihad and da'wah together which helped to open the doors to victories." [9]

In Western countries, *dawa* aims not only to instil Islamist views in existing Muslims but also to convert non-Muslims to political Islam. The ultimate goal is to destroy the political institutions of liberal democracies and to replace them with top-down theocratic Sharia law. Political Islam's absolute power holds appeal for anyone interested in totalitarian political power, whether they are genuinely religious or not, and whether they are Muslim or non-Muslim. Religion's potential as a tool for the establishment and maintenance of political power must not be overlooked in any complex assessment of political Islam.

Dawa is subversion from within – the instrumental abuse of religious freedom and democracy to undermine that very freedom. For this reason, *dawa* is able to operate under the protection of liberal laws that cover religious freedom, giving it much more room to manoeuvre than, say, fascism.

The failure of liberals to address Islamists' civilisation-jihadist process (their term)[10] owes less to Europeans' unfulfilled or latent need for religious morality than to the clever ways in which Islamists have sold their ideological product. As stated in their own strategy memoranda, the process is going to work by becoming "a part of the homeland" in which it lives, "stable" in its land, "rooted" in the spirits and minds of its people, "enabled" in the live [sic] of its society.[11] The document states:

> The Ikhwan must understand that their work in America is a kind of grand Jihad in eliminating and destroying the Western civilization from within and "sabotaging" its miserable house by their hands and the hands of the believers so that it is eliminated and God's religion is made victorious over all other religions.[12] [emphasis mine]

The "sabotaging" of their (Westerners') own miserable house by their (Western) hands is clearly underway.

Well-organised Islamist groups assume representative status on behalf of all Muslims, simultaneously marginalising Muslim reformers and dissidents.[13] Ayaan Hirsi Ali's own marginalisation is a case in point. Despite her heroic status as the victim of a religious witch-hunt that saw her artistic collaborator Theo Van Gogh murdered in an Amsterdam street, and irrespective of her clear identity as an exemplary Muslim moderate who fully endorses liberal secularism, Islamists have succeeded in marginalising Hirsi Ali and stripping her of both Muslim and non-Muslim supporters who should be her natural political allies. In addition to shutting down her voice, they also desire to kill her, and have issued a fatwa to this end.

Besides branding Muslim reformers and actual moderates like Hirsi Ali as "Islamophobic" or as "Uncle Toms" or "house niggers" and relegating them to the margins, a second strategy is *hijra*: taking control of immigration trends to transform Western societies.

A third strategy is to reduce women to the status of reproductive machines for the purpose of demographic transformation.

Fourth is the advantageous use of progressive parties in democratic societies, using their emphasis on "inclusion" to force the acceptance of Islamist demands in the name of peaceful coexistence.

Fifth is to exploit the good will of self-consciously progressive movements, effectively co-opting them.

Finally, Islamists increase their hold over the educational system, including some charter schools, faith schools and home schooling.

Other methods that have worked well in the United States are the use of prison chaplaincies to focus on recruiting African-American men, as well as other ethnic minorities. African-Americans are the number one target group for conversion by the *dawa* network. Nearly a quarter of all Muslim Americans are converts. According to J. Michael Waller of the Institute of World Politics, Muslim inmates comprised between 17 and 20 per cent of the US prison population in 2003, but most of them arrived in jail as non-Muslims. According to his research, 80 per cent of inmates who find faith while behind bars convert to Islam. Among recent targets of Islamist infiltration were the Women's March and Black Lives Matter. Identity politics work because victim status appeals to liberal progressives, which is a key strategic locale for annexation.

Influential Sunni cleric Yusuf Al-Qaradawi has explained that the West is to be conquered not by the sword but by ideology and through '*wassatiyya*', a strategy through which Muslim communities have their own religious, educational and recreational establishments in the West. He urged Islamists in the West "to have your small society within the larger society" and "your own Muslim ghetto."[14] Islamists committed to *wassatiyya* explicitly regard the West as territory to settle or colonise through immigrating, out-breeding non-Muslims and converting as many people as possible to the tenets of political Islam.

One reason Westerners so persistently underestimate the potential dangers of radical Islam is the fact that these more insidious political threats are far more difficult to identify than acute threats of physical violence. The Dutch Intelligence Agency AIVD has flagged the gradualist character of *dawa*: not everyone is convinced that Islamism's isolationism and its development of parallel social structures may constitute a problem.

In contrast to Muslim-majority countries, Western governments are seemingly unaware of the tight nexus between Islamists' ideological strategy and *dawa*'s front organisations. Westerners see only the charitable or humanitarian side of *dawa* efforts, while remaining blissfully ignorant of its subversive side.

Understanding *dawa* requires acknowledging the reality of political Islam. Political Islam is not just a religion, explains Hirsi Ali. It is a political ideology, a legal order and a military doctrine associated with the campaigns of the Prophet Muhammad. Like any theocratic movement, it rejects the distinction between religion and politics, mosque and state. It implies a constitutional order fundamentally incompatible with the rule of law in Western democracies. It favours a caliphate over legally accountable and removable elected representatives.

To advance their goal of imposing Islamic law (Sharia) on society, radical Islamists employ a wide range of mechanisms, of which violent *jihad* is only one, relatively minor, example. Hirsi Ali is adamant that we ignore at our peril the ideological infrastructure that supports political Islam in both its violent *and its non-violent forms*. Working in the guise of religious missionary activity, Islamist organisations often enjoy not just freedom from interference, but also official sponsorship from government agencies who regard them as religious "moderates" simply because they do not engage in violence. This makes what they actually do far more insidious and destructive than violence, which earns only very short-term victories and is openly and obviously hostile to its targets. *Dawa* is the opposite – it works precisely because it does **not** manifest as an obvious enemy to the institutions and political structures that it aims to eradicate. Quite the opposite; it mimics and infiltrates them, using their language and mobilising their energies.

The use of jihad and terrorism only serves to make ultra-conservative politically extreme organisations appear moderate, simply because the latter do not openly practice violence. Their positioning alongside their violent counterparts creates the appearance of relative non-violence and is used to change the flavour of their politics, much the same way that a slice of apple pie might seem savoury after eating mouthfuls of raw sugar. Institutionally, nonviolent Islamist propagandists benefit from terror attacks committed by jihadists because of what is known as the "positive radical flank effect" whereby terrorist attacks make ideological Islamists engaged in *dawa* appear comparatively non-extreme or innocuous in the eyes of Western governments.

Islamists also use terror attacks to construct their victim narrative on behalf of *all* Muslims. Each new act of terrorist jihad is seized as an opportunity to go on the offensive against their critics. And each time they construct a straw man and then attack it: "*Look how all Muslims are branded as terrorists!*" They deliberately conflate their critics' legitimate resentment of jihadis with a general hatred of "Muslims" (an association which is *their own* strategic invention). They then attribute this conflation to "the far right" or "Islamophobes", thus creating the demand for yet more protection and immunity from legitimate scrutiny, which is invariably described as some form of racial discrimination. They erect an obviously bigoted conflation (i.e. that between Islamist jihadis and

"Muslims") and then transfer it to their critics, misrepresenting the *bad feelings* Westerners have *about violent jihadis* as bad feelings that Westerners *do not have* towards all Muslims. This trope also presupposes what it aims to achieve; namely that extremist religious conservatives speak for and defend "Muslims" (all Muslims). By these methods, Islamists stoke the flames of "Muslim grievance" against the West ... an attitude that ideological Islamists (but only some Muslims) already possess.

When Salafi-Wahhabist Islamism or jihad becomes the object of well-deserved anger, Islamists claim that "Muslims" are being attacked, thus misrepresenting the jihadist's version of Islam as the religion of all Muslims, which it certainly is not. Islamists are the only group who benefit from this fiction. It allows them to falsely accuse anyone who disagrees with Salafi-Wahhabism of "anti-Muslim bigotry", while also giving them grounds to castigate non-extremist Muslims as "sell-outs" or "dirty kuffars" (non-believers). This manoeuvre erases the distinction between Muslims and Islamists, effectively allowing Islamists to monopolise the Islamic faith. At the same time, they (or their acolytes) relentlessly accuse *Westerners* of confusing ordinary Muslims with violent Islamists − a conflation that they themselves have manufactured and propagated. The key difference is that *they* are permitted to lump all Muslims together in a defensive context, while anyone who wishes to criticise jihadists is accused of attacking "Muslims" and of being irredeemably bigoted.

Until we stop drinking this Kool-Aid, secular Europeans will be helpless against the spread of Islamism and its intolerant ideology. We must be clear that *Islamists,* not "Westerners", routinely represent Islamism as normative Islam. *Islamists,* not "Westerners", have been responsible for misrepresenting legitimate criticism of *Islamism* as an assault on "Muslims" simpliciter. This is *their* quintessential gambit, despite their highly effective transference of responsibility for it to "right-wing" Europeans, i.e. anyone who objects to what they're doing. "Westerners" have not invented the conflation of Salafi-Wahhabism and "Muslims". This blurring of the two is a conceptual tool deliberately constructed by Islamist extremists to give them leverage with Europe's opinion leaders and media class. Western liberal secularists have no interest in maintaining this fiction and a strong incentive *not to* do so.

When Ayaan Hirsi Ali was set to do a public speaking tour in Australia and New Zealand last year, she had to cancel, citing "security concerns".

A widely-circulated video at the time featured various Muslim women, most of whom were donning conservative religious "modesty" dress, denouncing Hirsi Ali as an Islamophobe associated with the far-right. An online petition signed by 400 people accused her of being too "divisive". In one sense they were correct. Dividing extremist Muslims from ordinary moderates and liberal Muslims was part of her agenda. She is open about her opposition to Islamist ideologues and does indeed want to divide them from Muslim communities, rather than giving them carte blanche to lead Muslim citizens into an ever more radical and illiberal form of Islam. She speaks with the aim of helping ordinary people to identify Islamist political gambits, and has the relevant background, education and expertise to do so.

As a teenager, Ayaan Hirsi Ali sympathised with the views of the Islamist Muslim Brotherhood, and chose to don a hijab. She also agreed with the fatwa proclaimed against British Indian writer Salman Rushdie in response to the representation of the prophet Muhammad in his novel *The Satanic Verses.* In 1992 Ayaan travelled from Kenya to visit her family who were in Düsseldorf and Bonn, Germany. She eventually went to the Netherlands to escape an alleged arranged marriage. Once there, she requested political asylum and obtained a residence permit. Thirteen years later Hirsi Ali became an MP. She received repeated death threats over her challenges to Islam's treatment of women, and consequently spent time living under 24-hour police guard. Hirsi Ali left the Netherlands for the United States in May 2006 in the wake of a bitter row which broke out when she admitted lying about her age and name in her Dutch asylum request. She has continued to research and critique political Islam, most recently publishing a 105-page report titled **The Challenge of Dawa** for the Hoover Institute.

When ordinary Muslims, wishing to distance themselves from intolerant manipulators, praise Islam as "a religion of peace", the extremists seize representative status for this glorious religion whose image has been sanitised by their Muslim opponents. Jihadis do the dirty work and ordinary Muslims (and their Western sympathisers) then sanitise their image. Illiberal theocrats are Islam's self-appointed representatives and posture as defenders of "Muslims" as though this were a single homogeneous group. The wording of the petition against Hirsi Ali exemplifies their presumption to speak for all Muslims: "Against a backdrop of increasing global Islamophobia, Hirsi Ali's divisive rhetoric simply serves to increase hostility and hatred towards Muslims," the petition read. Hirsi Ali is not opposed to liberal Muslims, but only to

Islamism's stealth theocrats. The ordinary secular Muslim's well-meaning attempts at distancing themselves by claiming that most Muslims are peaceful only ends up serving Islamists and has effectively become a powerful weapon in their rhetorical armoury. This is not the intention of ordinary Muslims, but the effects are the same.

Hirsi Ali is clear in her policy recommendations that protection of the religious freedom and rights of Muslim individuals who are *not* engaged in Islamist *dawa* must be integral to her recommended policy shift. But she is adamant that the now obvious failure of two previous U.S. administrations to effectively counter radical Islamism resulted from their insistence on separating moderate, tolerant Islam from a supposedly tiny minority who practice "violent extremism". This theoretical separation only assists the agents of *dawa*.

Hirsi Ali explains that the policy of drawing a sharp distinction between a "tiny" group of extremists and an "overwhelming" majority of moderate Muslims has been one of the most damaging strategic errors since 9/11. The insistence that radical Islamists have "nothing to do with Islam" has only led to further policy errors. She recommends instead that those who wish to stop the spread of political Islam make a more effective distinction between 'Mecca Muslims', whose roots lay in the spiritual phase of Islam's historical development, and 'Medina Muslims' who give more weight to Qur'anic verses revealed after Muhammad's move to Medina, which represent the political and militaristic phase of his later career.

In the Medina of Muhammed's time, the focus was on collective submission, not individual rights. These concepts were enshrined in Sharia law manuals that remain valid to this day. Generally, Islamic activists who favour the strengthening of Sharia law in society, rather than those who would prefer to reform and modernise it, have prevailed in Islam's internal ideological battle – at least so far.

Some estimates put the proportion of the world's Muslims who are Islamists at 10-15%. Out of 23% of the global population, that implies more than 160 million individuals – not a number that fits well with the "tiny minority" rhetoric. Clarion Project, the US-based political Islam monitoring organisation, published statistics that further bust the myth that extremists are a miniscule set of unaffiliated individuals aggrieved over a lack of employment opportunities or craving a stronger sense of identity. According to European counter-terrorism coordinator Giles de Kerchove, there are as many as 35,000 "radicals" in the UK, and of those some 3,000 have been on MI5's radar. Since the new millennium, 126 people have been killed in the UK in terrorist attacks, according to figures from the Global Terrorism Database.

A fundamental problem, says Hirsi Ali, is that the majority of otherwise peaceful and law-abiding Muslims are unwilling to break ranks and repudiate or even so much as acknowledge the theological warrant for intolerance embedded in their own religious texts. While there is an important emergent group of "modifying Muslims" the statistics show that assimilation to secularism has not happened and in fact the change is in the other direction, with almost 60 per cent of European Muslims surveyed claiming that Muslims should return to the roots of Islam and 65 per cent believing that religious rules are more important than the laws of the country in which they reside. More than a fifth of Muslim Americans say that there is a great deal or fair amount of support for extremism in the Muslim American community.

Every time a person of influence recites, "Islam is a religion of peace" Islamists are given great PR and more protection. As Denis MacEoin has argued:

To see extremist Islam as a "perversion" of Islam misses an important point. The politically correct insistence that radical versions of Islam somehow pervert an essentially peaceful and tolerant faith forces policy-makers and legislators, church leaders, rabbis, interfaith workers and the public at large to leave to one side an important reality. Flatly, Islam in its original and classic forms has everything to do with today's radicals and the violence they commit. The Qur'an is explicit in its hatred for pagans, Jews and Christians. It calls for the fighting of holy war (jihad) to conquer the non-Muslim world, subdue it, and gradually bring it into the fold of Islam. Islam has been at war with Europe since the seventh century.[15]

It is rather odd, therefore, that Western leaders from Barack Obama to David Cameron and Hillary Clinton have all repeated the axiom "Islam is a religion of peace" as if they were qualified theologians, thus giving the official imprimatur to "peaceful" Islam, a religion that has been monopolised by intolerant ultra-conservatives and theocrats with whom these Western leaders do business.

On June 14, 2017 a glaring example of this happened when US Defense Secretary James Mattis met with representatives from Qatar to sign a $12 billion arms deal to provide the nation with 32 Boeing F-15QA fighter jets in spite of a 9 June public statement by Donald Trump in which he stated that Qatar is a "high-level" sponsor of terrorism. The deal was originally authorised by Congress when Barack Obama was in office. However, Trump apparently took no steps to prevent the deal.

Then there was the year-long investigation by BBC Arabic and a Danish newspaper which uncovered evidence that the UK defence giant BAE Systems made large-scale sales across the Middle East of sophisticated cyber-surveillance technology, including to many repressive governments who used them to locate and crush dissidents during the Arab Spring. For five years starting in 2011, British arms giant BAE sold the systems to a range of oppressive states including Saudi Arabia, the UAE, Qatar, Oman, Morocco and Algeria, a new investigation just revealed. The systems will enable these governments to track the physical whereabouts of their citizens and read and listen to most communications.[16]

It should not surprise us, then, if the U.S. establishment gives Dalia Mogahed, Linda Sarsour, and Ibrahim Hooper their status as chief representatives of normative Islam. Hooper is the national communications director and spokesperson for The Council on American-Islamic Relations (CAIR), a group identified by the Justice Department as a Muslim Brotherhood entity and designated as terrorists by the United Arab Emirates (UAE).[17] Sarsour has been involved in campaigning against the award-winning movie *Honour Diaries*, which showcases the struggle of nine women's-rights activists, some of them Muslim, as they campaign against honour violence and female genital mutilation. She has also tweeted positively about Sharia law's interest-free loans while neglecting to mention its hudud punishments and inequality towards women, and has made derogatory public remarks about feminist ex-Muslim Hirsi Ali, whose liberal credentials far outstrip her detractor's.

Dalia Mogahed, a Muslim hijabi who was an adviser to President Obama for Muslim affairs and a member of the U.S.-Muslim Engagement Project's "Leadership Group", is an oft-cited specialist in Muslim-American relations and has supported Sharia law compliance as a form of "gender justice" for women.[18] She has constantly used her role as a chief spokesperson for Muslims to mainstream the claim that "Muslims" are victims of oppression and smears, thus poisoning the well for legitimate critics of Islamism, a tactic that is working in spades for the promotion of soft Islamism. She has also used the rhetoric of race to imply that Muslims are a racial minority equivalent to African Americans. A case in point was her response in the *New York Daily News* to the May 2017 terror attack at the Ariana Grande concert in Manchester. In her article, titled "Don't Ask Muslims to Condemn Terror", she argued,

> "Imagine if white folks were collectively suspected of condoning the actions of Dylann Roof, who walked into that black church in Charleston and shot and killed African Americans in supposed defense of the white race."

This kind of language will no doubt play well with an anti-racist liberal American audience, but it not only misrepresents as "white" all of those who want Muslim leaders to condemn terrorism, but also defines followers of a religious ideology as a *racial* group. This statement also had the usual effect of conflating all Muslims as victims of white bigotry, thus turning the "real" victims of the Manchester attack into Muslims *simpliciter*, when the truth is that the actual victims (maimed and killed) were mostly white British Ariana Grande fans.

The British establishment's relationship to "Muslims" is similarly slanted towards Islamist groups. Sophisticated soft Islamism disseminated by organisations like the iERA (Islamic Education and Research Academy), essentially the movement's public relations arm, promotes Islamist norms through the discourse of diversity, multiculturalism and inter-faith outreach.[19] Meanwhile MEND keeps the victimhood leitmotif spinning, defining its political aims as combating Islamophobia.[20] Despite being found to host hate-speakers linked to the Islamist movement, the iERA has not had its charitable status revoked by the UK's Charity Commission.[21] Hate speech is a problematic concept, but where laws against it exist they should be applied consistently.

Likewise, mainstream British newspapers have unquestioningly repeated reports issued by Islamophobia watchdog **Tell Mama.** The organisation claimed steep rises in "Islamophobic incidents" following the slaughter of drummer Lee Rigby in Woolwich in May 2013. **Tell Mama**, which in 2012 alone received £375,000 in taxpayers' money, made sweeping claims about "a sustained wave of attacks" but failed to mention that 57 percent of the 212 reports referred to "attacks" that took place only online, mainly offensive postings on Twitter and Facebook, or that a further 16 percent of the 212 reports had not been verified. Not all the online abuse even originated in Britain. None of it resulted in hospital treatment of any of the victims.

Even if we set aside the illiberal concept of emotional policing that "hate crime" implies (as applied to speech), there was no concrete evidence of a post-Brexit spike in "hate crime" either. As *Sp!ked* editor Tim Black has pointed out[22], this did not stop the media constantly repeating and alluding to it, without mentioning that the alleged spike was created by (1) the official[23] (and unofficial) solicitation of reports of hate crime after the referendum (because if you ask people to report something, you're obviously going to get an increase in people reporting something); and (2) the police hate-crime-recording criteria, which stipulates that "the perception of the victim [is]... the defining factor in determining whether an incident is a hate incident... The victim does not have to justify or provide evidence of their belief, and police officers or staff should not directly challenge this perception."[24] The authorities first suggestively solicited people to report hate-crime to a dedicated hotline after the EU referendum, then automatically treated all the reports as crimes regardless of evidence. If I were an Islamist propagandist, I know what I'd do.

The pseudo-Left, kowtowing to Salafi-Islamism's mythological Muslim monoculture and thoroughly enraptured by its victim narrative, stereotypes Europeans in ways that they would never accept vis-à-vis their uniformly innocent "exotic" counterparts. White Westerners, even those born after the 1960's, are homogeneously characterised as "colonialist", "Eurocentric" or "privileged" irrespective of their behaviour or social positioning. In an atmosphere of obsessive Western self-loathing over colonialism and imperialism, Swedish-Bangladeshi journalist Tasneem Khalil has taken a reflective step back to note that religion is itself a "gift" of colonialism.[25] Likewise, Moroccan-French journalist Zineb Al Rhazoui urged delegates at a 2017 Secularism Conference in London[26] to bear in mind that Islam is itself imperialist. Islam divides the world into two territorial entities: Dar al-Harb (the House of War) and Dar al-Islam (the House of Islam). Etymologically Islam means "submission" and all those who do not submit to Islamic Law are relegated to the territory of war and jihad. This is not Al Rhazoui's subjective interpretation but the content of the Quranic text itself.

Marnia Lazreg has also made the case for thinking of contemporary Algerian Islamism as a colonising force. Islamists turn colonialism into an ahistorical, demonised category with which all of their opponents, but especially post-colonial states are identified.[27] Meanwhile, their own mission is experienced as an alien force imposed on the lived Algerian Islam across centuries. It is itself a project of cultural and psychological colonisation, not unlike the French "civilising mission" of the its past.

However, Western Europeans will apparently go to any length to relieve their craving for redemption and to satiate their addiction to the good feelings that flow from amour-propre. In his book *The Strange Death of Europe*, Douglas Murray recounts a prescient insight from French novelist Michel Houllebecq's novel *Submission*:

> "...the novel's truest conceit is the depiction of a class of politicians across the political divide so keen to be seen above all as 'anti-racist' that they end up flattering and ultimately handing over their country to the worst and most swiftly growing racist movement of their time." (p. 283)

Anglo-American culture has allowed intolerance to become more acceptable than tolerance. Fear and intimidation have replaced political persuasion – civilised debate, argument, or even satire – as the way to "convince" opponents and change their behaviour. Both hard (terrorist) and soft Islamism (its apologia) have together turned even atheists into theocracy's spokespeople, even its proud, arrogant defenders. Although they will do so eventually, Islamists do not need to win political elections to dominate the culture. They have already changed our behaviour through intimidation and *ad hominem* attacks.

Few Western Europeans dare to criticise political Islam or extremism. They know the consequences only too well. At worst, genuine liberals face extra-judicial punishment. At best, they face ostracism and/or stigmatisation from colleagues, close friends or relatives. There is not even the possibility of being a martyr if the very people for whose values you choose to die think that you are against the values they hold dear. Islam has won the battle of ideas. It is only a matter of time before this suffocating conformity is transformed into full-blown theocracy through the ballot box and the blunt instrument of law.

Notes

[1] *An Open Letter to Imam Ajmal Masroor from Akmal Safwat, M.D., co-founder of Democratic Muslims of Denmark.*
[2] The Federation of Student Islamic Societies. Within the National Union of Students, FOSIS is now the biggest voting bloc by far, commanding more than a quarter of the conference floor. The President of the NUS, Malia Bouattia, is also its first Muslim. She has called for dismantling of the Government's counter-terrorism strategy, Prevent.
[3] Alexandra Topping, Nishaat Ismail and Shiv Malik, "British Muslims Condemn Terror Laws for Creating 'Witch-Hunt' Against Islam", *The Guardian*, Weds, 11 March, 2015, accessed on 18 June, 2017 at

https://www.theguardian.com/world/2015/mar/11/british-muslims-terror-laws-witch-hunt-islam-cage-hizb-ut-tahrir

[4] 'Muslim Community Writes to House of Lords Over the New CTS Bill' at Hizb ut-Tahrir Britain, January 26, 2015, accessed on 18 June, 2017 at http://www.hizb.org.uk/viewpoint/muslim-community-writes-to-the-house-of-lords-over-the-new-cts-bill/

[5] 'Amnesty International Responds to Questions About CAGE' at Amnesty International UK website, accessed on 18 June, 2017 at https://www.amnesty.org.uk/amnesty-international-responds-questions-about-cage

[6] Milne, Seamus, Woolwich attack: If the whole world's a battlefield, that holds in Woolwich as well as Waziristan, *The Guardian*, 20 December, 2013.

[7] 'Muslim Reformers Versus Islam Apologists: a Brief Field Guide' at *Conatus News*, June 14, 2017, accessed on June 18, 2017 at https://conatusnews.com/muslim-reformers-versus-islam-apologists/

[8] Malik, Kenan, See: https://kenanmalik.wordpress.com/2012/04/11/a-book-in-progress-part-15-politics-morality-and-the-haitian-revolution/

[9] Sheikh Ibn Baz, *Words of Advice Regarding Da'wah: From the Noble Shaykh*, (Birmingham: Al Hidaayah, 1998).

[10] According to a May 1991 memorandum written by Mohamed Akram, a.k.a. Mohamed Adlouni, for the Shura Council of the Muslim Brotherhood on the general strategic goal for the Muslim Brotherhood in North America, the process of settlement is a "Civilization-Jihadist Process" with all that the word means. [emphasis mine]

[11] Ibid. Accessed at: https://www.investigativeproject.org/document/20-an-explanatory-memorandum-on-the-general

[12] Ibid.

[13] Daniel Pipes, "Interview with Hisham Kabbani: 'The Muslim Experience in North America is Unprecedented,'" *Middle East Quarterly*, June 2000, www.danielpipes.org/6337/muhammad-hisham-kabbani-muslim

[14] Vidino, Lorenzo, "Aims and Methods of Europe's Brotherhood", MEMRI, special dispatch 447, December 6, 2002, www.memri.org/reports/leading-sunni-sheikh-yousef-al-qadaradhawi-and-other-sheikhs-herald-coming-conquest-rome , 22-44. See also Vidino, L., *The New Muslim Brotherhood in the West* (New York: Columbia University Press, 2010).

[15] MacEoin, Denis, 'No Tolerance for Extremism' at Gatestone Institute, June 16, 2017 accessed on 17 June 2018 at https://www.gatestoneinstitute.org/10536/tolerance-extremism

[16] BBC News, 15 June, 2017, 'How BAE Sold Cyber-Surveillance Tools to Arab States' accessed on 17 June at http://www.bbc.co.uk/news/world-middle-east-40276568

[17] 'CAIR Met With Congress 325 Times in 2016' by Ryan Mauro, *The Counter Jihad Report*, posted July 13, 2016. Accessed at https://counterjihadreport.com/tag/muslim-brotherhood/page/43/ on 6 June, 2017.

[18] 'Anatomy of a Smear', by Jeffrey Godlberg, Oct 26, 2009, *The Atlantic*, accessed at https://www.theatlantic.com/international/archive/2009/10/anatomy-of-a-smear/29022/ on 6 June, 2017.

[19] Sara Kahn, The Battle for British Islam, (London: Saqi Books, 2016), p. 64 and 'Evangelising Hate', *Council of Ex-Muslims of Britain*, 2014, http://ex-muslim.org.uk/wp-content/uploads/2014/05/EvangelisingHate_Report_Web.pdf

[20] Sara Kahn, The Battle for British Islam, (London: Saqi Books, 2016), pp. 66-68.

[21] 'The Charity Commission Should Revoke the iERA's Charitable Status' by *Council of Ex-Muslims of Britain*, March 7, 2017, accessed at https://ramblingsofanulsterscot.com/posts/iera/charity-commission-revoke-ieras-charitable-status/#more-6134 on 6 June, 2017.

[22] Black, Tim, 'Putting Brexit back in Its Box', *Sp!ked* Online, 3 April, 2017, accessed on 21 June, 2017 at http://www.spiked-online.com/newsite/article/putting-brexit-back-in-its-box/19634#.WUpvaYUr4fp

[23] The carefully worded, suggestive call for the public to report "racial hate crime following the referendum result" came from Deputy Mayor of London Sophie Linden's office. Linden said she and the Mayor were "working to raise awareness of the ways of reporting hate crime to the police" in order that they could take action in prosecuting perpetrators and support victims. Yet they were creating "victims" with this public call for reports, not discovering them. The site also re-directed people to report to Tell Mama, a pro-Muslim organisation that had previously (in 2013) been found to have falsely inflated its statistics in reporting of anti-Muslim hate crime. See https://www.london.gov.uk/what-we-do/mayors-office-policing-and-crime-mopac/our-strategies/hate-crime/reporting-hate-crime

[24] See: College of Policing, the Professional Body for Policing manual titled 'Hate Crime Operation Guidance' at http://www.report-it.org.uk/files/hate_crime_operational_guidance.pdf

[25] Speaking at the 2017 the *International Conference of Freedom of Conscience and Expression in the 21st Century* in central London, UK.

[26] The 2017 the *International Conference of Freedom of Conscience and Expression in the 21st Century* in central London, UK.

[27] Howe, Stephen, 'Aftershock' in *New Humanist* magazine, Sept./Oct. 2011, Vol. 126., No. 5, p. 29.

CHAPTER FIVE

STRIKING AT THE LAST BASTION:
FREE EXPRESSION

On 7 January, 2015 two Islamist terrorists armed with assault rifles entered the offices of the French satirical newspaper *Charlie Hebdo*, murdered twelve people and left eleven others injured. Police launched an intensive manhunt. When the two perpetrators were eventually located, they had taken several hostages. A shootout with police left the two men dead. Several days later, in a display of solidarity with the two million demonstrators who converged on Paris, forty world leaders appeared to defend freedom of expression and to mourn the dead journalists. The assault on *Charlie Hebdo* ignited a worldwide discussion on the meaning and significance of free speech and made the question of whether this principle is adequately protected in European nation states more urgent than ever.

By 2015 the right to free expression had already become quite precarious in Europe. Dutch jurisprudence experts Paul Cliteur and Tom Herrenberg from Leiden University have compiled a thorough study of how and why free expression has become such a tenuous right in modern Europe. *The Fall and Rise of Blasphemy Law* (Leiden University Press, 2016) charts the West's numerous legal concessions to religious fundamentalism over the course of almost four decades. The books ten contributing authors demonstrate why blasphemy laws have enjoyed an upsurge in the last quarter of the twentieth century.

Their analysis of case studies reveals two trends: first, the West's gradual dissolution of blasphemy laws and, over recent decades, the *de facto* revival of bans on blasphemy by extrajudicial executions, political pressure on Western states and the international community and the semantic re-branding of blasphemy laws under the auspices of "group defamation" or "inciting hatred". Through a series of compromises, liberal legislators have been persuaded to release their grip on the once all-important distinction between protecting people and protecting ideas and have sanctioned a casuistic conflation of the two.

Historian David Nash[1] has examined the history of blasphemy in the West from the medieval period. The secular-inspired liberalism of the French and American revolutions, says Nash, saw the blasphemer primarily as an ideological dissident. With religion no longer the Law of the land, authorities had to find other grounds on which to defend restrictions. In England, the Foote Case of 1883-4 proved decisive. The presiding judge (Justice Coleridge), established a new test of blasphemy which was based not on the *matter* uttered, but instead highlighted the wounding of the aggrieved individual's *feelings* (i.e. the manner). Effectively this was the beginning of a shift in the law from treating the material as blasphemous to asking whether it could be proven to offend.

British barrister Ivan Hare has outlined the history of blasphemy under the English common law from its development by the courts in the seventeenth century.[2] Chief amongst the puzzling elements of the English blasphemy law he examines is the resurrection of blasphemy law in the late twentieth century in the 1977 *Whitehouse V Lemon* decision, which reversed two of the most important progressive strides that had been made over the previous century, first, by requiring an intention to insult or cause offence and also by confining the crime to cases where a "breach of the peace" was likely to result. This second criterion virtually invites any offended party to stamp his feet as loudly as possible.

In March 2008, only some three months after the *Jerry Springer* decision, in which the High Court of Justice upheld a lower court's ruling that the play, "in context" could not be considered as blasphemous, Baroness Andrews introduced clauses into the House of Lords (by way of an amendment to the Criminal Justice and Immigration Bill), which would abolish the offences of blasphemy and blasphemous libel, thus ending 350 years of legal history. But the change was arguably a semantic one, and had little effect in principle because the Racial and Religious Hatred Act that had come into force on 1 October, 2007 had *already* by then conflated persons and beliefs in its definition of "religious hatred".

The replacement of straightforward blasphemy laws with "incitement to religious hatred" would ostensibly equalise the status of *all* religious groups before the law, but in so doing this move produced even worse new laws that conflated the concept of blasphemy with the concept of hate crime. Because this framing of the law implied that blasphemy was akin to racism, this reconfiguration of old laws gave a dangerous cultural legitimacy to laws that would have seemed incredible only fifteen years earlier. Hate crime (initially conceived to protect *biologically* defined minorities from discrimination), was amalgamated with protection of *ideologically* defined minorities. The racialisation of ideology became official.

For most of the twentieth century the laws of blasphemy were on the books but remained dormant as a "dead letter" while the culture modernised and progressed. However, by the century's end mass communication had brought multiple religions into proximity and supranational agencies came under increased pressure to address legal religious privileges. In addition, the West's prioritisation of individual liberties clashed with the Islamic emphasis on collectivism and community.

The maelstrom that followed the 1989 publication of Salman Rushdie's *The Satanic Verses* highlighted the need to confront the underlying inequalities in existing blasphemy laws. Finding themselves unwilling to relinquish blasphemy law *tout court*, which would have removed protection (and privilege) from state religion, European states opted instead to offer wider protection for minority religions to bring it up to par with the official state religion.

International Pressure

In recent decades polemics like the Rushdie affair have become an incentive for subverting the content and universality of the fundamental human right of freedom of religion and belief. Religious freedom has been absorbed into policies protecting the reputation of religions against defamation, which has severe consequences for the normative framing of this right. Author Mirjam van Schaik has provided a trenchant analysis[3] of resolutions and international documents drafted by the Organisation of Islamic Cooperation (OIC), the self-proclaimed representative body of the Universal Ummah: a community of more than 1.5 billion Muslims.

The OIC considers itself the "collective voice of the Muslim world" and is the second largest intergovernmental organisation after the United Nations. In 2011 the OIC created an advisory body, the Independent Permanent Human Rights Commission (IPHRC), which has the legal authority to oversee human rights in OIC member states. Since 2013 the OIC has had an official representative office for the European Union in Brussels. For several decades the OIC has disrupted the universality of the Universal Declaration of Human Rights and its framework.[4] The core of the OIC's view of human rights can be gleaned from its own Islamic human rights document, the Cairo Declaration on Human Rights in Islam (CDHRI), adopted in 1990, which declares that all human rights must be addressed from an Islamic perspective and all rights and freedoms are subject to Islamic law (Sharia).

In 2005, the OIC prepared a ten-year action plan for the Muslim Ummah to achieve its renaissance, in order to (inter alia) project the true image and noble values of Islam. Section VIII of the action programme stated that the 2005 establishment of the IPHRC had to be consistent with the principles of the much older Cairo Declaration, which did not even recognise the fundamental right of freedom of religion. This casts doubt on how far it represented a substantial "renaissance". The action programme made all human rights relative to Islamic law and specified that they must comply with it. The Ten-Year Programme of Action on the topic of human rights has since been extended to the year 2025.

The OIC's current charter was adopted in 2008, three years after the formation of the Ten-Year Programme of Action. The current charter was adopted by the Eleventh Islamic Summit in March 2008, which aimed to revitalise Islam's role in the world. It no longer refers to the Cairo Declaration and its notion of Sharia law. Perhaps this is not an accident. The wording of the new charter requires careful analysis because it has the appearance of adhering to the United Nations charter. However, on closer inspection, all of its commitments are explicitly constrained by the stipulation that such commitments need to be in accordance with the constitutional and legal systems of the particular member states. In general, these legal systems are theocratic and Islam is constitutionally entrenched. This exercise in political casuistry has only created *religious legitimacy* for the OIC members to escape their UN human rights obligations.

Equally relevant is article 1 of the new charter which states the OIC's objective "to protect and defend the true image of Islam" and to "combat defamation of Islam" – objectives that have been formally enshrined in their charter and lend them an air of legitimacy. Mirjam van Shaik contextualises the OIC's semantic constraints on human rights by examining **three key stages** that led to the introduction of the concept of "defamation of Islam" into the UN Human Rights Council. The first of these developments has to do with the defence of the image of Islam. The second involves consequences of the fatwa against Salman Rushdie, and the third consists in the reprimands several of the OIC member states received in various UN fora.

i. The image of Islam

The OIC's concerns over the image of Islam came into focus during the third Islamic Summit Conference in Mecca in 1981. During this Summit the members of the OIC agreed to

"develop ... mass-media and information institutions, guided in this effort by the precepts and teachings of Islam, in order to ensure that these media and institutions will have an effective role in reforming society, in a manner that helps in the establishment of an international information order characterised by justice, impartiality and morality, so that our nation may be able to show to the world its true qualities, and refute the systematic media campaigns aimed at isolating, misleading, slandering and defaming our nation." (Mecca Declaration, 25-28 Jan, 1981, Final Communiqué, para. 6)

Van Shaik points out that "nation" has to be understood in this context as Islam in general. Second, it is not the image of Islam for Muslims *within OIC countries* that is stressed so much as the perception of Islam by *non-Muslims* globally.

ii. Responses to Rushdie

In response to Rushdie's book, in 1989 the OIC called for all members of the international community to ban the book and "take necessary measures to protect the religious feelings of others." (Eighth Islamic Conference of Foreign Ministers, March 1989). Two years later the OIC adopted a unified stand on the attack of Islamic sancties and values and called for an international legal instrument to protect their religion. During the 1994 Summit the OIC reiterated their call to "project the correct image of Islam" and again at the Islamic Summit in 1997 they expressed their wish for a group of experts to take up this cause. Eventually this led to the launch of the "defamation of religion" resolution in 1999 in the UN.

iii. Reprimands and OIC Member States

Ironically, the calls for the protection of Islam's "image" in the world that so occupied the energies of the OIC in the nineties coincided with critical reports on incidents and state actions in several OIC member states from the UN special rapporteurs on Religious Intolerance as well as from the rapporteurs on Freedom of Religion or Belief. Saudi Arabia's response to the special rapporteurs was a fierce example of the ploy that has now become commonplace (I like to call it "the perp-victim flip"). Instead of responding to accusations of human rights violations levelled against them, Saudi Arabia went on the offensive, insinuating that *they* were the real victims: the "disturbing disinformation on Islam and the Islamic people" was "a sort of a new crusade". Yet the "disturbing information" was about how they had violated the human rights of individuals within their states. One cannot help but wonder whether the aforementioned group of experts had played a role in this new persecution-styled response to UN reports that conflicted with the "image" they wanted to project.

The OIC's 1999 introduction of their draft resolution on "Defamation of Islam" contained the all-important conflation of religion and race. The resolution adopted liberal language redolent of Western critiques of racism (hatred, intolerance, discrimination, intolerance, intimidation) but applied it to the protection of Islam (an ideology and set of values). Instead of dismissing the OIC's whole line of reasoning, the EU member states took an accommodating stance and decided to correct the exclusivity of religious protection by broadening the protection to *all religions*. This move gave the OIC room to introduce the religious defamation concept and in 2001 Pakistan, acting on behalf of the OIC, introduced a resolution titled: "Combating defamation of religion as a means to promote human rights, social harmony and religious and cultural diversity." Ironically, Pakistan today is one place where religious and cultural diversity are *least* tolerated and where so-called social "harmony" (uniformity) is a political fiction manufactured by violent suppression of apostasy and dissent.

Despite the fact that this resolution served to protect religions rather than the human rights of individual adherents of these religions, the resolution was adopted by 28 votes in favour with 15 against, and 9 abstentions. This set the stage for what would follow in subsequent years. References to the concept of defamation of religion increased considerably in the UN and the OIC stepped up efforts to criminalise religious defamation, despite the absence of any definition of "defamation" in any of their resolutions. The emphasis in the OIC's resolutions is on the protection of religions but fails to explain how one religion can profess its own beliefs without defaming the central tenets of other religions. By their very nature religions are defamations of other religions, and atheism or humanism are inherently defamatory insofar as they discredit the central tenets of belief. The rights of religious minorities are central to the mandate on freedom of religion, and the idea of protecting religions is at odds with the freedom of religion and with human rights in general. Freedom of religion is meaningless if it does not include freedom from religion. But individual liberties were to be demoted in favour of group belief systems. Religious defamation is an ambiguous concept that tends to allow the attenuation of human rights to be hidden within the vagueness of the concept.

Resolution 16/18 – when the walls came tumbling down

On March 24, 2011 The United Nations Human Rights Commission adopted Resolution 16/18. It was a crucial moment in the dismantling of the liberal concept of freedom of religion. The OIC had introduced the resolution on "Combating intolerance, negative stereotyping and stigmatisation of, and discrimination, incitement to violence and violence against persons based on religion or belief." This document has played a guiding function in the UN and received the backing of the United States, which stated that it was "pleased" and hoped the consensus would become a blueprint to "promote respect for religious differences" in the international community.[5] The Algerian representative, in what can only be described as a piece of bald-faced propaganda, described the move as a contemporary translation of Martin Luther King Jr.'s "I Have a Dream" vision.

Only several months after the adoption of resolution 16/18, the OIC's Council of Foreign Ministers adopted a new resolution on the topic of combating religious defamation and resolved to remain seized on the matter as a top priority at all OIC Summits and Councils of Foreign Ministers. In her trenchant analysis of the 16/18 resolution, Mirjam van Shaik observes that while there is no longer explicit reference to the "defamation of religion" concept, making it look as though the aim is to protect the individual rather than religions, there is still an implicit emphasis on one religion in particular and even more concepts are included which have more or less the same ambiguity as the defamation of religion concept (e.g. "derogatory stereotyping", "negative profiling" and "stigmatisation").

To facilitate implementation of Resolution 16/18, the Istanbul Process, a series of high-level meetings, was formed in July 2011. The first of these meetings was hosted by the OIC and chaired by Hillary Clinton. This was followed in December 2011 by another meeting (behind closed doors) in Washington, again co-chaired with the OIC. This time Clinton had a more prominent role and stated "together [with the OIC] we have begun to overcome the false divide that pits religion sensitivities against freedom of expression."[6] Annual sessions took place in London, Geneva, Doha, Jeddah and Saudi Arabia in the following years.

In 2013 the criminalisation of hate speech was put on the agenda, leading to more debates over the line between free criticism of religion and hate speech. Creative semantics and emotionally charged rhetoric had already been used to define free expression that could be interpreted as "denigrating" sacred symbols and personalities as "incitement to religious hatred", which was now being re-framed as a matter of identity: "It needs to be understood that people in some parts of the world tend to identify themselves more with a particular religion than elsewhere."[7]

A year after the adoption of resolution 16/18, the Islamic Educational, Scientific, and Cultural Organisation (established by the OIC) announced that the International Federation of Journalists "should respect Islamic religious symbols and halt desecration of them."[8] Mirjam van Shaik's research ultimately reveals a back-and-forth struggle between universal human rights and the supremacy of Islamic law *over* human rights. Her analysis shows that while the OIC have managed their image carefully to give the impression that they are falling closer into step with international law and human rights, the substantial direction of change has been in the opposite direction, with the international community gradually marching to the tune of Islamic demands while compromising the universality of freedom of religion.

International Cooperation on Migration

The Budapest Process is, according to its own website, a consultative forum with over 50 governments and 10 international organisations aiming at developing comprehensive and sustainable systems for orderly migration. It is one of the longest-standing cooperation frameworks on migration for Europe and its eastern neighbours and during its more than 20 years of operation, the Budapest Process has developed from an information sharing tool between European countries in a pre-EU enlargement setting to a far-reaching Europe-Asia forum for improving migration management.

According to 'The Heart of Asia – Istanbul Process' website, The United States and over 20 other nations and organisations serve as "supporting nations" to the process. On April 26, 2013, Almaty,

Kazakhstan, hosted the third Ministerial Conference of the Istanbul Process. The April meeting focused on the creation of "Silk Routes Partnership for Migration" to promote further dialogue and cooperation on the issue of migration. The Budapest Process (from 19 April, 2013) provided the groundwork for the following week's Istanbul Ministerial Declaration on *A Silk Routes Partnership for Migration*. The Declaration outlines its vision for integration thus:

II. Integration

a) Strengthening integration processes for migrants and refugees,

b) Working for the successful integration of migrants and refugees and their active participation in receiving communities through the provision of adequate integration tools and measures,

c) Supporting receiving communities in welcoming migrants and refugees as well as taking action to encourage their active participation in the social and cultural life of the receiving communities,

d) Promoting host governments' cooperation with civil society and diaspora communities in both monitoring and countering incidents of discrimination, racism and xenophobia.

The language here is vague enough that 'integration' can be understood as happening in either direction. While there is mention of countering discrimination, racism and xenophobia, there is no mention of countering religious extremism, terrorism, religiously-based homophobia, child marriage, honour violence, or female genital mutilation. It is not clear that newly arrived migrants or refugees are expected to integrate into the host culture, or whether the host culture will integrate **for** (into) *the migrant's* origin culture. No reference is made to factors that facilitate assimilation, develop *the migrant's* intercultural communication skills, or aid his adaptation to the new host culture.

Rather, the language suggests that the receiving culture will be the one that is actively "supported" in curtailing its attitudes towards new arrivals, and in "welcoming" the newcomers. This leaves many questions about the future direction of integration unanswered, which makes censoring public debate about it at this historical junction particularly incongruous with the democratic process.

Dutch blasphemy law and extrajudicial enforcement

Leiden University Dutch Legal experts Paul Cliteur and Tom Herrenberg have analysed Dutch blasphemy law, which entered into force in 1932 and was finally repealed in 2014.[9] The Dutch situation has to be seen in light of events surrounding the 2004 murder of Theo Van Gogh, which resulted in the Dutch pro-multiculturalism intelligentsia adopting a submissive attitude towards radical Islam. This was evident in the cases of Van Gogh, Ayaan Hirsi Ali and Pim Fortuyn – all of whom had been vocal advocates of Voltaire's full-blooded definition of tolerance. As Douglas Murray points out, "until he got to the subject of Islam, there was nothing remotely "right-wing" about Pim Fortuyn."[10] A homosexual and Marxist university professor who was a spokesman of almost any socially libertarian policy, Fortuyn only underwent this re-definition as "right-wing" by his political opponents when he began to win popularity in the run-up to the 2002 election.

The content-neutral tolerance for all ideas championed by classical liberals and social libertarians differs radically from the more anaemically conceived "multiculturalist tolerance". The latter prioritises polite silence and self-censorship over lively and sometimes vigorous debate. This more limited, selective tolerance has permitted "peace" to triumph over free expression…but at a cost. The irony is that the above-mentioned human targets of violent intolerance have been willing to pay the ultimate price for their liberty, while the multiculturalist "left" have been unwilling even to pay the modest cost of discomfort or embarrassment that comes with the occasional verbal tussle. Fortuyn (himself a homosexual) had, before being murdered, reserved the right to say, "Islam is a backward religion" but he also accepted that conservative Muslim imams and other orthodox religious believers had the right to say, "homosexuals are sick".

Around the turn of the new millennium, in Dutch academia, as in the rest of Western Europe, the study of radicalised religion fell out of fashion and was dwarfed by Edward Said's criticism of orientalism.[11] European students were taught how to be guilty of Eurocentrism but no one minded if Pakistanis, Afghans or Tibetans were home-centric. Liking one's own way of life, it seemed, was a sin for which only "the West" should repent. Academics seemed to lose interest in what was happening in the real world around them and became obsessed with the past, or a selective reading of it, that focussed exclusively on the West's conquests of other peoples and never on its contributions to civilisation or human rights. Critical commentary on the prophet of Islam was invariably framed as an "attack on Islam" to which the true Muslim (apparently a very fragile being) must respond with violence. This way of presenting the issue was in tension with 1960's Dutch freethinking iconoclasm and scepticism towards authority. The open, critical cultural climate was eroded by the importation of Puritanism that came with a new wave of immigrants to the country. But this was also a violent form of Puritanism, as Van Gogh's murder so graphically attested.

Cliteur and Herrenberg explain that there are two general ways in which liberal multiculturalists can respond to this new phenomenon. Either they can adopt a welcoming posture towards the legal suppression of blasphemy, either as a gesture of "multicultural etiquette" or, pragmatically, to avoid terrorist attacks. One way of choosing this conciliatory option without appearing to openly endorse blasphemy laws is to target blasphemous utterances by incorporating them into more extensive laws against "incitement to hatred on religious grounds" and "defamation of a group of people on the basis of their religion". The latter of these accommodations to blasphemy law might seem harmless enough. But the authors caution that this type of legislation contains the potential to develop into a resurgence of blasphemy prohibitions. Thankfully, the Dutch state moved in the opposite direction and revoked provisions that protect religion and religious symbols as such. The Dutch chose to repeal their outdated blasphemy law in 2014 rather than expanding or pretending to modify it.

Early warning signs

Many of the debates on the role of religious fundamentalism that have become familiar to us in the post-9/11 geo-political landscape were foreshadowed in *Death of a Princess* (1980), a dramatised documentary about the execution of a Saudi princess who was accused of adultery. Paul Cliteur, Laetitia Houben and Michelle Slimmen have argued that this case set a precedent insofar as it represents the first large-scale attempt to stifle freedom of speech in European nation states on the ground that the film's content would offend religious sensibilities. This case study provides a clear illustration of the way in which theocratic dictatorships have successfully exerted pressure on liberal democracies, through economic boycotts or other coercive measures. Although the execution of the princess amounted to an "honour killing", the Anglo-American oil company Mobil Oil pressurised the United States to cease distributing the film after it had initially aired in June 1980. Even the non-commercial

American Public Broadcasting Service (PBS), which received funding from Mobil Oil for other programming, came under pressure from the U.S. Secretary of State, who apparently attempted to persuade the channel to put economic interests above fundamental human rights.[12]

With alarming resonance, characters in the film who defend the Saudi regime's barbarity do so on the same grounds as today's multiculturalist defenders of Islamism. A character named Samira deploys the "No True Scotsman" fallacy, a tactic that has been used repeatedly against critics of Islamism by everyone from Barack Obama to David Cameron. Those who say that draconian punishments and intolerance for dissent have "nothing to do with true Islam" start from the unstated premise that religion, in its most basic nature, is good. Whenever something bad seems to be connected to religion, this is apparently *not religious*. On that basis, the character Samira can say without irony that Saudi Arabia "isn't a Muslim country".[13]

Then there is the character Elsa Gruber who argues from an incoherent combination of cultural relativism and universalism – another form of argument that has become ubiquitous nowadays. On the one hand, genuine liberals who object to Islamic barbarism on the basis of human rights are morally scolded for imposing their Western values in a non-Western context. But presumably this "Orientalism" is objectively morally wrong, because there is a universal moral value in … uh… allowing others to live according to their own values (i.e. liberal tolerance and free expression are good things). But the response to Westerners when they judge non-Western states (e.g. when the latter kill dissidents) is that there is something absolutely morally wrong in issuing such a verdict against other cultures. The righteous relativist does not just claim that judging other cultures is distasteful from a particular cultural perspective. Rather, he thinks it *objectively* wrong in principle. Hence, there is no such thing as a consistent moral relativist.

Another character in Death of a Princess, Ms. Quataajy, is a mouthpiece for the brand of victim-blaming that became typical of responses to the *Charlie Hebdo* massacre: the princess had "brought it on herself".[14] She "should have known" what would befall her. She is responsible for the consequences of her behaviour. Mobil Oil used the same twisted logic when trying to persuade the American Public Broadcasting Service to cancel *Death of a Princess*: We all know that our Constitution protects free speech, but the press has an obligation to "be responsible", and so on.[15] Implicitly, "responsibility" has nothing to do with calling out gross violations of human rights and infringements of the principles for which countless generations of political philosophers and social activists have fought. Accordingly, there was something "irresponsible" about illuminating the cruel death of a young princess who did *nothing* wrong other than choose to live her own life.

The Fall and Rise of Blasphemy Law authors Cliteur, Houben and Slimmen return to the question of what any of this has to do with Islam and whether the princess's execution was mandated by the religion. There are several possible responses. The first is to say that theo-terrorism has nothing to do with Islam. The other is to say that it has everything to do with Islam. *Death of a Princess* does not, in contrast to other controversial films about Islamic tenets, hold Islam responsible for the execution. It is mainly Arab culture, as interpreted by those in power, which is held accountable.

So, we return to the question of how to establish what exactly belongs to a religion and what doesn't. It appears that the answer is always "up to us", as Samira seems to believe in the film when she proclaims, "This autocratic regime has nothing to do with Islamic thought, feeling or ideology." The same mantra is today repeated by politicians like Barack Obama who say that deplorable practices like terrorist attacks have nothing to do with Islam. The Dutch authors point out that it would be closer to the truth to say that while terrorist attacks do not have everything to do with Islam, it is equally unrealistic to claim that they have nothing to do with the religion.

Thirty-five years on from the cancelled screenings of the film, the position of women in Saudi Arabia has not significantly changed. After the American broadcaster PBS announced that it would air the film, Mobil Oil Company (a financier of some of PBS's other programming) stepped up the pressure. On 9 May the Secretary of State sent a letter to the President of PBS complaining about the possible consequences of screening the film in which he acknowledged the objections of the Saudis. Ultimately PBS did not buckle. It broadcasted the film, although many of their affiliate stations delayed or cancelled it.

Commercial interests also played an important part in the Dutch discussion about screening the film. Dutch MP's stressed the negative political and economic consequences, and insinuated that "responsibility" for what they considered a bad idea lay with the broadcasters, who should not offend the religious feelings of the Saudi royal family.[16] While the

Dutch broadcasting corporation did not succumb to this pressure, the importance given to the religious feelings of the offended parties that had been introduced into the discussion would play a huge role in all of the controversies – the Rushdie Affair, the Danish Cartoon Affair, the Rudi Carrell Affair, and the Charlie Hebdo Affair — that were then still to come.

Since the 1988 publication of Salman Rushdie's *The Satanic Verses* and Khomeini's "fatwa", clashes between a culture of civil liberties and theocratic extremism have expanded beyond novels to cartoons and video clips. Something that came up over and over again in the discussion of Rushdie's book was the notion that, as someone who came from a Muslim cultural background, Rushdie should have known better. This idea was voiced – more or less explicitly – by Rushdie critics Hugh Trevor-Roper, John le Carré, Roald Dahl and John Berger. Critiques by the latter two shared common ground with Iran's parliament speaker at the time, who said the solution to the crisis was to seize copies of Rushdie's book and burn them.

Official government reactions to Khomeini's presumption to exercise control over an individual not belonging to his jurisdiction were surprisingly tame. Only novelist Anthony Burgess had the prescience to observe that the Ayatollah's order to kill Rushdie on British soil was tantamount to a jihad. "It is", he said, "a declaration of war on citizens of a free country and as such it is a political act."[17] Burgess's reaction highlighted the really relevant issue of national sovereignty while British politicians Margaret Thatcher and Sir Geoffrey Howe deflected attention to the book's contents instead, and in Rushdie's view, began to play both sides in order to appear to defend free expression while keeping diplomatic relations with Iran on track. It took Ian Davidson to steer the discussion back on course. Writing in the *Financial Times*, he commented, "the only questions that are immediately relevant are whether Mr. Rushdie was legally entitled under British law to write and publish his book, and whether Ayatollah Khomeini is entitled to incite the murder of Mr. Rushdie."[18]

The Fall and Rise of Blasphemy Law provides trenchant analysis of Rushdie's critics, which is all the more important because their basic arguments have been repeatedly used against the Danish cartoonists, *Charlie Hebdo* journalists and other critics or satirists of Islamic ideology ever since. While historical iconoclasts from Nietzsche to Holbach to Freud (all of whom characterised religion in ways that could easily offend believers) are lauded, their contemporary equivalents (Dawkins, Hitchens, Onfray, Harris) are despised. Jonathan Swift and Voltaire were not criticised for their "tone", while Rushdie was subjected to the red hot embers of scandal for his.

Other commentators seem to think that the size of the religion, or the length of its established status, is a legitimate criterion for placing its tenets beyond criticism. It is bizarre to suppose that the right to criticise a religion diminishes in proportion to the power it wields. *The Fall and Rise of Blasphemy Law* authors rightly ask why it should not be the reverse in light of Lord Action's observation that power corrupts and absolute power corrupts absolutely.

We might also analyse the disparity between our submissiveness to the demands of Islamists and our relative assertiveness in the face of secular dictators. Why should we not take "responsibility" and show deference towards the feelings of the Leader of the Democratic People's Republic of Korea when we happily do so vis-à-vis the Supreme Leader of the Islamic Revolution in Iran?

What Rushdie's early critics had in common was their presumption that their weak response to *The Satanic Verses* controversy was exceptional – it was *just one man's* personal liberty that was at stake – and their compromises would not lead to the erosion of political liberty in general. Today we know better. Indeed, the Rushdie affair can be regarded as the *locus classicus* of a social phenomenon new to modern Western societies: censorship by terrorism, taboo and intimidation.

Testing the Utilitarian Grounds for Censorship

The need to address Islam's religious privilege came into focus in February 2017 when Denmark's state prosecution service decided to enforce the blasphemy section of its Criminal Code by fining a 42-year-old man who burned a copy of the Koran and posted a video of the act in a Facebook group. The blasphemy fine was especially troubling since the Danish authorities did not prosecute in a similar case when Christianity's sacred text was burned.

Denmark is one of the most liberal countries in Europe. In 2005 its prime minister Anders Fogh Rasmussen defended the now infamous publication of twelve cartoons of Mohammed, stating, "In Denmark, the freedom of speech and the freedom of the press is not up for negotiation."

During his weekly media briefing the prime minister further noted that the crisis was no longer about the twelve drawings in *Jyllands-Posten*. "It's about everything else and different agendas in the Muslim world. It's obvious that extremist circles exploit the situation."[19] As Munira Mirza wrote in response to the British newspapers' refusal to re-print the *Jyllands-Posten* cartoons of Mohammed, "... sympathetic lefty anti-racists who believe censorship will protect Muslims are actually missing the point. Many Muslims want the same freedoms as everyone else to debate, criticize and challenge their religion."[20] Few people seemed to mind that censorship protected only the most intolerant Muslims.

Danish freedom of expression deteriorated considerably after 2005, in part owing to intimidation and a chilling climate of fear, in which de facto blasphemy laws were enforced largely via extrajudicial execution. (e.g. In January 2010, Danish cartoonist Kurt Westergaard was attacked by an axe-wielding Somali man who had taken offense to the cartoons of the prophet Muhammad. When the man burst into his Aarhus home Westergaard took refuge in a security room, which saved his life.)

In February 2017, Denmark's state prosecution service decided to enforce the blasphemy section of its Criminal Code by fining a 42-year-old man who burned a copy of the Koran and posted a video of the act in a Facebook group. The blasphemy fine is especially troubling since the Danish authorities did not prosecute in a similar case when Christianity's sacred text was burned. Jacob Mchangama, a Danish lawyer who founded *Justitia*, a civil-liberties group that monitors freedom of expression across Europe, called out the double-standard that gives Islam special protection and said the blasphemy charge was a giant step backwards for his country. In response to the ruling, it could reasonably be asked whether previous terrorist attacks in Copenhagen have softened Denmark's once-robust tolerance for protest speech of the Koran-burning variety. But in June 2017 Danish lawmakers at last ended the country's 334-year-old blasphemy law.

Mill's "Mankind Minus One"

John Stuart Mill argued that mankind does not have the right to silence the individual – even when his ideas or opinions are shared by no one else. In their trenchant analysis[21] of the demise of free expression in a world of "theo-terrorism", Dutch legal experts Paul Cliteur, Tom Herrenberg and Bastiaan Rijpkema apply J.S. Mill's insights on the tyranny of prevailing opinion to the pressing question of whether a liberal state should tolerate even massively unpopular speech acts like that of Terry Jones, or for that matter the Danish Koran-burner.

The 2010 planned Quran-burning by American pastor Terry Jones was met with almost universal repulsion, from both Islamist and liberal ends of the spectrum. As such, Jones's symbolic speech act furnishes an ideal case study against which Mill's argument might be tested. The "mankind minus one" situation confronts us with an apparent moral dilemma between (1) the positive value of free speech and (2) the negative effects of its violent consequences. The values to be weighed in the balance are liberty and free expression on the one hand, and peace and security on the other.

The wording of a 2011 *Guardian* poll question implied that, if you believe that Jones, in burning the Koran, should be held responsible for reprisals such as deaths of UN staff in Afghanistan, then this is because his act is "a provocative blasphemy against others' beliefs." The way the poll question was framed required respondents who answered "yes" to accept the (unstated) premise that murder of innocents is an "understandable" response to provocative speech. From an ethics perspective, it appeared that the "crime" of burning a sacred book was equivalent to the crime of murder. Any basic ethical theory should take proportionality into account, i.e. the severity of the punishment should be equal to, but not greater than, the severity of the crime. But the question before us is not whether burning a Koran is equally harmful to the "victim" as murder is to its victims. Rather, it is whether the utility (practical usefulness) of not burning the book will be greater than the possible benefits of Jones actually burning the book. To be clear, we are asking whether (a) placing constraints on offensive speech *OR* (b) allowing people to express offensive opinions, will lead to greater happiness overall for the greatest number of people.

In utilitarian ethics, intentions are considered unimportant. The question of an agent's intention(s) is set aside. Since intentions are not relevant, and only consequences are taken into account, persons can (also) be held accountable for unintended consequences, such as how others respond to their actions or speech. First, this approach contradicts our most fundamental intuitions about moral agency. It presupposes that everyone is responsible for everything, even undesired or unforeseen outcomes of their actions. This means that we are responsible for both our own actions and the actions of others (for example, Adolph Hitler's Mum would be held morally accountable for killing millions because she birthed a baby who went on to become the architect of a pogrom). To morally attribute the actions of murderers on the other side of the world to Pastor Jones is to disregard the agency of those murderers and to render them innocent of their own choices. Utilitarianism suggests (un-persuasively) that a person bears the moral responsibility for the unwanted consequences that others attribute to their speech acts.

On the other hand, governments and pseudo-liberals have stressed that while provocative speakers or artists have a legal right to express provocative ideas, they should choose not to exercise this right if social disruption, fear and/or suffering will likely result. This implies that the freedom to express controversial ideas is relatively less important than safety, security and public order. It also erects a false dilemma by claiming that we cannot have *both* freedom of expression and safety and security but must choose between these two values.

Rule Utilitarians[22] might look to the long-term consequences of such a position. They could ask whether the long-term impact of adopting self-censorship as a general rule (rather than just in one instance) will lead to the greatest happiness for the greatest number. If governments were to pander to the wishes of intolerant terrorists by placing legal limits on free expression, then terrorists would only be vindicated in the use of violence and emboldened to continue its use. Thus, even the pragmatic, outcome-centred focus of utilitarianism leaves serious doubts. Utilitarian reasoning places all of the cards in the hands of those who threaten to use violence. The short-term victories that make utilitarian responses to terrorism alluring are unwise both practically and principally.

Back to the British Context

Rumy Hasan, a senior lecturer at University of Sussex, also provides insightful analysis of tensions between blasphemy law and freedom of expression in modern multicultural Britain.[23] In the wake of the Rushdie Affair, Hasan observes how public figures in Britain accepted and even helped to promote a gradual conflation of race/ethnicity with culture/religion. The political climate encouraged respect for (and recognition of) culture and religion, which were subsumed within discourses of race and ethnicity. This became a central part of the multicultural doctrine. This reasoning, he argues, became the slippery road to the extension of blasphemy laws. In the clash between freedom of expression and ethnic minority sensibilities, the former gave way to the latter.

The Satanic Verses affair had an extremely chilling effect on freedom of expression in a way that was specific to Islam and Muslims such that satirising Islam became the new taboo. Britain had acquired, through extra-judicial means, a de facto blasphemy law as self-censorship became the default position in the media, the arts and academia. The website *Islam surveyed* revealed that in January 2016 *The Guardian* decided to curb comments on certain subjects. Mary Hamilton, the executive editor of audience opinion, took the decision to close three topics to comments from the audience: race, immigration and Islam. This was blatant suppression of free speech, which is ironic because the *Guardian* describes its comment section as "Comment is Free" while in reality its censorial stance appears to be based on the offence of blasphemy.

Importantly, in the multicultural discourse migrants were not expected to conform to the norms of their host society, but conversely the indigenous society was required to show positive esteem for the migrants' cultures and religions. Exceptions to the norms of European culture became the new norm, and any attempt to hold on to the host culture's values came to be regarded as a grievous harm akin to racism. The underlying assumption was that for ethnic minorities, religion is far more important to their identity than cultural values are to anyone else in British society. This resulted in one-way tolerance that blatantly breached universalism. Hasan identifies this as a crucial factor in the increasing alienation of indigenous whites.

Like Mirjam van Shaik, Rumy Hasan has analysed the semantic shift that occurred in the 90's and post 9/11, when Muslim groups began campaigning to extend blasphemy law to curb perceived "Islamophobia". In 2004 the British National Party leader Nick Griffin was arrested for describing Islam as a "wicked, vicious faith" but was cleared of inciting racial hatred on the grounds that Islam is not a race or ethnicity. The Labour Party by then had come to rely on a de facto "Muslim bloc vote" to win key constituencies. Probably as a matter of political expediency, says Hasan, Labour introduced new amendments to existing legislation that would function as blasphemy provisions. In its 2005 general election manifesto, the Labour Party promised to introduce a Bill designed to outlaw "incitement to religious hatred". Without any serious debate, the role of religion was given decisive importance in the national identity. Euphemistic language such as "protection" and "tolerance" was used and the promised Bill was duly passed by Parliament in the form of The Racial and Religious Hatred Act 2006, which went into force on 1 October, 2007.

As with international legislation, the language is sufficiently vague to effectively outlaw virtually anything a believer finds offensive. The wording of sections 29B(1) and 29J are in conflict, and either could potentially cancel the other out – the question remains which one will be given precedence. The former stipulates that a person is guilty of the crime if he "displays any written material which is threatening" and "intends thereby to stir up religious hatred". The latter states, "Nothing in this section shall be read or given effect in a way which prohibits or restricts … expressions of antipathy, dislike, insult or abuse of particular religions or the beliefs or practices of their adherents." Hasan points out that the Act is, in effect, an extension of "race" to encompass "religion", which is why it was named the "Racial and Religious Hatred Act".

Muslim leaders in Britain, organised under the Muslim Action Forum (MAF), have also attempted to formulate a legal strategy to prevent insulting and derogatory publications depicting their Holy Prophet Muhammad. They started a petition signed by over 100,000 Muslims promoting this kind of censorship under the banner of "Global Civility". This euphemism adds another term to the ever-expanding lexicon deployed to curb free expression in a multi-faith society in which the minimum requirement is not to give offence to religious adherents.

The *Guardian*'s topic-specific selective censorship (described above) is consistent with the general approach of the UK media, as evidenced by the refusal of any mainstream media outlet to publish or show the Danish cartoons when the controversy exploded in 2005. Taking offense has become the first refuge of the censor and the media meekly complies. Hasan poignantly cites *On Liberty*, in which Mill reflects on the inconsistency in wanting free discussion while objecting to it being "pushed to an extreme". If the reasons for allowing extreme cases of free expression are *not* good then they are not good for any case at all, since free expression is intended *a forteriori* for those ideas which are up for debate, not for ones that are considered to be so certain as to need no further discussion. Hasan concludes that restoring the freedom of expression enjoyed four decades ago will require courage and determination, as well as the participation of the mainstream media and academia.

Online Censorship

In what can only be described as the ultimate irony, the German Chancellor's Cabinet on 5 April, 2017 approved a new bill that punishes social networking sites if they fail to swiftly remove content their laws make illegal, such as hate speech or defamatory fake news. Under the proposed new legislation, Facebook, Twitter and other social media networks will face a fine of up to 50 million Euros if they fail to remove content deemed as "hate speech" or "defamatory fake news".

Rationalising the censorship, German Justice Minister Heiko Maas stated, "Just like on the streets, there is also no room for criminal incitement on social networks."[24] He further justified the tough new rules by stating, "The internet affects the culture of debate and the atmosphere in our society. Verbal radicalisation is often a preliminary stage to physical violence." Due to its Nazi past, Germany bans public Holocaust denial and any overt promotion of racism.

Maas went on to say that measures to combat hate speech and so-called "fake news" will ultimately have to be taken at the European level if they are to be effective. The bill was widely described as a prophylactic against the kind of online invective that has allegedly risen since the recent entry of large numbers of migrants into Germany.

A Brief Analysis of Terminology

Those who defend Europe's internet censorship laws make constant reference to the illegality of the speech in question. There seems to be a vicious circle of question begging: when asked exactly what constitutes "hate speech" the reply is "illegal forms of speech", and when asked *why* these kinds of speech are illegal, the answer is that they are hate speech. The only thing that lends this definition some vague semblance of content is "incitement", a concept that assumes adult individuals are not responsible for their own actions anyway, since other people are apparently to be blamed for making them do things. The government would be better off not mentioning this deterministic concept if it really wants to find anyone guilty, since the idea of vicarious guilt (or transferred guilt) completely demolishes the bedrock premise of European law; namely, that individuals are responsible for *their own* behaviour and not for other people's choices or acts.

Holocaust Denial

Sacred truths that cannot be transgressed by heretics become no different from the dead dogmas of religious orthodoxies. Treating the

Holocaust as so sacred that questioning the facts automatically makes the questioner a criminal or a psychopath is to assume not just that the guardians of orthodoxy are certain, but that they are infallible. If they are so certain (or indeed infallible) about the facts, then why do they harbour a dread fear of defending them? When historian David Irvine sued Deborah Lipstadt of Penguin books for libel after she had labelled him a "Holocaust denier", the ensuing trial resulted in expert assessment of the historical evidence. By letting this alleged "Holocaust denier" have his say and his day in court, new evidence *for* the existence of Auschwitz emerged. It was through the process of testing the sacred truth of the Holocaust that the mainstream view was reinforced. Had there been inaccuracies in our knowledge of the facts, there would be no harm in bringing them to light. Even when we possess truths that no reasonable person could doubt, this is no guarantee that we have the whole truth. History has shown time and again that our most sacred beliefs can be mistaken or incomplete.

Unpleasant Realities

According to German Federal Criminal Police Office (*Bundeskriminalamt, BKA*) data (page 14), there has been a sharp rise in sex crimes by migrants (*Zuwanderer*) between 2013 and 2016. In the first three quarters of 2016, migrants committed 2,790 sex crimes, or around ten per day. Meanwhile, German police have allegedly been deliberately omitting any references to migrants in crime reports, making it impossible for German citizens to understand the scale or proportion of migrant crime. German Police forces have increasingly demanded that government-friendly police statistics not be "manipulated."[25] In January 2017 a 22-year-old migrant from Tunisia turned himself in after police in Karlsruhe published a surveillance camera image of the man, who is suspected of sexually assaulting five women there. Karlsruhe police asked German media to delete any images of the suspect. A note for editors stated: "The legal basis for publishing the surveillance photos has been dispensed with. We strongly urge you to take this into account in future reporting and to remove and/or make changes to existing publications."[26]

Between 2008 and 2014, the overall number of police-recorded offenses of sexual violence increased by 16.6 % across the EU-28 (data available for 25 jurisdictions).[27] After a fall in the number of police-recorded offences in 2009, the incidence of police-recorded sexual violence in the EU-28 rose slightly each year during the period 2010–12 but increased more rapidly in 2013 and 2014. For example, in 2014 (data available for 28 jurisdictions) the number of police-recorded offences of sexual violence in the EU-28 rose by 12.2 %.

Following the arrest of a 17-year old Afghan refugee whose DNA had been found on the body of a 19-year-old German student who died in Freiburg after being raped and murdered, far-right AfD co-chief Joerg Meuthen, said: "We are shocked by this crime and at the same time we see that our warnings about the uncontrolled arrival of hundreds of thousands of young men from Islamic-patriarchal cultures are written off as populist."[28] The perpetrator had arrived in Germany in 2015.

An extensive survey by the Chatham House think tank conducted in 10 European countries (United Kingdom, Belgium, France, Germany, Greece, Austria, Hungary, Italy, Poland, and Spain) between December 2016 and January 2017 based on the statement: "All further migration from mainly Muslim countries should be stopped" found that, overall, across all 10 countries, an average of 55 per cent agreed that all further migration from mainly Muslim countries should be discontinued.

In September 2015 when a wave of Syrian refugees was entering Germany, Chancellor Angela Merkel was caught on a hot mic (at a UN luncheon) pressuring Mark Zuckerberg about anti-immigrant social media posts. The Facebook CEO was overheard responding that "we need to do some work" on curbing anti-immigrant posts about the refugee crisis. "Are you working on this?" Merkel asked in English, to which Zuckerberg replied in the affirmative before the transmission was disrupted.

The United States – Selling "Blasphemy Law" at Home

On April 4, 2017, the US Senate passed Senate Resolution 118, "Condemning hate crime and any other form of racism, religious or ethnic bias, discrimination, incitement to violence, or animus targeting a minority in the United States".

Senate Resolution 118 calls on

"...Federal law enforcement officials, working with State and local officials... to expeditiously investigate all credible reports of hate crimes and incidents and threats against minorities in the United States and to hold the perpetrators of those crimes, incidents, or threats accountable and bring the perpetrators to justice; encourages the Department of Justice and other Federal agencies to work to improve the reporting of hate crimes; and... encourages the development of an interagency task force led by the

Attorney General to collaborate on the development of effective strategies and efforts to detect and deter hate crime in order to protect minority communities..."

The resolution refers to hate crimes against Muslims, Jews, African-Americans, Hindus, and Sikhs and was sponsored by Senator Kamala Harris and co-sponsored by Senator Marco Rubio, Senator Dianne Feinstein, and Senator Susan Collins.

Perhaps unsurprisingly, the resolution was drafted by a Muslim organisation, EmgageUSA (formerly EmergeUSA) and the Muslim Public Affairs Council (MPAC).[29]

On April 6, almost identical wording was introduced under House Resolution '. Res. 257, "Condemning hate crime and any other form of racism, religious or ethnic bias, discrimination, incitement to violence, or animus targeting a minority in the United States". A House Resolution can be reintroduced as legislation.

H.Res. 257 argues for

"...the development of an interagency task force led by the Attorney General and bringing together the Department of Justice, the Department of Homeland Security, the Department of Education, the Department of State, the Federal Bureau of Investigation, and the Office of the Director of National Intelligence to collaborate on the development of effective strategies and efforts to detect and deter hate crime in order to protect minority communities".

The House Resolution was referred to the House Committee on the Judiciary on April 6, 2017 and afterward was referred to the Subcommittee on Crime, Terrorism, Homeland Security, and Investigations (on April 21).

These resolutions, especially the part of the House Resolution calling for the establishment of an "interagency task force...to detect and deter hate crime in order to protect minority communities", appear to resurrect H.Res. 569 (first introduced in December 2015). H.Res.569 condemned "violence, bigotry, and hateful rhetoric towards Muslims in the United States". Probably because it so obviously prioritised Muslims over everyone else, it did not pass. But the rewording of H.Res. 257 moved to include most of the major ethnic and religious minorities in the United States, weaving "Muslims" into the mix of other biologically defined minority groups in yet another conflation of ideology and race. For this reason, the new legislation has a far better chance of passing.[30]

The problem is not in the state protecting minorities, which has been a staple of liberalism for decades. Rather, it is in treating an ideologically defined group as equivalent to a biologically defined group. Freedom of religion is an important liberal value that secular states have protected by means of legal instruments such as the First Amendment to the United States Constitution. Freedom *of* religion simultaneously and reciprocally protects freedom *from* religion. While everyone has the liberty to practice a religion of her choice, individuals also enjoy protection from religious coercion, and must be equally free not to practice any religion at all. To be pressured into silence on other people's beliefs is tantamount to being forced to defer to that religion's belief system. Effectively, it is to be made to obey a blasphemy law. Disagreement is not hate. It is a form of respect for others to be honest with them, even when your views differ from theirs. In a civilised society, disagreement does not lead to violence or censorship. It leads to liberty and tolerance.

Notes

[1] See Nash, David, 'Blasphemy and the Law: The Fall and Rise of a Legal Non Sequitur', Chapter 2, pp. 27 – 48, in Cliteur, Paul and Herrenberg, Tom, Eds. *The Fall and Rise of Blasphemy Law*, Leiden University Press, 2016.
[2] See, Hare, Ivan, 'The English Law of Blasphemy: The Melancholy, Long, Withdrawing Roar' in Cliteur, Paul and Herrenberg, Tom, Eds. *The Fall and Rise of Blasphemy Law*, Leiden University Press, 2016, Chapter 3, pp. 49 – 69.
[3] Van Shaik, Mirjam, 'Religious Freedom and Blasphemy Law in a Global Context' in Cliteur, Paul and Herrenberg, Tom, *The Fall and Rise of Blasphemy Law* (Leiden University Press, 2016), pp. 177 – 209.
[4] Ibid., p. 179.
[5] 46th Meeting, HRC Extranet, Sixteenth Session, Draft resolutions, decisions & President's statements, A/HRC/16/L.38. Cited by van Shaik, Mirjam in Cliteur, Paul and Herrenberg, Tom, *The Fall and Rise of Blasphemy Law* (Leiden University Press, 2016), p. 199.
[6] 'Clinton Seeks to Smooth Islamic Defamation Row', Reuters, July 15, 2011.
[7] In a statement by His Excellency the Secretary General at the 3rd Istanbul Process Meeting on the follow-up of Implementation of HRC Resolution 16/18, 20 June, 2010.
[8] Flah, Loubna, ISESCO calls for the enforcement of UN Resolution on Defamation of Religion, *Morocco World News*, September 24, 2012. "Equally, the ISESCO underscored the importance of linking freedom of speech with **responsibility** and avoidance of double standard. Therefore, it called for boosting communication among media institutions and organisations as well as journalists

in Member States with their fellows in the West in order to promote **respect of cultural diversity** and to curb **racial discrimination**, as well as defamation of religious beliefs and religious symbols." [emphasis added]

[9] Cliteur, Paul and Herrenberg, Tom, 'On the Life and Times of the Dutch Blasphemy Law (1932-2014)' in *The Fall and Rise of Blasphemy Law* (Leiden University Press, 2016), pp. 71 – 110.

[10] Murray, Douglas, *The Strange Death of Europe, Immigration, Identity, Islam*, (London: Bloomsbury, 2017), p. 136.

[11] Cliteur and Herrenberg (2016), p. 100.

[12] Cliteur, Paul and Herrenberg, Tom, Eds. *The Fall and Rise of Blasphemy Law*, Leiden University Press, 2016, pp. 115, 118, 128, and 130.

[13] Ibid, p. 124.

[14] Ibid, pp. 118-119.

[15] Ibid, p. 120, esp. p. 133.

[16] Ibid, p. 130.

[17] 'The sins of a holy terror. Once it would do intellectual battle but Islam now prefers to draw blood,' in *The Globe and Mail*, 17 February, 1989. Cited in Herrenberg and Cliteur, 2016, p. 142.

[18] 'Why British Diplomacy Cuts a Poor Figure in Iran's Holy War: It is Britain which should have severed diplomatic relations rather than accept conciliation,' in *Financial Times*, 9 March, 1989, Citation from Herrenberg and Cliteur (2016), p. 145.

[19] 'Danish prime minister defends handling of prophet cartoon crisis,' *Asarq Al-Awsat*, February 21, 2006 (English archive. Accessed online on 29 June, 2018). 21, February, 2006 *Pravda Report* Online, accessed on 25 June, 2017 at http://www.pravdareport.com/news/world/21-02-2006/76288-0/

[20] 3 February, 2006, *Sp!ked* online, www.spiked-online.com

[21] See Cliteur, Paul and Herrenberg, Tom, Eds. *The Fall and Rise of Blasphemy Law*, Leiden University Press, 2016, chapter 7, pp. 157 – 175.

[22] **Rule utilitarianism** is a form of utilitarian ethics that says an action is right as it conforms to **a rule** (not just a discrete act) that leads to the greatest good, or that "the rightness or wrongness of a particular action is a function of the correctness of the rule of which it is an instance."

[23] See Hasan, Rumy, 'Blasphemy, Multiculturalism and Free Speech in Modern Britain' in Cliteur, Paul and Herrenberg, Tom, Eds. *The Fall and Rise of Blasphemy Law*, Leiden University Press, 2016, chapter 9, pp. 209 - 233.

[24] Grieshaber, Kirsten (Associated Press), 'Germany Approves Bill Curbing Online Hate Crime, Fake News', *US News & World Report,* Online Edition, April 5, 2017.

[25] https://www.welt.de/regionales/duesseldorf/article114003255/Wie-die-Polizei-Statistik-Verbrechen-verheimlicht.html

[26] http://www.presseportal.de/blaulicht/pm/110972/3545343

[27] http://ec.europa.eu/eurostat/statisticsexplained/index.php/Crime_and_criminal_justice_statistics#Recorded_crime_for_sexual_violence

[28] http://www.ibtimes.com/rape-murder-german-student-reignites-criticism-open-door-policy-2455655

[29] MPAC has historically had ideological ties with the Muslim Brotherhood and, according to a special report by the Investigative Project on Terrorism titled 'Behind the Façade: The Muslim Public Affairs Council', MPAC has a history of broadcasting a message of Anti-Semitic hate, has given oxygen to the defensive "war on Islam" theory, defended financiers of terrorism, presented U.S. counter-terrorism efforts as a politically-motivated form of persecution and has publicly defended at least a dozen suspects of terrorist activity within the United States.

[30] Bergman, Judith, 'U.S. Trying to Criminalise Free Speech – Again', at Gatestone, June 20, 2017.

CHAPTER SIX

DIVERSITY AT UNIVERSITIES?

The B vocabulary consisted of words which had been deliberately constructed for political purposes: words, that is to say, which not only had in every case a political implication, but were intended to impose a desirable mental attitude upon the person using them. Without a full understanding of the principles of Ingsoc it was difficult to use these words correctly. In some cases they could be translated into Oldspeak, or even into words taken from the A vocabulary, but this usually demanded a long paraphrase and always involved the loss of certain overtones. The B words were a sort of verbal shorthand, often packing whole ranges of ideas into a few syllables, and at the same time more accurate and forcible than ordinary language.

-George Orwell, 1984

The promiscuous deployment of "No Platform" policies at UK Universities is indicative of the way that the once rare legal exceptions to free speech have been transformed into all-purpose offense-prevention vaccines. In his book *Trigger Warning: Is the Fear of Being Offensive Killing Free Speech?, Sp!ked* editor Mick Hume observed that the use of such policies by student unions in the mid-70's was directed against racist and fascist ideas deemed too extreme. This was already problematic for many leftists of that era. But nowadays "No Platform" policies represent an all-pervasive pampering culture that Hume says would be better described as "No Argument" – a refusal to countenance any views not consonant with the status quo. As Greg Lukianoff of the Foundation for Individual Rights in Education (FIRE) has observed, the increasing incidents of students and faculty *dis*inviting speakers regarded as too controversial has resulted in an academic environment in which students crave freedom *from* speech and from speakers with whom they disagree. Feelings trump other trifling principles such as intellectual freedom or the free exchange of ideas. At London's School of Oriental and African Studies (SOAS) the culture of over-protection has morphed into the demand for protection even from "potentially racist" white male teachers.

Perhaps it was no coincidence that this headline appeared in the *Times of London* on January 15th, the day before Martin Luther King Jr. Day:

> *"Black students' progress is being stalled by university tutors who are '60-year-old white men' and 'potentially racist'"*

In a report, cleverly titled "Degrees of Racism", the SOAS student union demanded that, "all academics must be prepared to acknowledge that they are capable of racism". The set of "potentially racist" tutors is exactly all tutors, so this demand is about as useful as an ashtray on a motorcycle. All academics (indeed all adult human beings) are capable of cannibalism too, but that in itself is no reason to conclude that they will be likely to cannibalise students or anyone else. Presumably some other subset of academics is *not* capable of racism … and I'm guessing this would be, uh, black minority ethnic (BME) professors.

The report's unstated premises are (1) that the only potential victims of racism are BME students and/or (2) that the only potential perpetrators of it are white tutors. Even if we accept the premise that most racism has been perpetrated by white people, the argument would still be invalid. The reasoning goes something like this:

- Most known racists have been white.
- Mr. X is white.
- Therefore Mr. X is probably a racist.

The structure of the argument is identical to this:

- Most known terrorists have been tea-drinkers.
- Ishmael is a tea-drinker.
- Therefore, Ishmael is probably a terrorist.

We are being asked to accept the conclusion that most white people are probable racists on the basis that most known racists have been white people. The reasoning would be valid only if being white were a sufficient condition for being a racist. Many factors, such as culture, religion or poor education can account for racism, and there is no evidence of any one-to-one correlation between racism and being white *per se.*

But then reasoning is not what matters here. The SOAS students' accusations appear to be less about formulating arguments than using emotive buzz-words as propaganda ploys. Who could resist such emotionally-charged appeals to universal taboos like "racism"? Newsflash: assertive self-righteousness does not make you right. More often, it is the last resort when your arguments are bankrupt. Essentially, we are being encouraged to treat as a suspected racist any teacher who is not black or from a minority ethnic group. To understand how racist *this is*, just imagine the reaction if we were asked to treat as a suspected terrorist any tutor who is not white European, or as a suspected sexist any tutor who is not female. SOAS student union representatives might retort that I am changing their wording from "potential" to "probable". But unless they wanted us to think that white teachers are *more likely* to be racist, their report and their demands would be pointless. Their report serves to *problematise* the teaching of BME students by non-BME teachers in the UK, so "potential" must mean "likely" or else the problem disappears.

The student union also claims that "unconscious bias" is rife at the school. Is there any reliable way to measure this claim? The student union's demands are not a response to any actual incident or accusation made against any particular teacher at SOAS. It is a blanket charge that is impossible to assess in light of its vagueness and shows scant interest in what words like "racism" mean. If racism means everything – from "having more in common" with Westerners than Arabs to being a card-carrying member of the KKK – then it ceases to mean anything. Racism is an important issue; using the word cynically to end political debate before it has even begun, or to poison the well, only trivialises it's meaning and reduces it to a cliché, blunting its forcefulness against genuine cases of institutional or systemic discrimination. Anti-racism should be a vivid, living ethic, not a dead dogma that we unthinkingly apply more promiscuously than a two-peckered billy goat. The political use of the "racism" trope has begun to resemble weaving a shark net with mesh as tight as cheesecloth, and then calling everything that gets caught in it a "shark".

The students' report also claims that white tutors allow white male students to dominate class discussions. Before drawing hasty generalisations from this, we might wish to assess this claim a bit further. For example, we might ask how many of the white tutors who allegedly "allow" white male students to dominate class discussions are female. If the number of female professors is reasonably high, we might conclude that any number of factors, including a Western cultural climate of male entitlement, might explain the dominance of white males. (By the way, acknowledging this does not mean that non-Western cultures do not also foster a climate of male entitlement.) Other culture-specific factors, such as cultural taboos about inter-generational "disrespect", could also account for differences. Not all white European students have the kind of deferential attitude to adult authority figures that their parents or grandparents did.

But the student union's report goes on to claim that white tutors also have lower expectations of black and ethnic minority (BME) students because of "racist stereotypes of people of colour as less capable, or lazy". This speculation about the interior psychological expectations or motivations of tutors is impossible to evaluate.

However, one thing is sure, it is odd that the racism of low expectations, when fostered by the regressive left in sympathy with BME activists *in defence of* exceptional protections for non-Western and/or theocratic culture warriors, garners no such complaints of "racism". In fact, it is quite the opposite. As British-Iraqi counter-extremism specialist Haydar Zaki has argued, if the far-right's orientalism can be summarised as "Muslims are barbarians", the far-left's neo-orientalism claims "Muslims are barbarians, but it's just who they are, and/or it is 'their culture'." Some Muslims, by taking offense to even harmless satire of their religious beliefs, collude in white peoples' patronising attitudes towards them, and feed the "racism of low expectations" by refusing to show resilience in the face of arguments directed at their beliefs in same the way that other people might be expected to do.

The regressive left scrutinises every infraction of women's rights except when it is promulgated by Islamists (under the auspices of "Islam"). Well-meaning lefty social justice warriors (SJWs) revere an image of Muslims as unable to (and therefore not expected to) reconcile universal human rights with their Islamic faith. "This form of racism pains me," says Zaki, "It assumes Muslims like me are too regressive for the beauty of human rights, which are reserved for non-Muslims." Not only have multiculturalism's do-gooders been reluctant to challenge ultra-conservative Islamist theocrats, they go further and accuse anyone who has the courage to do so of "racism" or "Islamophobia". Ironically, they pour scorn even on moderate Muslims and feminist Muslims who argue for human rights against Islamist theocratic repression.

The racism of low expectations goes hand-in-hand with multiculturalist policies that grant aspects of minority culture or ideology special immunity, treating its adherents as fragile infants. Rather than treating members of minority cultures as adults capable of submitting their beliefs to public scrutiny and defending them in response to critical examination, they are handled with kid gloves. By contrast, liberal tolerance (which entails vociferous disagreement, debate, satire, and active engagement with opposing ideas) shows respect for the other by treating him/her as an adult capable of resilience in the face of disagreement. In other words, it treats them as equals.

The SOAS Students Union report makes sweeping demands, including compulsory classes for academics to combat their so-called "unconscious bias", BME hiring quotas, and the granting of long-term contracts to staff so that "all staff feel able to confront each other's racism" without threat of repercussions. This looks like a sure way to embolden those who are wont to abuse the "race" gambit as cover for the importation of illiberal ideologies like Wahhabism into Universities. The report's title "Degrees of Racism" is ironic in light of another report, published by the Centre for Social Cohesion in 2009, titled "Degree of Influence", which listed a number of donations to SOAS from Saudi Arabia and Iran.

SOAS's Centre for Islamic Studies was established in 1995 with the help of a £1 million donation from King Fahd of Saudi Arabia to establish a chair in Islamic Studies. The Saudi ambassador told the audience in a speech that: "The endowment of this chair should be seen as part, and a very important part, of the kingdom of Saudia Arabia's efforts to present the beliefs, thinking and culture of Islam to the non-Moslem world." One estimate is that during the reign of King Fadh (1982 to 2005), over $75 billion was spent in efforts to spread Wahhabi Islam. The money was used to establish 200 Islamic colleges, 210 Islamic centres, 1500 mosques, and 2000 schools for Muslim children in Muslim and non-Muslim majority countries.[1] The schools were "fundamentalist" in outlook and formed a network "from Sudan to northern Pakistan".[2] In June 1995, thirty senior academic staff members at SOAS signed a petition protesting the university's acceptance of the King Fahd donation. Commenting on the petition, one of the signatories said, "We wanted to protest about the fact that such a large sum of money was accepted from such a source without consultation. Saudi Arabia is known to have a certain agenda on Islam and there could be implications about accepting money from such a source."[3]

SOAS also received £35,000 from the Iranian government and from a charity closely linked with the Iranian government in order to fund two studentships over a three-year period, starting in 1999. Independent Iranian academics at SOAS said that they would be intimidated by the presence of people with links to Iran's state security forces.[4] In a letter of protest, 74 international academics said the funding raised serious issues about academic integrity and freedom at SOAS. Nineteen professors, nine department heads and over a third of the academic board said the externally sponsored posts "should be subject to the school's established appointment procedures, including observance of equal opportunity and procedural transparency".[5] SOAS director Sir Tim Lankester defended the donations.

SOAS also received 1.25 million from Sheikh Mohamed bin Issa Al Jaber in 2001, who has been accused of labour violations at Jadawel International's Dhahran and Riyadh compounds (an allegation which the Sheikh denies). Al Jaber's donation mostly funded the establishment of The London Middle East Institute (LMEI), the purpose of which was, according to Al Jaber's website, to provide "a centre of expertise and resources for academics as well as for the world of business, government, the media and NGO's". Among his unspecified donations to the Institute was the endowment of a Professorship in Middle East Studies at SOAS, the holder of which is also designated as the director of the LMEI, which its own homepage described as "closely linked to SOAS".

According to the Arabic-language newspaper *al-Quds al-Arabi,* SOAS professors were angry that Professor Muhammad Abdel Haleem had been appointed to the professorship, especially as the new post had not been advertised either inside or outside the university (although Sheikh Mohamed bin Issa Al Jaber vigorously denies any direct influence over the appointment of Professor Haleem). It also said lecturers believed that the donation could influence SOAS's teaching. Abdel Haleem was also one of seven trustees at the controversial King Fahd Academy in London, which operates "under the support and supervision of the Embassy of the Kingdom of Saudi Arabia in London" and admitted to using textbooks that two independent translators for BBC Newsnight said called Jews "apes" and Christians "pigs"[6] Given SOAS's lack of responsiveness to academics' protests about the excessive influence of ideologically orientated foreign gifts, it seems rather rich for BME students at SOAS to direct their suspicions exclusively at the university's non-BME academics.

The SOAS student union report quoted black undergraduates, one of whom asked rhetorically, how he/she could "have rapport" and "feel comfortable talking to" a 60-year-old white man" given that, "our experiences of life are so different and you're coming from completely different places." Imagine the response if a white British student were to say the same about a BME teacher. The assumptions about uniformity of experience seem based on the belief that skin colour or age is the main factor around which human experience revolves – which is a totally reductionist view, not to mention racist and ageist. But worse, it demonstrates a kind of tribalism that is antithetical to what education is all about, which is the exchange of ideas between people who may be different culturally, ethnically or generationally but who can transcend their own experiences and learn from one another as human beings who share a common ability to reflect and to reason. Universities are supposed to be places where people can be exposed to new and different ideas — other than the ones in which they have been nurtured from birth. If there is one thing that literature, cinema and art foster, it is imaginative self-transcendence and empathy with others. Ideas do not belong to any single cultural or ethnic group.

Ideas can be shared, and, through our common human faculties of reason and imagination, we are able to understand other languages, reflect on traditions and consider them on their own merits, rather than solely in respect of their origins in certain groups. By engaging with young people exclusively through the prism of "their own" values or traditions, we only reinforce their sense of difference and separation from wider society. The assumption that only people with shared religious, traditional or cultural backgrounds can fully relate to one another is an essentialist notion that isolates groups into ghettos and sends the message that "Western ideas" are not really for them or (conversely) that "oriental" ideas are too foreign for Westerners to contemplate or value. People identify with experiences, ideas and beliefs, not only with skin colour or ethnicity. This makes the timing of the report on the eve of Martin Luther King Jr. Day even more ironic, since King famously stressed (in his *I Have a Dream* speech) his hope that his four children "will one day live in a nation where they will not be judged by the colour of their skin but by the content of their character." If the SOAS cry-bullies were correct, then we would have to assume that white students cannot learn from an old black man like MLK, or *any* older black pedagogue, which kind of defeats the whole point of their proposal to appoint more BME teachers to SOAS. Should Toni Morrison stop teaching white students at Princeton as well?

This attack on white teachers is just the latest example of what can only be described as a sustained, low-level offensive against the 1960's-styled liberalism that extended civil rights to blacks, women, and LGBT people and provided the groundwork for one of the most progressive, anti-authoritarian eras in human history. From campuses to courtrooms, an ongoing piecemeal dismantling of political liberalism's core principles and institutions is underway, partly thanks to student-led movements that are the product of an aggressive multiculturalism. Young faux-liberal social justice warriors no longer seem to know what liberal values are, so they can hardly be expected to recognise when their good intentions and energies are being co-opted to abolish or attenuate them.

In regard to religion, the National Union of Students (NUS) operates a policy of preventing what they regard as offensive and disturbing – in effect, blasphemous – to the religions of ethnic minority students. As in the wider society, this particularly applies to Islam. Whether forcing students of the LSE Atheist, Secularist and Humanist Society to remove "Jesus and Mo" T-shirts or attempting to silence ex-Muslim Maryam Namazie's speeches to students at Warwick University or Goldsmiths College, a climate of intimidation prevails. Amnesty International and INDEX on Censorship have also maintained complicit silence in offering no public support to those satirising or critiquing Islam in the UK even though Amnesty did take a principled opposition to the banning of the play *The Bible: The Complete Word of God (Abridged)*.

The SOAS student union report called a 10% gap in attainment between white and BME students "significant", even though it is less than the sector average of 15.3%. They use this statistical gap to shift the burden of proof to Universities in general, stating, "We are open to ideas about how best to address this issue." The assumption that the issue of attainment is directly related to their unfounded allegations about race is yet another claim that needs closer analysis. This has not stopped them using their unsubstantiated claims as leverage to pressure universities to comply with their demands. However, the burden of proof rests with *them* – the plaintiffs – to show that white University professors are racist and that this has caused an attainment gap. Unless they can show that these sensationalist headline-grabbing claims amount to anything more than hot air, universities have no obligation to redress their grievances.

The Assault on Free Speech at American Universities

In a *Dissent* magazine article of April 25, 2016, Dr. Marcia Chatelain, PhD., Associate Professor of History and African American Studies at Georgetown University, called free speech a "straw man". She misleadingly referred to the free speech lobby as "right wing". While some right-wing speakers have expounded right wing views under the *protection* of free speech, the principle itself is anything but right wing. The principle requires that the state must remain neutral with respect to content, so that freedom to express ideas applies equally to all speech and all speakers. This neutrality prevents the state from assuming an infallibility that it does not possess. Additionally, it stops the state (or a powerful majority) from dictating morals to individuals about matters that are private and not significantly dangerous to others. Many things that people regard as distasteful or even morally repugnant are nevertheless protected insofar as they do not cause significant harm to others. Examples are activities like eating pork, consenting adult sex outside of wedlock, using contraceptives, watching porn, watching FOX News, smoking in your own home, drinking alcohol, reading tasteless books or wearing a mini-skirt.

Freedom of expression is one of the key pillars of liberal political philosophy and has long been defended by the progressive liberal left. But deception works in mysterious ways and Chatelain's article was a case in point. She presented attacks on freedom of expression at universities as completely innocuous, describing them variously as a humble request to "celebrate Halloween respectfully" (in reference to students taking offense to Mexican styled fancy dress as offensive "cultural appropriation") or to consider students' "fear and anxiety in the face of racist and homophobic threats".

Emotionally-charged appeals to cliché taboos like disrespect, intimidation, racism and homophobia are seductive. The whole point of defending the freedom to argue is that the use of emotive buzz words is a propaganda ploy, not an argument. The very brand of prejudicial language Chatelain deployed is a key tool in the propagandist's armoury because it's rhetorical force can be sufficient to end discussion and silence debate. It attracts liberal sympathies because historically liberals have defended minorities that have been victims of powerful cultural and institutional discrimination. Chatelain used loaded terms abundantly to persuade her readers that proponents of free expression must be flogging bad things (racism, homophobia, disrespect) that any reasonable person (like herself) would reject. Interestingly, she omitted the word "sexism" from the opening of her article – the emotional appeal section — as it does not conjure the "right" kinds of emotions. Feminism was not a very sexy concept at the time. It is one of those Western ideas that seem to clash with religious cultural practices. People feel mixed about attacking sexism, as they are not sure whether or not culturally-backed sexism is *really* sexist, whereas there is unanimous agreement that racism is wrong because only white people do it. The implication Chatelain seemed to be putting across was that racism is so obviously wrong that anyone who would support **that** kind of free speech must be **that** kind of person (right wing/racist). "Sexist" doesn't push the lefty groupthink auto-sympathy button as readily as "racist" and "homophobic" do. So she left it aside.

Chatelain also used tendentious rhetoric in describing offensive language, ideas or speech as "threats". This word insinuates a direct connection to a violent *act*, and violent acts *are* illegal for good reasons. Using words that conjure the image of a violent action is misleading in this context, however. Liberals draw a line between free speech and the kinds of acts that might be truly harmful to a person, and not just to his or her feelings. Speech is only a threat when someone says they are going to carry out illegal acts against you, in contexts where this is a real likelihood. This very seldom happens in university lecture halls and few speakers on campuses would have any incentive to risk the legal consequences of actually assaulting members of the audiences to whom they speak. Then there are more personal and informal interactions. These might hurt the feelings, pride or "worldview" of other students, but only in the same way that being made to take bad-tasting medicine or to work out vigorously hurts the body. That is, listening to such views is uncomfortable but enduring them (tolerating them) does no damage to the "victim's" permanent interests as a progressive being ...probably quite the opposite. All ideas, even bad ones, stimulate thought. They force us to ponder *why* we disagree with them, and whether we are right in so doing.

As a young person at school and even at university, I was subjected to generous helpings of sexism and homophobia. Sometimes it made me resent the people who promoted such backward ideas and I would have preferred that they not express their views in public (some of them were my teachers). But none of their ignorant speech seriously harmed me, and I suspect it had the opposite effect. Exposure to their ideas made me want to expand my exposure to other (better) thoughts and ideas, and to develop my own. It encouraged me to argue back (which I was free to do) and to hear more views from different thinkers, and better ones. I got busy teaching myself how to analyse ideas I disagreed with. That's what university is all about.

There is another important issue raised by the emotional appeal to buzz words like "racist", "homophobic", "sexist" or "Islamophobic". If we have not actually heard an argument it is impossible to assess whether these hot-button terms correctly *apply* to the ideas expressed. We beg the question if we say that an idea is racist, Islamophobic, or sexist in advance of having listened to the view. How do you know that argument X is racist? Is it racist because racism is bad and you "just feel" that this argument might also be bad? One should be expected to prove, not just assume, that an argument is an instance of sexism, homophobia or racism before wielding this stigmatising language against it. Furthermore, why are we so afraid of homophobic or racist ideas, when these ideas are among the easiest in the world to argue against? In a social context where we are free to argue back, poor arguments ought to give us the least worry, not the most.

If we cease to care what words like "racism" actually mean, and instead just apply them as blanket dismissals of all controversial speech, then we have lost the plot. We are no different from Bible-toting fundamentalists who need not explain anything since the mere fact that it is in the Holy Book means that it is infallible. The racism taboo is being used cynically to manipulate liberals into supporting illiberal policies and the over-zealous hunting of "racism" is watering down the definition of racism and making many ordinary disagreements into forbidden thought crimes.

Chatelain also used misleading language when describing censorship on campus as mere "calls to improve campus diversity and equity". This was a huge inversion of the situation. Censorship would do the exact opposite: it would limit diversity of viewpoints and ideas on campus to those we already "just know" are acceptable. This is really just a recommendation to short circuit discussion of alternative views and challenging opinions.

But her assault on free expression didn't stop there. She also pulled rank. "We", she asserts (in her role as a campus academic), "are the ones who do the hard work of trying to maintain our communities in the face of ideological and social discord." Yes, that is *exactly* what her article aimed to do – to maintain a community of like-minded people and to protect it from "discord" (i.e. disagreement with them) that might disrupt the harmony of ideas within its borders. A university should be a place where "discord," albeit not violence, can flourish, which is why freedom of speech is appropriate there more than anywhere.

"Our ideas", said Chatelain, "are only effective when they emerge from substance, not straw." But surely what makes an idea substantial is that it has withstood the testing that comes from a healthy clash with other viewpoints. Untested ideas can have no substance, which is apparently why she had to appeal instead to emotional rhetoric and her own status as an academic. Next, she launched a sort of panegyric on 'the university', reminding us that college campuses are exceptional places, unique and "unlike other public and private spaces" because ideas that circulate there infuse all of the university and are like a beacon to the rest of the world.

If there is any way in which universities really are exceptional to the rest of the spaces and places on the planet, then it is because they are supposed to be places where people can be exposed to new and different ideas — other than the ones in which they have been nurtured from birth. Yet the lofty ideal of higher education, says Chatelain, rapidly disintegrates along "fault lines of race, gender, class, sexual orientation, ability and citizenship". Wow! – those ideas again: the ones that are supposed to be so sacred that any rational being would automatically kowtow before them. Where's the actual argument? There just isn't one. So instead she waxed into a quasi-religious incantation, urging her reader to take heed since the "words we utter on campus … carry the weight of a mutual agreement we share to enrich and illuminate the mind and the self." What does this even mean? It appeals to a sense of community bond that no one has actually contracted to, despite her insinuation. And worse, it transforms anyone who dares to dissent into some sort of anti-social infidel. What it fails to understand is that communities are not homogeneous blocs of uniformly similar people, who all agree on values and share a set of identical interests. In such static 'communities' individuals and their rights get trampled.

The word "unsafe" and phrases like "culture of hostility" surfaced again soon after this to remind the reader what is at stake. Any failure to obey will result in dire consequences and the tacit suggestion was that dissenters are some species of violent criminal. The aim of the "victims" then is the reasonable, innocuous one of "asking for civility". This misrepresents speech as violence, as a harmful act. Speech is not tantamount to assault or battery, but the metaphorical language she used implied it over and over again. When speech does feel most harmful and most like it has the force of a blunt instrument, it is in an atmosphere where there is no possibility of dissent. Where speech is repressed, and heterodoxy forbidden, and where violence or the coercive force of the law are used to suppress unorthodox ideas – only then do words and ideas And yet this is what Chatelain's article calls for. Any genuine examples of ideas actually injuring people always involve this combination of coercion and the violent suppression of dissenting views.

Chatelain wrapped up her remarks by noting that the possession of a right to free speech does not entail a right to protection from scrutiny, a view to which defenders of free speech on campus would wholeheartedly agree! In fact, that is what they said in the first place: she had just finished arguing the opposite. Implicitly such ideas as Chatelain espouses *are* exempt from scrutiny, however. This is why, despite her wish to censor it, free speech is so important: even ideas like "racism" that we take for granted are eternally wrong need to be tested from time to time so that we remember *why* we reject them, and so that we do not apply them unscrupulously to those who may be innocent.

Chatelain reminds us that disagreement, refusal to listen and protest are all acceptable. Yet this is exactly what her opponents (defenders of free speech) have said all along, so why is it better now that she has hijacked it as ammunition against them? Maybe since her arguments didn't work, she decided to borrow those of her opponents? If she is pretending that free speech defenders would not agree with that point, then *she* is attacking a straw man.

Lastly, Chatelain attacks the tendency to constantly argue "the other side" of a point. This balancing of ideas is deceptive, she claims, because all too often this gambit is resorted to as a panacea when critical thinking starts to get too painful. Willingness to play the diplomat or to dissuade us from our hard-won convictions is an approach she says we should eschew. Yet this approach sounds an awful lot like the sort of "civility" on campus that Chatelain suggested we ought to *promote* by abandoning free speech that is too "painful" to *her* pet causes. Somehow Chatelain stumbled to the conclusion that the defence of free speech is so "empty" that the universities must resist the pressure to give into it. One could say the same of her reasons for doing so.

Blinded by (Bad) Science

In another attempt to use the "racism" card to shut down free speech, a *Big Think* headline of May 14, 2017 warned readers that *"Prejudiced People Invoke 'Free Speech' to Mask Their Racism, Says Study"*. Like all regressive pseudo-liberal propaganda, author Paul Ratner's article uses kernels of truth to present overarching falsehoods. The true part of his argument is that some people who claim to be in favour of "free speech" do not really care about free speech in principle, but just defend it when said "free" speech is in broad *agreement with their point of view*. The false part of Ratner's article is that those who defend a consistent principled freedom of speech (i.e. freedom of expression for *all views*, including the ones they personally find repugnant) secretly harbour racist sentiments. His article suggests that we should be worried, since "racism" is the hidden motive of most defenders of free speech.

Not only is this empty speculation about the collective psyche of the free speech lobby. It is also bolstered by an example of bad science. The alleged prejudice of free-speech advocates is backed up by exactly one "scientific study" from the University of Kansas. What is not mentioned in the article is that the study itself is completely biased and circular in its methodology. Here's what we were told:

> The study consisted of eight experiments with hundreds of participants, who were recruited from Amazon's Mechanical Turk service. They were made to respond to news of racist incidents or situations like someone getting fired for racist speech. The reactions were scored according to the standard Henry and Sears Symbolic Racism 2000 scale.

> The researchers observed a positive statistical correlation between racial prejudice and standing up for racist attitudes by arguing the need for "free speech". Interestingly, those who scored low on prejudiced opinions actually avoided standing up for free speech in race-related situations.

At first glance this all seems pretty reliable. But on closer inspection, the study is flawed because (according to the premise of the research) one major criterion for defining a person as "having a racist attitude" was that they would defend someone against an employer who wanted to fire them on the basis of racist speech. In other words, if someone defends freedom of speech (even for racists) then the presupposition is that they must *be* racist themselves. This methodology begs the central question because there are other reasons – besides tacit racism – why liberals, including black liberals, defend freedom of expression even for ideas they find repugnant (like racist speech). It would only be true that all defenders of racist speech acts are necessarily racists IF all people who defend absolute freedom of speech were also racists, which they are not. The article thankfully concedes this… but only after creating a mental link between free speech advocacy and the "science" suggesting that it is racist.

Subjects were defined as having a "racist attitude" if they responded negatively to someone getting fired for exercising their freedom of expression. The notion that a principled defence of racist speech is tantamount to a positive endorsement of "racism" was a premise of the research, not an outcome or a "finding". It was an *a priori* assumption, not an *a posteriori* observation. This is a major flaw because the starting *premise* frames all of the "results". Worse, this pseudo-science is being used as the basis for spurious smears against people who defend free speech, thus poisoning the well.

One of the UK's leading anti-racists, Trevor Phillips, in his book *Race and Faith: The Deafening Silence* (Civitas, 2016), argued against this simplistic policing of speech and supported freedom of expression for racists. He had the foresight to see that any limitation of free speech "is, in the end, an erosion of the last defence available to minorities in a diverse society." (p. 54) Phillips, who is British, argued that Parliament should renew and formalise a presumption in favour of freedom of expression. This means that the current accretions and caveats on freedom of expression should be replaced by legislation ensuring that only forms of expression that directly encourage physical harm (not mere offence) be subject to legal restriction.

True liberals (as opposed to their ersatz impersonators) know this and have historically been unwilling to jettison essential freedoms whenever they become inconvenient or emotionally "painful". They know only too well that, if they relinquish these hard-won liberties, they will not be able to resort to them later on, when *their own ideas* may be the ones that have fallen out of fashion.

Notes

[1] See, Gold, Dore, *Hatred's Kingdom: How Saudi Arabia Supports the New Global Terrorism*, Regnery Publishing, Inc. (Washington D.C., 2003). See also: House, Karen Elliott (Knopf, 2012), *On Saudi Arabia : Its People, Past, Religion, Fault Lines and Future*, p. 234: "A former US Treasury Department official is quoted by Washington Post reporter David Ottaway in a 2004 article [Ottaway, David *The King's Messenger* New York: Walker, 2008, p.185] as estimating that the late king [Fadh] spent `north of $75 billion` in his efforts to spread Wahhabi Islam. According to Ottaway, the king boasted on his personal Web site that he established 200 Islamic colleges, 210 Islamic centers, 1500 mosques, and 2000 schools for Muslim children in non-Islamic nations. The late king also launched a publishing center in Medina that by 2000 had distributed 138 million copies of the Koran worldwide."
[2] Council on Foreign Relations, accessed on January 15, 2017 at https://www.cfr.org/religion/mideast-threat-s-hard-define/p4702
[3] 'Troublesome Gifts – A Saudi Arabian Donation Has Outraged Staff at The School Of Oriental And African Studies', *Guardian*, 20th June 1995.

[4] 'Uproar as SOAS takes Iran cash' at *Times Higher Education*, December 10, 1999. Accessed online on January 15, 2017 at
https://www.timeshighereducation.com/news/uproar-as-soas-takes-iran-cash/149196.article

[5] Ibid.

[6] See: 'BBC *Newsnight*, Friday February 9th, 2007', for the interview in full, www.youtube.com/watch?v=-0-jadXUKWM&feature=related

CHAPTER SEVEN

HOW THE LEFT GOT LOST

Cast your minds back to 1996. That year, in Manchester, UK, an IRA bomb injured over 200 people and devastated a good part of the city centre, Robert Mugabe was re-elected president of Zimbabwe despite a mere 32 percent voter turnout, Boris Yeltsin won re-election as Russia's president amidst claims of corruption, the Nintendo 64 video game was released in Japan, rape victim Sarah Balabagan was caned in the United Arab Emirates, *The Ramones* played their last gig, Dolly the Sheep, the first mammal to be successfully cloned, was born at the Roslin Institute in Scotland, the U.S. launched Operation Desert Strike against Iraq, and filmmaker Stacy Title released a low-budget indie film about regressive "liberals" that went virtually unnoticed.

In hindsight, *The Last Supper* is probably the most prescient film of its decade, if not the 20th century. Set in the household (and garden) of five liberal post-grad students in small town Iowa, the film is a prophetic morality tale about what happens when would-be champions of the liberal principle of tolerance fail to hold themselves to its demands.

The five smug academics have a weekly Sunday night ritual of inviting a different guest to dinner as a stimulus to topical debate and intellectual sparring. It is all rather civilised until the night when a stranger named Zach provides roadside assistance to law student Pete after the latter's car breaks down. As their expected guest has cancelled, the five housemates invite Zach to stay and dine with them instead. Desert Storm "War" veteran Zach doesn't share the graduates' worldview, to put it mildly. The veneer of civility quickly crumbles once Zach begins to expound his right-wing views, including that Hitler "had the right idea", that black people have quick tempers and that liberals are feckless "pussies" who never actually do anything other than whine. Things spiral out of control when Zach pulls a knife on Marc, threatens to rape his girlfriend, Paulie, and later breaks Pete's arm. In a moment of panic, Marc stabs their redneck guest in the back, killing him.

Feeling trapped at the prospect of a murder rap they don't deserve, the graduates bury the deceased bigot's corpse in the garden and set off on a path of righteous "activism" against Zach's brand of right-wing ignorance, which they justify as a remedy to the ineffectual passivity of which Zach had accused them. Before Zach's corpse has even grown cold, the group convene a panic-stricken rationalisation based upon the following hypothetical: "It's 1909. You're in a pub in Austria, having a Schnapps with a stranger, a young art student with one testicle. Let's say his name is Adolph. Now Adolph at this point in his life has done no wrong. He's not bitter. He's not angry. He's committed no crime, he does not bring knives to the dinner table, he's not killed anybody, he certainly hasn't started a world war. Do you kill him? Do you poison his Schnapps to save all those millions of innocent people?" This hypothetical forms the catalyst for the housemates' reconfiguration of their collective guilt into a public service and prophylactic against the social ills of chauvinism and bigotry. "Zach was Hitler" and they've made the world a better place by shutting him up, permanently.

Together the five form a pact to eliminate evil by literally exterminating (via poisoned wine) any table conversant that expresses, at first, right-wing ideas but later just conservative views and, ultimately, any ideas they happen to find distasteful. Their intolerant approach to other peoples' intolerant *ideas* seems to illustrate a paradox in the liberal conception of tolerance: defenders of the tolerant liberal state seemingly refuse to tolerate intolerant ways of life that conflict with their own. However, this apparently fatal flaw in liberal tolerance is a chimera. The Iowa housemates are not liberals, because they do not champion the tolerant liberal principle of free expression (which is content-neutral), but only those viewpoints in which the content is broadly liberal/tolerant. The classic liberal political philosophers (Locke, Mill, Paine) had faith in reason and persuasion as the best means of combating the influence of pernicious, illiberal ideas. The Iowa pseudo-liberals distrust human reason and think they have an exclusive monopoly on it.

When we first encounter the housemates at the beginning of the film, four of them are squirming in front of the television as a reactionary demagogue named Norman Arbuthnot spouts hateful opinions about feminists. Arbuthnot is the arch-enemy of progressive values, a Marine LePen or (at the time) Rush Limbaugh-like mouthpiece for populist bigotry. Despite wincing at his sexist rants, they acknowledge that they "should be helping" Paulie prepare their dinner, yet none of them do, which foreshadows the hypocrisy that will tarnish their progressive self-image throughout the narrative.

Their self-contradiction comes full circle by the end of the film when, through a chance encounter, they manage to snare "big fish" Arbuthnot in their poisonous net. But as the dinner conversation unfolds, they find to their astonishment that Arbuthnot's views are less extreme than their own, and that he is the real champion of liberal tolerance, despite his admittedly prickly public persona and inflammatory rhetoric. Arbuthnot explains that the extremes of both parties grab all the headlines, but "the real decisions are made by moderates". When Luke, the graduates' ring-leader, says to Arbuthnot that his views are extreme, and "extreme views incite people to extreme measures" Norman replies that he "can't be held responsible for every nut case who thinks I mean something when I mean something else." He explains that he needs to say outrageous things in order to "cut through" and be heard, since he's not an elected representative but just a concerned citizen who sees certain things wrong that he wants to comment on. He is being the voice of dissent, following in the footsteps of Jefferson, Monroe and Paine, who were all critics. In response to this, Paulie voices the pseudo-liberal's worst fear: that Arbuthnot may become too influential and that his followers hate anyone who disagrees with him or his opinions. This is the ultimate irony, since the five would-be liberals do just that.

What is odd about Paulie's objection is that the grad students, who are in the best possible position to use their expensive college educations to formulate counter-arguments, don't seem willing to do so. Instead they want a paternalistic short cut that will pre-empt "dangerous" (unorthodox) speech before it can be aired (or, God forbid, evaluated). This of course presupposes that they are infallible guardians of wisdom and truth. They so prefer this illiberal brand of paternalism that they abandon the classical liberal emphasis on human reason altogether and, instead of using it to persuade their opponents, adopt the apolitical method of coercion (violence). They are too cynical about human nature and the value of genuine diversity to actually live up to its demands. Their brand of "diversity" has been transformed into a rigid orthodoxy that proclaims the unambiguous and uncritical acceptance of "difference" and "the other" *tout court* – not because of the merits of "the other's" viewpoint(s) – but merely because the person or group who expounds it is different to "us". And yet, this policy (paternalistic protectiveness towards perceived "others") has become, to use Mill's description, a "tyranny" espoused by the majority. In other words, it is not protection for "them" or for a vulnerable minority but is itself the master discourse: all decent, reasonable people "just know" that "difference" is always right and morally good, irrespective of ideological content. Consequently, anyone who disagrees can only have one kind of motive: the bigoted (i.e. wrong) kind.

Moreover, the housemates seem to think that the Arbuthnot's followers are somehow especially susceptible or vulnerable vis-à-vis his persuasive powers. But as Arbuthnot says, "Followers of Nelson Mandela commit murder. Followers of Ghandi kill people, …" Arbuthnot says these were great men, but neither they (nor he) can control what people do. "People do what they want to do." While Arbuthnot acknowledges that there are some harmful people on both the extreme left and the extreme right, he suggests that "the more extreme those opposites get, the more moderate this society becomes, because when you average out all those extremes, you come out with a society that is pretty well anchored in the middle. And that's what we all want, isn't it? A society where all of us can live? All races, all religions, all views living together … In any society, no matter how big or small, you're going to have dissent, I mean look at the five of you. Can you honestly say you agree on everything?"

When they put their Austrian pub hypothetical to Arbuthnot, he says he would "absolutely not" poison Hitler but would instead "talk to the man, try to show him the error of his ways to the best of my ability, challenge his ideas, exchange thoughts, provoke change by intelligent debate." Given the unexpected turn this dinner conversation has taken, the five excuse themselves to convene a spontaneous meeting in the kitchen to "prepare dessert" (i.e. to debate whether there is really warrant for exterminating their arch-enemy given that his views are making a lot of sense). The trouble is, they are no longer capable of debate, even amongst themselves. They have cynically abandoned reasoned argument because they just know that they are right. Luke, unable to tolerate dissent, pulls a gun and threatens to kill them if they swerve from their planned course of action.

The collective protagonists are minorities with ostensibly left-wing values. As such, they are identity politics personified – perfect proxies for today's "safe space" crusaders and champions of no-platforming. By contrast, Norman Arbuthnot expresses views that most moderate liberals today would probably consider offensive at best and repugnant at worst. Yet he is not intolerant. He is not preventing anyone else from responding to his views, nor is he prepared to punish dissenters or coerce compliance. He is simply expressing offensive ideas. Free expression – even of ideas that are blasphemous, challenging, tasteless, unorthodox, sacrilegious, disturbing, forbidden and taboo — is something that genuine champions of tolerance have always defended. J.S. Mill, the architect of liberal political philosophy, advocated for "absolute freedom of opinion and sentiment on all subjects, practical or speculative, scientific, moral, or theological", however immoral the opinion or sentiment may seem. (*On Liberty*, 71)

Indeed, the fatal flaw or paradox is on the other foot: today's strident illiberal champions of exclusively "liberal" speech *content* like to remind us that "Euro-centric" or "Western" political forms are dangerous and misguided, since there is no universal truth... except of course *their* truth that 'there is no universal truth and no common human rights'. That view is true, and so infallibly true that anyone who expresses the least doubt about it or even wants to debate it must be silenced.

The concept of "intolerance" means more than verbal objection to others' views. Tolerant people *do* object to other people's views, often in quite vocal and acerbic ways. Tolerant people also fully accept (and endorse!) all manner of non-violent dissent, satire, ridicule and criticism. Tolerance implies a willingness to engage in debate and argument, and to withstand offensive views.

By contrast, intolerance implies rejection of the other's fundamental right to dissent, and so denies him self-determination. Intolerance implies an unwillingness to abide the offensive, taboo, or unorthodox opinions of the age. Intolerant individuals or groups dictate how others must live and what they may or may not say. This is what makes the Iowa housemates intolerant even as they imagine themselves to be champions of diversity.

Back in 2000 I interviewed Elinor Tatum, editor of *The New York Amsterdam News*, a Harlem-based African-American newspaper with progressive roots dating back to 1909. The previous year, she had been on the receiving end of a shit storm after defending the right of the Ku Klux Klan to hold a demonstration in New York City. The mayor, Rudolph Giuliani, had attempted to divide-and-conquer his liberal critics by denying the white supremacist organisation a permit to hold a small rally in the city with their traditional white hoods. His aim was to force liberals into a false dilemma that would tempt them to abandon their traditional commitment to absolute freedom of expression for all ideas by pitting it against their bedrock anti-racist sympathies. During his tenure, the mayor had trampled on all manner of free expression that was critical of him or his policies, so banning demos was par for the course. Less obvious than Giuliani's "sanitizing" of New York City was the price paid in civil liberties for this brave new muzzled metropolis. His constant clashes with New Yorkers' First Amendment rights earned him the *Thomas Jefferson Center's Lifetime Muzzle Award*. While he combated the kinds of petty crime that is visible to tourists, the maverick mayor had also stacked up a record-long list of First Amendment law suits against his administration and became notorious among black New Yorkers for giving his police force carte blanche to harass and abuse black "suspects". During Giuliani's tenure, the number of deaths in police custody grew so high that the NYPD stopped releasing statistics on it. Notorious police misconduct incidents like the shooting of Amadou Diallo and the torture of Abner Louima have gone down in the annals of New York City history.

Tatum, like Norman Siegel of the New York Civil Liberties Union, had taken the heat from former allies (Tatum from some members of the black community and Siegel from certain Jewish New Yorkers) in order to defend the principle of free expression that she knew would protect *all* minorities, including ethnic minorities, in the long run. Both Tatum and Siegel were seasoned civil rights activists with long pedigrees of anti-racist advocacy and civil liberties activism. They knew that Giuliani was presenting liberals with a false dilemma. Yet, to many of their liberal allies at the time, they seemed like turncoats. Tatum told me that she and her associates "realised that if we had a double standard we could not rightly stand up for any organisation that we believed in, if we couldn't stand up for an organisation that we abhorred what they said … that is the true test of civil liberties." Meanwhile Giuliani, the seemingly "liberal" defender of NYC from the scourge of the KKK, had established a double standard, allowing demonstrations he liked (such as a rally to celebrate the New York Yankees World Series victory) but disallowing those he disliked (such as demos by the New Black Panthers, taxi cab drivers, or AIDS advocacy organisations).

Tatum was right. Tolerance is not an attitude that one adopts depending upon the content of speech or the personal qualities of the speaker. Tolerance aims instead at structural equality. Because it is a principled approach, it applies equally and consistently to all forms of speech and to all speakers, regardless of the content or good taste of their expressions. As it turned out, the principle of free speech prevailed in NYC, and some twelve Klansmen held a pathetic demonstration in downtown New York City, while more than two-hundred counter-demonstrators gathered opposite to exercise their Constitutional right to protest. This was a triumph of how freedom of speech should work. Civil rights lawyer Norman Siegel advised both groups and when some protested him (for legally representing the Klan in their First Amendment rights case) by picketing his apartment building with insulting signs and chants, he also defended their right to do so and told the security guard at his apartment building not to call the cops on them.

As a principled form of forbearance, tolerance is distinct from weakness, indifference or a passive laissez-faire attitude. German philosopher and political theorist Rainer Forst defined tolerance as a three-stage approach involving (1) objection to a belief or action, (2) an acceptance component, such that positive reasons for tolerating the belief or action trump negative ones, and (3) limits to our acceptance, such that some beliefs and activities are regarded as intolerably wrong. In order that we can distinguish it from an arbitrary or apolitical approach, there must be some specified limits to toleration. The reasons we give for rejecting certain kinds of beliefs or activities must outweigh the reasons for accepting them.

Liberals in the United States (and to a lesser extent in the U.K.) have followed J.S. Mill's harm principle in drawing the line between objectionable-but-tolerable ideas/activities and those that are simply intolerable, and therefore illegal. While the pseudo-liberals in *The Last Supper* seem to think it is not good to let people do "bad" (but harmless) things, or even to hold "immoral" ideas, Mill argues the opposite: "The only purpose for which power can rightfully be exercised over any member of a civilised society, against his will, is to prevent harm to others. His own good, either physical or moral, is not a sufficient warrant." (*On Liberty*, 68) There are famous difficulties in determining what counts as "harm to others" but liberals have traditionally maintained a very narrow understanding of harm to encompass only those activities that physically injure or constrain others or damage their "permanent interests as progressive beings". Offence does neither. Plato suggested the reverse, i.e. that Socrates, in being a "stinging insect" on the body politic, provided a healthy stimulus to the Athenian status quo. Dealing with, and being forced to think about, ideas that we disagree with or that offend us only makes us better thinkers and more resilient individuals. It allows us the opportunity to change our mind. Our beliefs would never evolve if they never had to undergo any testing against the merits of other – opposed – ideas. We should be thankful for opportunities to learn from this clash with diverse ideas, not brittle and defensive.

The Austrian-British philosopher of science, Karl Popper (1902–1994) also understood that a limit on tolerance is integral to its definition. He recognised the danger in censoring intolerant attitudes and thought it preferable to counter them with rational argument and keep them in check by public opinion. However, he saw that "Unlimited tolerance must lead to the disappearance of tolerance. If we extend unlimited tolerance even to those who are intolerant, if we are not prepared to defend a tolerant society against the onslaught of the intolerant, then the tolerant will be destroyed, and tolerance with them." [*The Open Society and its Enemies*, 1945] Popper maintained that society has a right to suppress intolerant attitudes if their spokespersons refuse to engage in rational argument and refuse their followers the right to hear alternative views.

So, tolerance must have limits. But *The Last Supper* illustrates what happens when the line is drawn at offensive speech and shows why this threshold is far too low. They key to tolerance is reciprocity, which is guaranteed by structural equality, not by policing content. If we draw the line at the mere *expression* of repellent *ideas*, then we have refused to extend to others the same privilege we want for ourselves. All of us, even the most authoritarian religious zealots, want the freedom to pursue values that are genuinely our own, and to be sovereign over our own minds. This is why classic liberal philosophers have had a higher threshold for offensive speech. They would limit only *actions* that interfere with the reciprocal liberty of others to live according to their beliefs.

Structural equality puts a legal brake on the kind of hypocrisy and double standards exercised by intolerant individuals. Because it aims only at a fair framework within which all variety of ideas can be expressed, rather than the promotion of some particular ideological content, liberalism can and does accommodate illiberal worldviews, within limits. Religious zealots can and do live freely and thrive within liberal democracies, up to the point that they coerce unwilling others to conform to their worldview. By contrast, liberals and progressives can never and will never be free to pursue their own ways of living within illiberal theocracies like Saudi Arabia. The limits that liberal states place on the freedom of illiberal ideologies are there to protect the equal freedom of others but not to constrain the individual zealot in the expression of his beliefs or the practice of his ideology or religion.

The housemates in *The Last Supper* champion a unilateral (not reciprocal) form of tolerance vis-à-vis the content of beliefs. This makes the ostensibly "progressive" ideas they champion into dead dogmas, believed not with the conviction that arises from critical thought, reflection, and the tussle with opposing ideas, but from the group-think mentality of Orwell's Oceana.

CHAPTER EIGHT

HOW WESTERN FEMINISTS GOT HOGTIED

Western feminists are in one hell of a bind vis-à-vis misogynistic aspects of Islam. On the one hand, they (Western feminists) are scolded for assuming that Muslim women cannot fight "their own" battles. On the other, they are chided for "othering" Muslim women, as though Muslims were some alien exotic culture whose *culture must be fundamentally different* from our own. When Western feminists critique Shari'a law, honour violence, female genital mutilation (FGM) or religious dress, they are told that their own Christian culture has behaved similarly or worse, but in the next breath they are reminded that Muslim women are "*uniquely* placed" to understand the religious patriarchy of "their" culture because it is impenetrable by Western women's minds or "lived experiences". However, if Western religious culture does similar things, then the opposite is true: Westerners can and should draw relevant comparisons between Christian, Jewish and Islamic male chauvinism.

Whatever they may say vis-à-vis Islamic patriarchy Western feminists will be shamed. When a seventeen year-old Birmingham hijabi was threatened with death by ultra-conservative Muslims in March 2017 after being caught on camera "twerking" in Muslim religious dress, non-Muslim feminists attempted to lend her their support. However, they were scolded for assuming that Muslim women cannot defend themselves. On the other hand, Ayaan Hirsi Ali, Sara Khan, Rahila Gupta and other women of Muslim background have expressed disappointment at the *lack* of support afforded to them by Western liberals and feminists.[1] But far too often, non-Muslim feminists are told that they lack authority to speak on such matters, since Muslims or ex-Muslims are "*uniquely* placed" to understand and "*accurately* discern" the position of individuals like the Birmingham hijabi. On the other hand, in contradiction to this, Western feminists are told that "Muslims" (in general) deserve every shred of support that mainstream society can afford them, since they are victims of Western cultural hegemony. They are told that the reason Westerners don't intervene in harmful cultural practices like FGM is because the victims are black. This suggests that Westerners *should* interfere with the other's culture more than they presently do. The messages are more mixed than a bag of All Sorts™.

I fail to see how this conflicting and internally contradictory set of demands and expectations will lead to anything other than complete silence about conservative Islam's religious or cultural strictures on women and girls. It silences and isolates women from *both* cultures, driving them apart by classic divide-and-rule tactics, preventing female solidarity across the cultural divide. Neologisms like "intersectionality" accomplish the same end, reminding white Westerners that they lack sufficient victimhood experience to join in the correct kind of solidarity with Muslim or Asian women, who always have more authority to speak on issues of "cultural" patriarchy. This also seems to assume that Western Europeans or American do not have any culture.

In 2017, I publicly expressed support for the Muslim and ex-Muslim liberal secularists who opposed Britain's Sharia courts.[2] A Muslim woman friend who wishes to remain anonymous told me in confidence that she was appalled that some Western women were endorsing (in conjunction with conservative Muslim women) Shari'a courts in the UK, but she also confided that she was afraid to express her views publicly from fear of retaliation from members of her community. This friend is a confident, outspoken, self-employed member of her community. I was genuinely surprised to learn that she had succumbed to intimidation.

Western feminists are in a bind. One minute they are scolded for "othering" Muslims, the next minute they are told that they cannot conceivably share any common ground with them anyhow. This constant vacillation has several consequences:

(1) It weakens liberal feminism from *within*, thereby eliminating the need for illiberal religious ideologies to attack feminist principles from the outside. Direct assaults on liberal values or feminism only tarnish the image of the assailant. Islamist patriarchy avoids this 'image problem' by resorting to identity politics, which works by splitting liberals' loyalties – forcing a false dilemma between two core liberal values: racial equality and feminism.

This effectively dismantles opposition to the dominant patriarchal ideology from within, preventing women from forming a united front. The ploy works by transforming every feminist conversation about patriarchal power into a conversation about "racism within the women's movement" or about how "white feminists dominate the discussion". Internal conflicts devour the women's movement, sapping its energy so that it never gathers sufficient momentum to be a united force against the *actual* (common) enemy: patriarchy. This strategy has worked time and time again to derail solidarity between women of diverse ethnic backgrounds. The differences *between* feminists are always stressed over and above their common socio-political status vis-à-vis patriarchy and its delivery vector: religion.

(2) As mentioned above, would-be Western defenders of Muslim women's rights are kept in a state of permanent anxiety through role conflict. Role conflict occurs when there are incompatible demands placed upon a person such that compliance with both would be difficult, if not impossible. The demands on the subject vacillate between two poles so frequently that she never knows where she stands or how to comply with expectations, which constantly shift from one pole to the other, making her guilty whether she defends Muslim women or not. If she is indifferent to their plight under patriarchy then it appears that she is guilty of neglect, and possibly racism. On the other hand, if she does defend them against Islamic patriarchy, she is "patronising" and usurping their agency to speak for themselves: she stands accused of having a "white saviour complex". The result is that the subject becomes stressed, anxious and diffident to the point of complete self-doubt and incompetency. She is paralysed.

(3) So ambitious is their contrition and craving to atone for unconscious sins against their perceived victims, that Western feminists will do almost anything to compensate. No longer must she protect her Muslim sisters from the sins of Muslim male chauvinists. Her main role is re-directed to protecting them from her own Western chauvinism. Sweet relief comes when she is showered with praise and admiration after standing up for the "correct" Muslims: namely, the (conservative, religious) ones who say that Muslim women *do not need anyone else* to stand up for them, because they are not oppressed by religious laws and customs. The irony in this would be risible if it weren't so utterly destructive of women's empowerment.

Islamists have dominated the East-West "feminist" discourse at universities, which is where most of the rhetoric about who is allowed to speak for whom has been disseminated. Threats and violent opposition are unnecessary when you can control your subject using positive reinforcement. In operant conditioning, a form of behaviour modification that teaches subjects the "correct" behaviour by means of rewards and punishments, the controller reinforces the desired behaviour by means of pleasant rewards. Positive reinforcement appeals to the desire to feel good or to earn intangible rewards for performing the "correct" behaviour. Pleasant emotional outcomes result from chirping from the P.C. script, making it far more likely that the behaviour will be repeated again in the future.

Ad Hominem, **Reversed**

The Ad Hominem ("at the man") fallacy is a diversion tactic that has worked in spades for regressive illiberal politics. The substance of this fallacy is to redirect criticism away from the argument and towards the person making it. This fallacy has been deployed time and again to suggest that some types of people lack authority to speak on certain issues because of their gender, ethnicity, culture or nationality (i.e. because of their "privilege").

The reverse of this is that *only* certain "types" of people can understand particular issues, or have sufficient experience or expertise to pronounce upon them. On this view, the quality of an individual's argument is less important than the qualities of the person making it. This makes superficial and irrelevant aspects of identity (race, gender, age) the primary determinant of a person's reasoning capacities. If this is not a racist idea, then nothing is.

As I have suggested in chapter 1, identity is not determined by biological sex or skin colour. Indeed, it is not determined at all, but chosen. Being a feminist is all about supporting public policies that treat women and men as equals, legally, morally or ideologically. Believing that men and women should share common rights, opportunities and civil liberties does not require having a vagina, nor does it require any particular cultural background. Being anti-racist does not require having brown skin or growing up as a victim of racism. If it did, Western feminists would not be so susceptible to the kind of manipulation by guilt that Islamists have exploited. Regardless of what is between their legs, or what policies their community may prescribe, individual human agents decide (using the stuff between their ears) what to value, and the degree of importance they will give to their biological sex, their religious upbringing, their national traditions or cultural customs.

White American abolitionist John Brown (1800-1859) pushed the boundary of acceptable thoughts and activism regarding slavery by engaging in armed opposition to slavery, even to the point of killing. His ideological influence was immense. Brown's violent acts made mere verbal abolitionism seem less radical (remember the "positive radical flank" tactic? - see above p. 58) and paved the way for its acceptance. After their initial revulsion to his views, both Northerners and Southerners were fascinated to hear what he had to say. Brown was willing even to go to the gallows for the emancipation of slaves. In his speech before the court, on Nov. 2, 1859, just before the judge sentenced him to die, Brown stated that the Bible itself had instructed him to "remember them that are in bonds as bound with them."

Historians and artists tainted Brown with insanity from the time of his death until the civil rights movement of the 1960's, at which time, Americans finally recognised that one did not have to be insane to die for black peoples' human rights. In some ways, the accusations of "madness" and misrepresentations of Brown remind me of the character assassinations levelled against Western feminists who advocate for Muslim women's full human rights today. Individuals who advocate for the most disenfranchised minorities ahead of their time can expect to become objects of public scandal and misrepresentation. They can find themselves marginalised and silenced to an extent that resembles the situation of those for whose rights they agitate. Few would tolerate the treatment of women in conservative Islamic culture if the same were instead reserved for, say, a racial minority group.

The regressive left has turned on their Muslim sisters, not because they don't care about them, but because Islamism's propagandists have misdirected their good intentions, steering their sympathies towards a false "victim", and away from real ones. Consequently, opposing ultraconservative Islam becomes rhetorically tantamount to "Islamophobia", which only begs the question whether "Islam" can accommodate anything other than its most authoritarian forms. This would only be the case if all Muslims were Salafi-Wahhabists, which they are not. Every time we buy into the "Islamophobia"-police's pretence to represent "Muslims", we support Islamic ultraconservatives' hierarchy of oppression that gives gender equality a lower status than religious "rights" (i.e. privileges). Effectively, religious rights trump all other rights. They also pose a false dilemma by implying that we can only defend feminism *or* "Muslims", never both.

The "Mind-Body-Spirit" Industry:
Lobotomising a Generation of Women

In July 2017 *Google* released its new "Inner Strength" App under the rubric of MINDBODY, alongside a zillion similar "time saving" Apps with titles like "Calamababy", "Lipstick Lounge", "Waxing Hub" and "Relax at Home Massage". The irony is that the more women obsess on inner strength, the more docile and dumbed-down they become in the outer world. The ever-expanding galaxy of commercialised Mind-Body-Spirit products and propaganda has created possibly the most politically disengaged generation of women in human history. Women account for half the Western population, and they are so busy focusing on their "personal growth" and physical appearance that they neglect their education and civic responsibilities and instead collaborate in their own exclusion from the outward-looking social sphere where the decisions that affect them and their families are being made. The fatuous world of adult colouring books, "mindfulness", and personal growth has all but eclipsed women's participation in the technical and political spheres.

Look at the insulting "women's interest" section of any magazine rack and the depressing array of titles directing women towards infantilising preoccupations that females are expected to find fascinating: relaxing fragrances, crafty home decorating techniques or (literally) navel-gazing yoga poses. These body-obsessive, mind-numbing activities serve to normalise women's political marginalisation and domestication. The gendered assumption that women and men even have separate interests is being promoted and expressed through retailer's divisions of everything from children's toys to adult magazines, apparently without consumers' recognition that these assumptions about men and women are *producing* the separation of men and women into two different species in the first place, not merely catering to them.

The commodification of women's minds, bodies, and spirits (i.e. their wills and desires) has epitomised an advertising industry that promotes female insecurity and conformity, and then sells women back their self-esteem at the price of a whole range of unnecessary "feminine" products that keep women as poor as they are dumb. The relegation of women to the inward-looking, domestic realm is not an expression of women's "inner nature" but of cultural conditioning by this industry of insulting "feminine" hogwash, and thus far women have been sufficiently gullible to "buy" it, both with their wallets and with whatever mental capacities they still possess.

Mind-Body-Spirit is an industry that functions very much like religion. It offers women (as a culturally and politically disenfranchised class of citizens) false hope and a sense of belonging as substitutes for actual power. It provides them the semantics with which to articulate a purely mythological *feeling* of "spiritual empowerment", and membership in an inner group of like-minded "enlightened" women who share similar lifestyles revolving around physical beauty, fashion, reproduction, child-rearing and the home, which only produces a *sense* of being virtuous or "empowered" while simultaneously offering no substantial benefits at all in the real world. This empty "spirituality" only feeds female complacency with the patriarchal *status quo* and its sexist division of labour.

Alongside this passive embrace of their own false consciousness, women also take a Panglossian view of actual religious male chauvinism. Women from oppressive Islamic religious cultures are regarded with the utmost respect for their submission to Islamic Sharia law, which gives a woman's testimony half of the validity of a man's and favours men across the board on all family matters, from child custody to male polygamy and inheritance "rights". Western women see their Muslim "sisters" (and their male superiors) not as "others" but as kindred spirits. They harbour a well-meaning but utterly naïve fantasy that people whose culture and religion are opposed to Western women's liberation and equality will be forever malleable if only shown sufficient love. The Pollyanna fantasy of joining hands and singing "Kumbaya" with religious fundamentalists who would sooner kill women than offer them equal rights or even reproductive control over their own fertility makes American and European women blind to the real plight of Muslim women living under Sharia law.

Bolstered by the feel-good philosophies of Mind-Body-Spirit, Western women have been deluded into embracing a phoney "tolerance" for everything – even the most abusive and irrational sexism – when they should be responding with righteous anger, like the women at the vanguard of 1960's feminism and the 1970's women's liberation movement. *Real* tolerance does not require "being nice" – it entails all manner of satire and objection to things you disagree with, short of censorship or violence.

The "just be nice" approach is grounded in the belief that women from other cultures are perfectly content with their own cultural situations, and that peaceful coexistence is inevitable. They overlook the possibility that the reason cultural mixing between European and religiously conservative Muslim women is *not actually happening* is that religious Muslim women either do not really possess much social autonomy or disapprove of them, view their lifestyles as "haram" and look forward to the day when *all* women will be wearing modesty dress and obeying Sharia law. Western women are failing to act in solidarity with Muslim feminists and secularists in the obtuse belief that doing so would make them xenophobic, a myth that conservative Islamists love to stoke with their victim narratives about how *all* Muslim women are under constant attack by xenophobic Europeans, when a great many Muslim women would argue (if given complete liberty to do so) that they face far more danger from religiously conservative Muslim men.

The saddest part of this narcissistic culture of "inner strength" and outer powerlessness is that the luxury of enjoying the freedom to choose this self-immolation *voluntarily* has come at such a huge cost to strong, courageous women of past generations. Women's liberation is a privilege that many Muslim women today risk their lives to achieve under threat of death. Despite this, many European and American women think they are following in the footsteps of great feminists of past generations when they defend regressive religions or merely post slogans on social media or wear a "this is what a feminist looks like" T-Shirt – yet another symbol of the way that all attempts at resistance to the dominant culture have been commodified and sold to them so that consumerism and empty gestures become the only responses to real-world problems.

Even when women *do* actually step out of their interior bubbles to do something active in their real, three-dimensional communities, this is instantly transformed, on social media, into a virtue-signalling advertisement *about* the act. Time spent advertising one's virtues to a virtual community of like-minded cheerleaders for the cause replaces time spent in the actual world doing things that might bring about real change. One starts to wonder whether the motive of all activism is really to change aspects of the real world, or merely to change one's status update on *Facebook*. Real-world actions have ceased to be ends-in-themselves and must constantly be made into opportunities for narcissism and self-image improvement, in a virtual world that consumes the would-be activist's energies as she fixates on her image *as* "activist" as yet another aspect of her personal appearance.

Until women wake up, smell the coffee and disengage from this nexus of consumerism and false consciousness, the real world will continue to be both a dangerous and hostile place for women.

Petty Policing of Language

The way the regressive left and some feminists have fixated their attention on policing verbal and visual language demonstrates a petty fundamentalism about words and images that is especially troubling in light of how important language and rhetoric really are. Words and images *do matter*, and they matter quite a lot. If they didn't, I would not have spent the last decade or so writing myriad articles and essays in defence of free expression.

In her 1993 Nobel Laureate acceptance speech, Toni Morrison recounted the tale of a wise old woman, a rural visionary reputed for her prophecies. One day a group of youths bent on disproving her clairvoyance come to her home and attempt to exploit the one disability that sets her apart from them: her blindness. "Old woman", one of them taunts, "I hold in my hand a bird. Tell me, is it living or is it dead?" When the woman does not answer, the young visitors cannot contain their laughter, whereupon she interrupts them, replying in her soft but stern voice, "I don't know", she says. "I don't know whether the bird you are holding is dead or alive, but what I do know is that it is in your hands. It is in your hands." Morrison explains what she takes the old woman's answer to mean: "if it is dead, you have either found it that way or you have killed it. If it is alive, you can still kill it. Whether it is to stay alive, it is your decision. Whatever the case, it is your responsibility." The blind woman shifts attention away from assertions of power to the instrument through which that power is exercised. Morrison uses the parable to draw a parallel between the small bird and language and between the woman and a practiced writer.

The old woman is worried about how language is handled, put into service, even withheld from her for certain nefarious purposes. She "thinks of language partly as a system, partly as a living thing over which one has control, but mostly as agency – as an act with consequences." Morrison notes that language is susceptible to death. For her, a dead language is "unyielding language … Like statist language, censored and censoring. Ruthless in its policing duties, it has no desire or purpose other than maintaining the free range of its own narcotic narcissism, its own exclusivity and dominance ... Dead language actively thwarts the intellect, stalls conscience, suppresses human potential." It is also sentimental, exciting reverence in schoolchildren, providing shelter for despots, summoning false memories of stability, harmony among the public. Oppressive language, says Morrison controversially, does more than represent violence; it *is* violence; does more than represent the limits of knowledge; it limits knowledge.

I understand Morrison to mean that words are not ends in themselves. They are a language; tools or instruments by which agents further certain ends. When we read a word or an image, we must ask what purpose or role it plays in the context of its use. We can ask what kinds of ends it serves, and what the agent's intention is in wielding it. The social justice "word police" may have good intentions but they are prone to commit the **fat oxen fallacy**: the belief that he who drives fat oxen must himself be fat.

Every representation of sexism is not sexist, nor is every representation of racism a racist representation. *Birth of a Nation* is not just a depiction *of* racism; it *is* a racist film. As such, it has even been used over the years to recruit people to the Ku Klux Klan. On the other hand, *Twelve Years a Slave* also depicts racist behaviours and speech, but in a film which is not itself in the least bit racist. On the contrary, by its depiction of racism, it has gone a long way to discrediting racists and their bankrupt ideology. *Thelma & Louise* depicts sexism (a lot) but is a feminist movie about two women who reject patriarchal America's "justice" system and would rather drive off a cliff than be subjected to a sexist legal system. Paul Verhoeven's film *Elle* depicts a woman who desires her rapist and yet is deeply feminist film *about* internalised patriarchal violence and its devastating effects on women.

The inability to distinguish the words and images in films from the uses to which they are put has led to a blunt sanitizing of language and visual culture that only closes down debate and critical perspectives and stifles progress. It kills language and assumes that words are sacred shibboleths or monoliths that can only ever be used in one single way. In his book *Race and Faith: The Deafening Silence* (Civitas, 2016), lifelong anti-racist Trevor Phillips argued, rightly in my opinion, that Parliament should renew and formalise a presumption in favour of freedom of expression. This means that the current bans on freedom of expression should be replaced by legislation ensuring that only forms of expression that directly encourage physical harm (not mere offense) be subject to legal restriction. In practice, Phillips accepts that this might mean that people are permitted to address him as "nigger" (or to me as a "dyke") but they would be prohibited from, say, pointing at him and instructing others to "get that nigger" or to point at me and shout "kill that filthy lezzer". In other words, they can offend us, but they may not credibly threaten us with physical harm.

I am reminded of an interview with the actor Roy Scheider, who played detective Buddy "Cloudy" Russo in *The French Connection*. Scheider remembers watching the movie in a cinema in uptown Manhattan very near the border with Harlem, where the audience was racially very mixed. When detective Jimmy "Popeye" Doyle (Gene Hackman) says to Cloudy, "Never trust a nigger" black people – perhaps surprisingly – burst into applause. At last, an honest representation of police racism! They cheered this line probably because it represented something that resonated with them, something honest and truthful about the world as they experienced it. It was a refreshingly honest depiction of how (many) cops behaved and spoke between themselves. When Cloudy responds, "He coudda been white." Popeye Doyle simply says, "Never trust anybody."

My point is that the "N-word" in this instance was not being used to *promote* racism. It was a movie that was *about*, inter alia, a racist cop. Similarly, the made for television series *Roots* features characters that use ugly, abusive language about "negroes". But the film's characters utter these epithets to show viewers what it was like *to be* one of those "negroes", not to applaud racism. In a similar vein, *The French Connection* merely shows, in an honest way, the ruthless and amoral attitude of cops and the pervasive bigotry that formed the cultural backdrop for the film.

French Connection director William Friedkin had his start working in the TV documentary format and decided to apply its stylistic techniques to a narrative film, making it as realistic as possible. Friedkin is himself no bigot. His earlier film *The People Vs. Paul Crump* (1962) almost certainly saved the life of its eponymous black inmate and exposed the systemic racism and brutality of the notorious Chicago police as well as leading to a revaluation of a penal system that prioritises retributive "justice" over rehabilitation. The documentary is an impassioned plea for mercy on behalf of a black prisoner whom Friedkin believed was innocent. As it turned out, Friedkin was wrong, and the prisoner confessed to the murder many years later.

Notes

[1] Reporting on the *2017 International Conference on Freedom of Expression and Conscience* in London, Rahila Gupta wrote that "Black and minority ethnic (BME) feminists in the west, and particularly in Britain, have never received support from those who should have been their natural allies – the left – in their struggle against religious fundamentalism, particularly Islamic fundamentalism." See Gupta, Rahila, 'Where is the line between Islam and Islamism?' at *Open Democracy* (50.50), 27 July, 2017. Accessed at https://www.opendemocracy.net/5050/rahila-gupta/islam-islamism-freedom-expression on 8 Aug. 2017.

[2] For more about this, see Flora Bagenal, UPI Women & Girls Hub, "Britain Probes Sharia Courts' Treatment of Women", June 28, 2016. Accessed online on 12 February, 2017 at http://www.upi.com/Top_News/World-News/2016/06/28/Britain-probes-Sharia-courts-treatment-of-women/8961467141637/

CHAPTER NINE

IS JUDGING ISLAM POSSIBLE?

Pluralist multiculturalism and identity politics have left a powerful legacy that has created a crisis of liberal values. Liberal values were well on their way out of fashion at the end of the last century. Few liberals give value to human rights anymore. After all, "rights" are implicit in liberal universalism and inclusivity, and as such constitute embarrassing forms of "cultural imperialism".

As I argued in chapter 2, multiculturalism is not just a synonym for cultural diversity. *Pluralist* multiculturalism is the view that universal suffrage, equal legal status and entitlements, and equality of opportunity are not sufficient. In addition, its advocates believe that citizens in liberal democracies ought to be *obligated to recognise and positively respect* members of a cultural minority, should be prohibited from offending them, and must participate in the protection of their sacred customs. This means that we have a burden of positive regard (rather than indifference) towards other cultures, and this need not be reciprocal.

Pluralist multiculturalism requires legal privileges or exclusions that enable particular cultural groups to maintain their distinctive identities or practices, undiluted by the norms or laws of the host culture to which they have chosen to emigrate. A prime example of this occurred in 2013 when British Judge Peter Murphy allowed a Muslim woman from London to appear in court and enter a plea without removing her full-face veil.[1] After much backroom wrangling over the legal issues, Murphy and his critics reached a compromise, ruling at Blackfriars Crown Court that the accused woman could also stand trial wearing the veil but must remove it only when giving testimony and then could give testimony directly to the judge while remaining behind a screen to shield her from public view while giving evidence.[2]

Liberal multiculturalism, of which I am an advocate, supports diversity within a broadly liberal framework, and therefore rejects intolerant or authoritarian cultural practices that violate the equal rights of others[3] to pursue their own vision of the "good life". Many liberals agree that this liberal form of multiculturalism better protects individuals within minority communities, unlike pluralist multiculturalism which protects groups but often leaves individuals within minority communities vulnerable to forms of cultural tyranny.

One problem with protecting groups *as such* is that dominant community leaders tend to speak on behalf of "the community" as a whole, whether or not their views are really representative of individuals within the community. This just replaces one form of cultural imperialism with another. It does nothing to address the problem of cultural imperialism (hegemony, dominance) in principle.

Pluralist multiculturalists place a greater emphasis on diversity than on equal rights and opportunities for all. Part of the pluralist multiculturalist agenda is to push for value pluralism and moral relativism (i.e. the view that different moral beliefs – both those that respect self-determination and authoritarian, theocratic or fundamentalist ideologies that do not – are equally legitimate). Accordingly, pluralist multiculturalists argue that we need to question everything in such a way that no one belief system is permitted to dominate.[4] They like to remind us that we live in an age where old political certainties have been eroded while new identity politics have thrived.[5]

The moral relativists who promote a subjective understanding of "truth" nevertheless assume that their relativist view on the matter is *correct*, or at least morally superior to that of their "Eurocentric" opponents, who are likely to be described as somehow involved in a "paranoid right wing project" of one kind or another.[6] The didactic moral relativist claims that all moral judgments are relative or subjective, and then turns *that belief* into an objective morality that all of us should live by. From such a perspective, it becomes a kind of "sin" to be anything other than a relativist. Accordingly, if one attempted to deploy an objective or universal view of human rights, one would run the risk of being accused of intolerance or colonialism. This is somewhat odd given the impressively wide-ranging signatories to documents such as The European Convention on Human Rights and The Universal Declaration of Human Rights[7].

Those who fear the rise of far-right reactionary parties in the UK and Europe rightly insist that political realities must inform any Western critique of Islam and that misrepresenting Muslim people in any simplistic way is dangerous. I share with multiculturalists the view that any constructive dialogue needs to be nuanced and respectful other peoples' reciprocal rights. We must also bear in mind the hypocrisies and global political crimes committed by our own regimes.

However, in practical terms there are fundamental disagreements over just *how* to achieve a constructive dialogue. As a liberal academic theologian and teacher of political philosophy, I want to address the question of how Western liberals can enter into any dialogue about Islam and its impact on women's rights, LGBQI rights and human rights unimpeded by the kind of fanatical political correctness that has only served to obstruct cross-cultural exchanges and mutually empowering relationships. Arguably, liberal values are consistent with, indeed essential to, protecting the values of toleration and diversity that multiculturalists ostensibly cherish.

It is important that we dissect some of the prevalent views and arguments used by pluralist multiculturalists to defend Islam from the sort of critical examination that might be levelled against any other religion or ideology in a modern liberal state. We should also bear in mind that criticisms of Islam come from Muslims or ex-Muslims as well as from outsiders who are not practicing Muslims. So, the question of whether Islam can be judged is also about whether Westerners can ever be justified in lending support to Muslims when they share critical perspectives in common.

Some doubt that it is even possible for non-Muslims to judge Islam, or aspects of it. Cultural relativists assume that groups cannot psychologically or imaginatively cross cultural barriers, presumably because the concepts deployed from within one culture cannot translate to another. This presupposes that people are incapable of understanding the beliefs or values of others sufficiently to assess them. Not only would this type of cultural "captivity" make the sharing of knowledge between different people obsolete, it also seems to make an un-testable claim about the psychological capacities of others. We should have reservations about such a sweeping relativism that makes the study of other cultures or other people's experiences (their literature, their poetry, their religious texts, their films, their humour) obsolete for all but the convert. It is as though, in order to really understand another person's outlook, you must also agree with it entirely or be so immersed in it that you could not doubt any of its customs or claims. Few people born into a culture even experience that kind of uncritical harmony with their own cultural traditions. Imagine our response if an American woman in 2017 said that a piece of literature was not worth reading solely because it was authored in 1950 by an African male. We would rightly think that this woman is a narrow-minded philistine.

Literature and art are about seeing, not only literally but also with our imaginations and minds. Words do not belong to anyone, and nor do ideas. The goal of literature is to take readers beyond the limits of their own lives and past experiences and, as Mark Rowlands has so beautifully described it, "to see your own limitlessness in the life of another."[8] Rowlands invites us to think of literature as "the imaginative extension of compassion, one procured by detailed, painstaking methods." He claims that the enormous success of this art form can be attributed to the strength of our desire to see:

> "We endure with fictional characters. We care about what happens to them. And we know, all the while, that [they] are not real. No one really knows why this is so: all attempts to solve this paradox are,... problematic." Literature can draw us so deeply into paradox only because it exploits the ability to see oneself in the other...

> In literature, the ideas are living, breathing, respiring, perspiring, woven into the fabric of a person's life, in all of its limitless wonder, and unintelligible apart from that life."[9]

The idea that individuals lack any consciousness apart from their cultural identities seems to entail a belief that no one *within* a particular culture ever doubts its customs or beliefs or finds them oppressive or alien to his own values or sense of self. Furthermore, the staunch relativist denies the possibility that the experience of immersion in some *other* (e.g. non-Muslim) culture could have significant parallels with aspects of the Muslim's experiences. Apparently, meaningful dialogue cannot be based on the outrageous assumption that we are all human, and as such might share common emotional or psychological needs that translate between cultures. For the relativist, there is no common ground of humanity or condition that could transcend culture, customs or country. The idea that one person's cultural experience might be comparable to another person's (from another culture) is beyond the pale.

Is it really true that cultures are incommensurable, or indeed that they are even internally homogeneous systems? Relativism neglects the fact that individuals can and do belong simultaneously to *many cultures* or sub-cultures and that people can *choose* to prioritise or to demote which aspects of culture will form their identities. As an example, within the category "Muslims" there exist male Muslims and female Muslims, Shias and Sunnis, straight and gay, middle class and working class, old and young, hardliners and reformers. The identity politician, in placing a person's culture above her individuality, seems to reject the possibility that a Western Christian woman may have a great deal more in common with a Muslim woman because of their shared gender, or shared homosexuality, or common love of chess, than she may have with a heterosexual Christian Englishman.

As an antidote to the allegedly "top down" moral realism that liberal universalism implies, some pluralist multiculturalists argue that a more complete form of respect for the "other" is needed – one that goes beyond imagining oneself in an other's situation to actually imagining oneself *being* someone fundamentally *different from* oneself.[10] The demand seems to be to abandon one's own moral convictions and values, and to psychologically supplant them with those of the other. Even if we agree that it this theoretically possible, the thought experiment seems to sidestep the problem rather than to solve it. In either direction it flows, this imaginative leap into the other's sandals seems to eradicate the self completely.

However, let us suppose for the sake of argument that an advocate for the liberal value of tolerance were able to abandon her values and supplant them with fundamentalist Islamic ones. Then let us compare the reverse situation in which, say, a fundamentalist imam exchanges his authoritarian theocratic values for liberal values like autonomy, self-determination and religious freedom. Having adopted liberal values, the fundamentalist would lose nothing, except his power to control *other peoples'* lives. Within a liberal framework, he would still be free to follow his own conscience, worship his own god, and adopt dietary restrictions and mandatory dress codes, with the minor constraint that he could not impose these religious constraints *on others* who do not share his beliefs.

On the other hand, the liberal, having adopted the fundamentalist imam's values, would now be forced to submit to rules that constrain her in what she can wear, what she can eat and drink, who she can associate with, what she can say, how she can behave, who she can marry, who she can copulate with and exactly how she can do it. She would have a lot more individual liberty to lose than the imam, who would forsake only liberties that belong to other people anyway. As J. S. Mill puts it:

"There are many who consider as an injury to themselves any conduct which they have a distaste for, and resent it as an outrage to their feelings; as a religious bigot, when charged with disregarding the religious feelings of others, has been known to retort that they disregard his feelings, ... But there is no parity between the feeling of a person for his own opinion, and the feeling of another who is offended at his holding it; no more than between the desire of a thief to take a purse, and the desire of the right owner to keep it. And a person's taste is as much his own peculiar concern as his opinion or his purse...

(*On Liberty*, 1859)

As women know only too well, fundamentalist religions (not just Islam) tend to insert their legal tentacles into *all* aspects of life, not least of all those that concern matters that liberals consider private.

My opponents will say that this argument fails since the liberal-turned-fundamentalist is *voluntarily* subscribing to her fundamentalist religious belief, so that she doesn't and cannot experience these religious commitments as "constraints". This riposte, however, does not address the issue in dispute – which is the relative compromise being made by each of these ideological positions in demanding that others "respect" them in the positive sense that requires us to go beyond mere non-interference to full adherence to the others' worldview. My point is that liberalism can accommodate the *voluntary* practice of Islamic (and other) fundamentalisms, while religious fundamentalism cannot accommodate the voluntary practice of anything else.

The riposte to my thought experiment also assumes what it needs to prove, which is that *all* Muslims *voluntarily* adopt these constraints on their liberty, a claim that is hard to reconcile with the existence of social stigma, honour-based violence, cultural taboos, and economic control that accompany dissent or prevent it from occurring in most places where Muslims are the majority or exert family pressures on individuals. There are social customs and taboos that can constrain an individual's development as completely as any form of political oppression, as John Stuart Mill saw only too well. Mill observed that society issues its own mandates that can exert a formidable social tyranny over the individual, especially as it "leaves fewer means of escape, penetrating much more deeply into the details of life."[11] Mill addressed the "magical influence" of custom, stating that it becomes second nature to us, despite being "continually mistaken for the first".

Another argument says that Westerners cannot judge Islam in isolation from culture and historical, political and ethnic factors. Consequently, Islam has no clearly defined meaning. Not all Islam is fundamentalist. Rather, Islam's meanings constantly shift depending upon the context and the speaker(s). Western liberals ought to be suspicious of this constant flux. Certainly, there are many Muslim moderates who are not fundamentalists and not intolerant. There are also Muslim apostates. My misgivings about the plasticity of Islam are not based on a wish to over-simplify it or to lump all Muslims into a monolithic group. But all too often the plasticity of Islam is conveniently deployed to silence all meaningful debate about Islamic cultural practices and their effects on individual Muslim persons. Whenever a critic of Islamic religious doctrines or practices attempts to single out for criticism some aspect of Islam that *is* intolerant or even violent, the response is invariably that the behaviour in question isn't *really* Islamic or is somehow not representative of Islam. Any Islamic practice that would be open to critical scrutiny (e.g. terrorism, jihad, honour-based violence or mandatory female veiling) is immediately relegated to the 'misrepresentation of Islam' category.

This, of course, implies that there *is* a **real** Islam, i.e. an authentic interpretation of Islam to which the false "misrepresentation" can be contrasted. However, the defender of the seemingly Islamic practice under scrutiny simultaneously claims, inconsistently, that there is *no real Islam*, since Islam cannot be discussed in isolation from all of its shape-shifting contexts of use. The pluralist multiculturalist implicitly *supports* the idea of an *accurately defined* Islam **if** the context is *defending* Islam from Western critics who are caricatured as never getting Islam quite right, or not right enough to criticise how it operates in any specific context, at any rate. Yet these same defenders of Islam deny that there is any accurately defined "Islam" when critics attempt to oppose forms of Islamist authoritarianism, sexism, homophobia, or intolerance. What this means, ultimately, is that the assertion of "real" Islam (correctly defined) can be used by Islam's defenders but never by its detractors, even if the defenders are not Muslims themselves and not experts in Islam. Detractors, on the other hand, had better *at least* be Muslim, if not specialists in Islam, or they simply aren't qualified to have an opinion.

Nebulous equivocation over the *real* Islam begins to remind one of Orwellian Newspeak, invented by the Ministry of Truth precisely to make a heretical idea literally *unspeakable*. This pre-emption of any criticism of Islam as inherently "biased", "racist", "Islamophobic" or "simplistic" forecloses all dialogue on things Islamic except amongst faithful initiates or their defenders.

One could argue that criticism of Islam should only be allowed if it is *informed* criticism. While this is certainly preferable for commentary on any subject, all too often the demand for more accurate or complete information forecloses debate over the most contentious Islamic beliefs or practices by sliding into the perfectionist fallacy: unless you know *everything* about Islam, you can't know *any*thing about it. The censorship of a re-screening on Channel 4 of Tom Holland's documentary *Islam: The Untold Story* in 2012 was a key example of this approach to informed "debate". Unless you have the "right" information, from the "right" institutional sources, you are unqualified to speak on the subject of Islam. Holland received death threats in addition to Iranian State media calling his film an insult to Islam and the Islamic Education and Research Academy (IERA) accusing Holland of making "baseless assumptions".

Culturally sensitive Westerners are laden with guilt about their own "cultural insensitivity" (racism?) while apparently seeing their sexism as negligible. We must ask why the Islamist's right to self-determination vis-à-vis Western law is more important than the right to self-determination of some who live under *its* religious legal strictures. In some cases, the former "right" nullifies the latter. The idea that sexism is only "wrong" because of Western liberal culture's assumptions, but not wrong in any universal way that could make a patriarchal religion's discriminatory practices objectively unethical, applies equally to the West's taboo of racism. The liberal value of egalitarianism that makes racism a cultural abomination is, according to the relativist's outlook, just a cultural "construct" with no independent validity and no objective moral claim on anyone else. This being the case, relativists really need to stop being so "culturally insensitive" towards racists. It is almost as though they want to colonise the whole world with anti-racist ideas, God forbid!

J.S. Mill, the architect of liberal political philosophy, defended freedom of expression on all matters (even for partial truths or mistaken views) because we seldom possess the entire truth. Even if we are supremely confident that society has got it right on some particular question, and that the alternatives are ludicrous, it is healthy to withstand the expression of false viewpoints because it forces us to hold our beliefs actively, rather than in the lazy manner in which one might cling to dead dogma. If we regard our most reasonable values in the manner of blind faith, we risk becoming as narrow-minded as the acolytes of Westboro Baptist Church.

While it might be preferable for non-Muslims to consult Muslim scholars about Islam, rather than assuming we know all about their sacred texts or customs, the kind of cultural sensitivity that is supposed to inform genuinely respectful relations *between Westerners and Muslims* apparently does not apply to relations *between Muslims* themselves. Do anti-racist liberals or Islamists ever suggest that Muslim men ought to actually interview a wide cross-section of Muslim women and then, based on that inductive process, draw conclusions about women as a group? No. It is just accepted that, if a select group of all-male Islamic "experts" begin from deductive, *a priori* theological accounts of what women (as a group) are like, this definition is eternally valid insofar as it is the culturally dominant one. These too are stereotypes, but ones that apparently don't bother the faux-liberals that defend Islam from its evil "racist" detractors. While culturally sensitive liberals have a commendable desire to curb the stereotyping of Muslims by Westerners, they fail to apply the same standards to the stereotyping of sub-groups of Muslims by one another, and they fail to see that there are many motives for wishing to criticise Islamic teachings or practices other than latent racism.

A British survey about people's perceptions of the word "Islam" revealed that a large majority of respondents recorded negative associations with the word.[12] This might be unfortunate. But I would wager that, if you did a similar survey about British peoples' perceptions of the word "feminism", you might get an overwhelmingly negative response too. Each year in my classroom I survey my students on their perceptions of "feminism". Students of both sexes who are from a variety of cultural and religious backgrounds consistently express an overwhelmingly negative set of connotations with the word. Yet no one from the pluralist multiculturalist camp has ever suggested that feminists can't be ridiculed or publicly scorned or offended.

Feminists and homosexuals are supposed to "put up and shut up", because they should "tolerate difference" when it is apparently confined to other cultures. However, for them to expect the same from fundamentalist Muslims is "intolerant" and a cultural imposition. Yet most liberals who embrace multiculturalism would be more than happy to express disapproval of Westboro Baptist Church, a fundamentalist Christian church that became notorious for its outspoken homophobia. Most Americans and Britons do not share a culture with Westboro Baptist

Church's members, who live in Kansas, USA. The only difference in their attitudes and willingness to express disapproval of *these* religious bigots is that Westboro Baptist's homophobes are white.

A 2016 ICM poll of British Muslims revealed that over a third of respondents (39%) agreed that wives should always obey their husbands. This is deeply offensive to feminists, but in a tolerant society they have to deal with being offended. The majority of British Muslims (52%) held homophobic views and agreed that homosexuality should be illegal in Britain, while 47% thought that homosexuals should not be allowed to work as teachers. Again, no one has ever suggested that homosexuality has to be positively "respected" by religious believers (and protected from "defamation") just because such views offend homosexuals. Unless the religious homophobia comes from rural white Americans, in which case "culture" apparently has nothing to do with it.

My point is not that we have to choose between one form of bigotry and another. Western liberals need not remain in a deadlock over whether or not tolerance and respect for religious minorities trumps respect for women or homosexuals. After all, religious women and Muslim homosexuals fall into both categories. *Liberal multiculturalism* offers a framework within which Muslims can live according to their faith, be prevented from coercing others to do so, and remain free to offend, and be offended, by others in an open, dynamic, sometimes uncomfortable (but genuine) dialogue. This is what political liberty looks like. It is not always pleasant, but genuine political freedom is too precious to sacrifice on the altar of "politeness".

This model worked, with minimal violence, for decades before September 11, 2001, which "changed everything". But human beings are in charge of what they choose to change, and how they respond to "events". Despite the demagoguery, there is no compulsion for them to respond in reactionary ways that erode the most workable and fair model of government they've had so far.

Notes

[1] http://www.express.co.uk/news/uk/571042/Muslim-niqab-Supreme-Court-Neuberger-court-full-face-veil
[2] http://www.bbc.co.uk/news/uk-england-24112067
[3] N.B. – Often these 'others' are within the same minority community.

[4] For example, see Nina Power's comments in *The New Humanist Guide to Getting Along*, Winter 2013 Issue, Features, Vox Pops, p. 46.

[5] See for example Daniel Trilling's editorial mission statement in the Winter 2013 edition of *The New Humanist*, p. 5.

[6] Ibid.

[7] The following countries voted in favour of the Declaration: Afghanistan, Argentina, Australia, Belgium, Bolivia, Brazil, Burma, Canada, Chile, China, Colombia, Costa Rica, Cuba, Denmark, the Dominican Republic, Ecuador, Egypt, El Salvador, Ethiopia, France, Greece, Guatemala, Haiti, Iceland, India, Iran, Iraq, Lebanon, Liberia, Luxembourg, Mexico, Netherlands, New Zealand, Nicaragua, Norway, Pakistan, Panama, Paraguay, Peru, Philippines, Thailand, Sweden, Syria, Turkey, United Kingdom, United States, Uruguay and Venezuela.

[8] Rowlands, Mark, *A Good Life: Philosophy from Cradle to Grave* (London: Granta, 2015), p. 3.

[9] Ibid.

[10] The London-based educator John Holroyd, for example, has recommended this and explains his concept of 'dialogicality' with reference to Giambattista Vico's (1668 – 1744) notion of 'sympathetic imagination'.

[11] Mill, J.S., *On Liberty*, Chapter 1: Introductory. (1859)

[12] Commissioned by the *Exploring Islam Foundation*, the 2010 online YouGov poll of 2,152 adults found 58% of those questioned linked Islam with extremism while 69% believed it encouraged the repression of women.

CHAPTER TEN

THE HIJACKING OF GENDER

In the second decade of the twenty-first century, the most ultra-conservative religious regimes in the world greeted the transgender movement and transgender people with unreserved acceptance, despite their steadfast objection to homosexuality and feminism. This exceptionally warm welcome ought to have rung alarm bells among liberals and progressives. In Pakistan, political parties, interest groups and other political organisations are required to respect Islam and "public morality", an obligation that gives homophobia official state sanction. Despite this, in 2009 the Pakistani Supreme Court ruled that the government must take proactive steps to protect transsexuals from harassment and discrimination. In 2010, Pakistan's Supreme Court officially granted a "third gender" designation to transgender individuals and protection from discrimination. The same ultra-religious Pakistani government censored the website Queerpk.com from being viewed in late 2013. The Supreme Court, however, has in recent years taken steps towards recognizing transgender peoples' basic rights.

In a joint statement by the Archbishops of Canterbury and York issued on Thursday 27th July, 2017 to mark the fiftieth anniversary of The Sexual Offences Act 1967, the two clergymen called for a *"ban on the practice of Conversion Therapy aimed at altering sexual orientation"*, and but also recognised the *"need for transgender people to be welcomed and affirmed in their parish church"*. To see why these two statements are conflicting and indeed deeply misleading requires us to go back a few steps and to undertake a closer analysis of the "transgender" concept and its assumptions.

Gender used to be a progressive liberal concept. Baaddassss feminists like Simone de Beauvoir used it to distinguish what's between your legs (sex) from what's between your ears (gender). You were born with the former. The latter you were taught. What was put between your ears got there by means of patriarchal cultural indoctrination through parenting, religion, television and film, books, merchandise and toys, teachers, coaches and music. In short: life imitates art (and cultural artefacts), …and art imitates life. Culture is constructed through creative human design, but this design does not happen in a vacuum. Human culture "constructors" are also *products* of the cultures into which they have been born, and may reinforce their culture's background assumptions, or resist them. Culture endures when its values and forms are reproduced by those who have been shaped by them; it crumbles when those who have been moulded by cultural conventions push back and reject aspects of their own cultural heritage that have outlived their usefulness.

This was certainly the case for Western feminists of the twentieth century. When women tried to work their way into roles or positions that were the preserve of men, propagandists of patriarchy resorted to "nature" to reinforce the patriarchal system. This tactic worked because the *cultural* landscape was so saturated with stereotypes that they did seem almost "natural". A theory of biological determinism was wheeled in to explain why patriarchy is not a political issue, or a cultural product, but biological necessity. Sociobiologists like E.O. Wilson insisted that patriarchy persists because genes anchor culture. This approach was nothing new. Freud had rooted patriarchal culture in the penis and vagina (mostly the almighty penis). Christian traditionalists had always attached patriarchal social arrangements to reproductive functions as given in "creation", defining women's social roles as mother and wife accordingly. Eve's transgression and punishment by God further reinforced the female's subservient relationship to her husband. To this St. Paul added a dash of New Testament authority, stating that women should "submit themselves to their husband" as to the Lord (Ephesians 5:22-23). The sacred institution of marriage was a human invention, but it sustained "God's" intentions.

Some stubborn feminists refused to go along with this kind of "naturalisation" of patriarchy and its concomitant biological determinism, instead seeing the explanation for male domination in social, cultural, theological, academic and economic institutions. Existentialists like de Beauvoir were loathe to accept explanations for human behaviour that claimed it is determined by some fixed "essence". Both she and her lifelong companion, Jean-Paul Sartre, insisted that character is formed by an individual in response to his circumstances, through his free choices. We find ourselves thrown here, *in situ*, confronted with our own free will, and our choices must be made against a background of facts that we cannot change, such as the biological sex into which we have been born. But what we "make" of this is up to us. While it is clear that only women can bear children, the implications of this are quite undetermined and the current social division of labour is only one of a variety of possible social arrangements available to us.

Just like ye ole feminists of yore, gay, lesbian and bisexual individuals once *transgressed* the gender stereotypes their culture had taught them. According to normative and widespread heterosexist gender myths, these queer folks were labelled "butch", "sissies", "dykes" and "fairies" – epithets intended to stigmatise anyone who refused to perform and dress according to the sexist *and heterosexist* gender roles they had been taught. "Fags" and "dykes" chose to reclaim these derogatory monikers, owning them and wielding them as badges of pride in the face of heterosexist gender's defenders. By turning gender norms into a form of theatre, drag performers showed that one could adopt and mimic gender roles irrespective of one's genitalia, thus exposing the fact that gender is *not* natural but a conventional form of role play which can be put on or taken off (an observation from which academic Judith Butler would later forge her career). Queers were incarnations of gender's failure to stick to real people. All of this was progressive, because it laid bare the sexually conservative fiction that all men share heterosexual personality attributes different to all women, and vice-versa.

Queers noted that gender was constructed around heterosexism (i.e. heteronormativity) and heterosexual "role play". Culturally normative male or female social roles (i.e. gender) become ritualised, fetishised and eroticised. Exaggerating differences between men and women, mystifying the opposite sex, and making sexual acts taboo served to heighten the excitement of penetrating the mysteries of the "other" and overcoming barriers to sexual fulfilment. Or, as Tom Digby has explained, proscription of non-procreative sexuality is greatly facilitated by differentially marking each of the persons who can fulfil each of the complimentary procreative roles through different clothing, hairstyles, behaviour patterns, language styles, and work roles. Additionally, the resultant oppositionality is then eroticised, such that heterosexism results in a constant tension between the elements of sexual attraction and inter-gender mystification, which then reinforces the oppositionality between the sexes and forms the material for many a romantic comedy.[1]

Post-War feminists exposed the way in which "male" had been defined as an ideal archetype, and "female" defined in opposition to it – as everything that was "not male". Similarly, homosexuals refused to see themselves as defective or disordered heterosexuals. Queers rejected the bifurcation of humans into exactly two opposite, mutually attracted heterosexual types.

For both feminists and queers of the late twentieth century, the natural was *repressed* by the social. But at the same time, the definition of "natural" was *produced* by cultural and theological assumptions and myths. Ideas about gender are not just outcomes of empirical observations; they are the premises of the "research". Consequently, when individuals did not conform to sexual stereotypes, they were allegedly "reversing" (presumably real, essential, fixed) gender roles, not exposing gender roles as fictions. But if individuals, when observed, do not actually conform to the social ideas/stereotypes of gender, then this ought to be taken as evidence that social ideas of gender are flawed. Instead, heterosexist gender's defenders treated gender roles as presupposed *a priori*, and evidence conflicting with them was interpreted as "abnormal" or deviant, not as an indication that the presupposed "norm" was flawed in the first place. There is a problem of circularity in the whole conceptual frame within which gender is "researched". John Gray's bestseller *Men Are From Mars, Women Are From Venus* is a study in this unscientific methodology.

The new transgender movement is not an extension of past efforts to deconstruct sexist and heterosexist gender mythology. Rather, it divides and conquers this once-powerful countercultural movement, hijacking its language and mimicking its political posture to disguise its opposite intent. Consequently, in the past several years "gender" has been radically re-defined and transformed from a set of conventions and constraints on what men and women can be or do, to an interior mental state or a definitive "identity". Educator and performer Chrissie Daz is right in saying that something fundamental has changed in the way in which gender is understood in the twenty first century, with the new transgender warriors representing a major paradigm shift in gender thinking over the last forty years.[2] An idea once wielded by the liberal left *against* conservative sexist and heterosexist stereotypes, gender has now been retooled as a weapon in the armoury of a regressive politics that is not only sexist but homophobic.

Today's transgender movement *reinforces* the myth that men and women are altogether different species of human beings, not just reproductively, but *mentally* – with different desires, different needs, different aptitudes, and different minds. Today's transgender spokespersons *support* the traditionally conservative naturalisation of "masculinity" and "femininity" as innate psychological states, intrinsic in the human subject as a deep and fixed psychological "identity" or arising from brain chemistry or other hormonal interactions of the body. The progressive idea that there is no uniform way that all boys *as such* (or all girls *as such*) necessarily feel or think has been scrapped. Instead of railing against a rigid heterosexist gender binary (as their rhetoric would suggest) the new Trans warriors assume that their innate sense of self ("identity") is inherently "masculine" or "feminine" *prior* to any socialisation. Apparently, the influence of cultural indoctrination is negligible. Gender has been de-politicised, naturalised and medicalised in the same stroke.

Trans-activists are forever using their neologism "non-binary" to re-tool gender, putting it into the service of a regressive sexual politics resembling the role it played before queers and feminists deconstructed it. Transgender's spokespersons forever claim that they, or their patients, are "non-binary". The noun "non-binary" contains a hidden assumption. To claim of oneself that one is "non-binary" is simultaneously to stake a claim to minority status. It therefore presupposes that other people, or indeed most people, **are binary**. But this is to assume exactly what needs to be proved. If nobody is binary, because the heterosexist myth that there are two big heterosexual categories of persons – with members of each camp presumably sharing not just the same genitalia, but a whole cluster of common personality traits – is absurd, then saying "I'm non-binary" is obsolete, redundant, and meaningless because *everyone* is non-binary.

Real gender critics of the past believed that the gender binary is a socially conservative myth. They accepted two biologically distinct *sexual* categories: males and females (and a small minority of intersex persons). But they treated as nonsense further division of the human species into two big, internally uniform, *personality* types based on shared reproductive organs. The fact that all women have vaginas or ovaries does not imply that all women have the same kind of "mind". By using the term non-binary (as a noun), the speaker implies that the non-binary person is different to the majority, who presumably *are* "binary". But if, as feminists and queers of the post-war period supposed, it doesn't make sense to group humans into two big heterosexual personality blocs, then *everybody* is non-binary so there is no need to proclaim that *you* are "non-binary" because it is redundant.

Saying that someone is "non-binary" is a lot like saying that someone is "non-unicorn". While it may be **true** to say that a person is "non-unicorn", it also implies something false, which is that some other group of creatures are "unicorns". But if there *are no unicorns*, then opposing humans to them by using the "non-unicorn" term is really misleading. Sure, we can talk about unicorns meaningfully because we know how to talk about fictional constructs. We can also talk about the tooth fairy and Santa Claus. But the ability to refer to something meaningfully does not mean that the referent actually exists (in reality). If it did, then our talk of tooth fairies would bring them into existence.

Gender is now a concept that *appears* to do the kind of political work once associated with the civil rights movement. In reality it reverses the logic by which civil rights were achieved. Civil rights activists of the past claimed that discrimination based on biological differences like skin colour or sex failed to acknowledge the equal humanity of all persons as moral agents. Grouping people according to common physical traits neglected their individuality and their character as persons. Groups of individuals were defined by reference to skin colour or genitals, not by human agency, character and behaviour. Thus were persons reduced to their bodies (or parts of their bodies) while the more important and distinctively human attributes of intellect and will (aspects that should ground an appraisal of character) were neglected.

Present day gender rights activists do not demand to be treated as individuals, nor do they see their character as a choice. They emphasise that they belong to a "minority" defined by gender identity, or sameness with others who share their allegedly "essential" condition as mentally "male" or "female" irrespective of biological genitalia. Whereas civil rights activists made biology irrelevant, transgender rights activists treat it as all-important. The "masculinity" or "femininity" of the trans subject's psyche is treated as an innate condition akin to hair colour or skin pigmentation. Young children are encouraged to *define* themselves as "masculine" or "feminine" by dint of their preferences in play, dress and mannerism. Since they are ostensibly a category of people defined by reference to this innate, essential difference, the argument is that they should not face discrimination any more than women or black/minority ethnic persons. However, whereas women and BME persons of the mid-twentieth century civil rights movement were keen to *disassociate* themselves from reductionist biological or essentialist definitions of their identities, urging others *not to* define them by reference to genitalia, skin colour or group stereotypes, today's transgender activists demand *recognition* of their allegedly innate difference, believing that membership in a biologically or essentially distinct group should entitle them to civil rights and legal recognition.

Adopting this determinist account of their "condition" (an innate gendered psyche) requires that we first accept religiously conservative premises about gender. Even if we allow, as transgender activists more recently claim, that gender is a choice – a *chosen* "identity" – then we should arrive back with the post-war progressive queers and feminists, and accept the logical conclusion that gender is meaninglessness fiction – since it is little more than a mythological social construct that can be "put on" or taken off (chosen and performed). Gender is not innate in us but a set of abstract ideas. But for trans-activists, the opposite has occurred: gender is something static and real, to be asserted and "owned". It is a meaningful and rigid category; indeed so real that it gives the claimant his or her *essential* "identity". It is allegedly a part of his or her inner "self" and at the very same time it is a choice, an identity that can be adopted at any point in one's life. But let us set aside these contradictory premises for a moment and just grant the transgender premise that gender is a real "thing".

As we saw above, one concept that is built into gender is the heterosexuality of men and women. However, if heteronormative gender means that being female includes being an erotic match for men, then lesbians might not identify very strongly with "femininity" (a female gender role), since they are not attracted to men and do not wish to be an object of male sexual attention. Likewise, male homosexuals will find it hard to "fit" into heterosexual masculinity with its accompanying erotic assumptions. Once binary gender has been essentialised and turned into one of two heterosexually-gendered fixed psychological states, this leaves only one option for biological females who feel a strong affinity with normatively "male" behaviours and/or sexual attractions – they must actually *become* biological males. They are no longer lesbians; now they are men trapped in female bodies. So we are back to the conservative religious view that gay persons are defective or dysfunctional heterosexuals. Likewise, if binary gender is conceptualised in the usual heteronormative way, then it would follow that a lesbian female could think of her attraction to other females as a "male" trait, and so she might re-define herself as 'masculine' (if she believes in the reality of gender). If women had an innate or chosen desire to "act like men" while being biologically female, they would be sick ("dysphoric"). The same goes for biological males who feel a stronger affinity to normatively "feminine" roles and sexual tendencies. In this context, it would be unsurprising if homosexuals felt confused.

Transgender's clinicians identify gender dysphoria (unhappiness) as an abnormal psycho-sexual condition. But if the dysphoria is really an *effect* or symptom of society's *misunderstanding* of **natural** human sexual biochemistry (including its homosexual variants), then the disease is not *intrinsic* in the "patient"; it is the outcome of a relationship *between* the "patient" and his surrounding (heterosexist) culture. Indeed, both liberal eugenicist Nicholas Agar and Christian bioethicists Michael J. Reiss and Roger Straughan construe disease as a socially constructed concept, or as a relationship between a person and society.

However, queer activists of the past argued that it is the nature of the relationship – not the nature of the patient – that makes the "patient" feel unhappy. A social "dis-ease" (uneasiness) with difference is re-conceptualised as a psychosexual abnormality within the constitution of the patient. The subject's "disordered brain" is seen as the cause of an unacceptable interaction of individuals and social organisations. The political consequence is that of deflecting criticism away from social institutions that might need reforming, and towards the aberrant individual demanding reforms. He must be altered to fit the institutions.

To get some purchase on how this works in practice, we need only consider the situation for queers in Iran. Iran is a sexist, intolerant, homophobic theocracy, where fundamentalist religious laws strictly enforce the hetero-normative status quo. The official state solution to homosexuality is to either (1) punish or execute those who practice it openly, or (2) "encourage" homosexuals to transition, surgically, to the "correct" sex so that they can fit back into the heterosexual norm, i.e., the only norm Iran tolerates. Consequently, Iran has the second highest number of sexual reassignment surgeries in the world, second only to Thailand.

This seems analogous to chemically lightening a black person's skin to make him more comfortable in a racist society, when what should be done is to tackle the society's racism. It seems politically regressive. Instead of rejecting or deconstructing the heteronormative binary, the medical industry seems to be facilitating the transgender individual's literal "deconstruction" of her*self* – literally her very body – so that she can re-make it in the binary heterosexist image required. This is violence masquerading as compassion.

This is not entirely dissimilar to the Soviet-styled "medicine" of the early 1970's, in which the Soviet state used violence only as a last resort in dealing with her dissenting intelligentsia who had begun to press for greater political freedoms. Psychiatric investigations and diagnoses of mental illness (typically schizophrenia) became the preferred instrument through which the dissident's incarceration in a psychiatric hospital could be achieved.

In light of the politically fraught historical relationship between the LGBQI rights movement and establishment political institutions, the current Transgender "treatment" trend might best be analysed in light of Michel Foucault's argument that the entire category of psychological disorders is the expression of power relationships within society. In a simplified form, Foucault's view is that madness is not a property of the individual, but a social definition projected by society onto a non-compliant proportion of its population.

The seemingly compassionate progressive medical and clinical "recognition" of the transgender "patient" may in reality be **reinforcing** the heteronormative binary that long caused suffering and alienation for a variety of gender queer people. Liberals need not object to informed, consenting adults surgically transitioning to a body they feel comfortable living in. However, perhaps liberal progressives should consider for a moment the rush to embrace this option uncritically, or as the *primary* solution for those who suffer gender dysphoria. This is especially so where children are concerned, since they have neither sufficient experience of their body's sexual potentials, nor adequate understanding of how socialisation works on their self-understanding, to give meaningfully *informed* consent to the procedure.

There is simply no way to test whether being unhappy with one's biological body is a by-product of dogmatic gender enculturation or the symptom of an innate condition, since all cultures indoctrinate kids with gender, albeit in a diverse variety of ways. There is no control group against which we could compare gender-indoctrinated individuals. But the Trans activists' claim that some biological females are *inherently* "masculine" while some biological males are *inherently* "feminine" assumes what it needs to prove: namely, that gender is natural and intrinsic in the psycho-sexual make-up of the individual, rather than a set of culturally circulated fictions that he or she has internalised.

On the other hand, if the "trans kid" is supposed to simply *choose* a gender and is granted the authority to define this for himself, the choice is still a selection from the heteronormative gender menu. Saying that the "patient" is doomed to unhappiness unless he can define his gender autonomously is a bit like saying that I am doomed to poverty unless I can choose whether to have an imaginary benefactor or to win an imaginary lottery. It would be so much simpler to just do away with imaginary sources of wealth since neither is real. Insisting on my "right" to escape poverty by claiming that I have a wealthy benefactor instead of a winning lotto ticket is meaningless if both are merely abstract concepts that only have currency in the real world because of outdated myths that create unnecessary social divisions.

While there is no problem accepting that sex and sexual orientation are essential or innate in our biological constitution, this does not commit us to accept an essentialist theory of **gender**. Indeed today's pseudo-liberal defenders of all things Transgender thwart progress by relinquishing the **nature / nurture** distinction that, in the past, the concept of gender served to illuminate.

In the context of gender identity politics, it becomes difficult to distinguish the homosexual from the transgendered person. The latter is conceptualised as a heterosexual male or female psyche/ "inner self" trapped in the "wrong" body.

But "wrong" according to whom, or what? Whether one is homosexual or heterosexual, binary gender norms represent a set of industrial strength constraints on how a person with male or female genitals may act. Homosexuality represents one good reason why a subset of people simply cannot feel "at home" in their bodies, given the sexual expectations built into socially dominant (heterosexist) gender norms.

But some straight people also find it incredibly hard to identify with the many behavioural expectations placed on persons of their sex. Some people simply find the gender constructs of "masculinity" and "femininity" too limiting or alienating. They struggle to adapt their interests and personalities to social expectations and generalisations about men and women. This is not a disease in those persons, but a symptom of social "dis-ease" with diversity (i.e. deviance from its norms).

All individuals are strongly "encouraged" to believe that they will be better off and happier if their ideas about their biological "selves" mesh with the culturally acceptable ones. Therefore, they too might be happier to transition than to cross-dress or to live with the constant rejection that haunts the non-conformist. In a liberal society, sexual reassignment surgery should not be off the table. However, it should not enjoy precedence over those who prefer to fight for social reforms. Gender reassignment surgery should be a decision taken by adults who are fully aware of the part that culture plays in their understanding of themselves as male or female persons.

To grasp the looming political implications of the current transgender rights trend, we need to be clear about how its core concepts function in relation to women's rights and LGBI rights, as well as to "liberal" eugenics. Transhumanists and so-called liberal eugenicists (Nicholas Agar, Julian Savulescu, James Hughes, Nick Bostrom, David Pearce, Gregory Stock, John Harris, Johann Hari, et. al.) combine their biopolitics with free market economics to arrive at an ostensibly "liberal" social policy on the use of biotech. These self-described "liberal eugenicists'" are arguing for unlimited and/or unregulated use of **reprogenetics**.[3] They distinguish reprogenetics from eugenics in that the latter implies state coercion with the presumption of benefit. The former would be voluntarily pursued by individual parents with the aim of improving their children according to their preferences. This is "privatised" or "free-market" eugenics (so there is of course a financial incentive to promote its use).

Most liberal eugenicists defend the right of parents to select the sexual orientation of their offspring. Social engineering traditionally done by means of discipline and punishment could soon be accomplished through biotech, pre-natal hormone treatments and/or genome editing. Reprogenetic interventions to inhibit homosexual desire/arousal would constitute a form of social engineering that is not therapeutic in any medical sense, but aims at constraining another individual's behaviour (without her consent) to the kinds of life goals that parents prefer. The future would be one in which homosexual persons would never rebel against the indoctrination of homophobic parents by "coming out" because they simply won't wish to do so. Inside the seemingly progressive Transgender Trojan Horse's belly is a regressive sexual politics that is prepared to use medicine and biotech to, first, surgically and chemically – and later, maybe even genetically – engineer us back to our traditional roles within the age-old heterosexual binary.

IF a biological cause of homosexual attraction exists, eliminating it will almost certainly reduce homosexual behaviour. To deny this is to pretend that voluntary sexual acts are unrelated to involuntary sexual attraction. The very purpose of reprogenetic interventions will be to eliminate individuals' voluntary homosexual behaviour by eliminating their involuntary biological predisposition for it. This will happen not by taking away the individual's free will, but by biologically steering the direction in which it is most likely to be expressed.

The new Trans movement (whether intentionally or not) removes the only barrier that would prevent parents being able to assume the patient's implied consent[4] for this kind of pre-natal eugenic "treatment" of his psycho-sexual "condition". In order to define and target homosexual orientation as a medical condition suitable for "treatment", it will first be necessary to distinguish this "treatment" from homophobic medical violence, which would be too objectionable. All that is lacking to make the distinction between medical violence and legitimate "treatment" viable is the assumption that the patient would happily consent to such a "treatment". In their haste to embrace "Transgender rights", well-meaning liberals and homosexuals are furnishing just that assumption.

A homophobic eugenics movement has searched for the holy grail of biological sexual orientation with the aim of finding a way to change it. If biotech companies ever do locate a biological cause(s) for homosexual orientation, all they will lack to be permitted to "cure" it is a conceptual framework that will allow homophobic genome editing or pre-natal hormonal treatment to appear benevolent. Since the "treatment" will be done to an unborn foetus, clinicians will need to pathologise homosexuality in such a way that parents can assume the patient's (offspring's) consent for its "cure". They could only make such an assumption **if** *existing* individuals with non-binary sexualities would consent to changing *themselves*.

The Transgender movement fights for recognition of the deviant's clinical "condition" and patients' "rights" to access medical assistance in transitioning back to a socially conservative definition of health. If some who have transitioned do not actually end up being heterosexual, they will have nevertheless supported the heterosexist notion that gender is, for some subset of individuals, an internal biological or otherwise definitive condition as well as one that causes them to feel bad ("dysphoric"). As voluntary patients who accept the theoretical medicalisation of their unhappiness, they will have played a role in the conceptual re-branding of socio-political issues as clinical pathologies. While Trans supporters are motivated by good intentions, they unwittingly help social conservatives to sell a eugenic agenda to the public, casting it as a form of enlightened compassion or tolerance for diversity.

There is no reason why we cannot have compassion for people who feel that they are trapped in the "wrong" biological body. What is troublesome is not how these individuals feel. Rather, the issue is how their feelings are being framed or interpreted, and this is partly owing to the socio-political contexts in which their feelings arise in the first place. As Sarah Ditum has argued, "the fact of suffering is not evidence that the sufferer has unimpeachable insight into the source of that suffering."[5] If societies were organised around the assumption that natural human sexuality (attraction) includes **both** heterosexual and homosexual variants, not only would this go some way to eliminating the stigma associated with being born intersex, it would greatly diminish homophobia and (to a large extent) sexism. And because it would also break down sexist myths about gender that alienate those who do not, and cannot, feel "at ease" with the social roles assigned to people of their genital sex, it would likely increase the well-being of those who presently feel they are trapped in the "wrong" bodies.

Notes

[1] Digby, Tom, 'Do Feminists Hate Men?', *Journal of Social Philosophy*, Vol. XXIX, Fall 1998, pp. 15 -29.
[2] See, Daz, Chrissie, 'Non-Binary Gender: Where the Mood May Take You' at *Culture on the Offensive*, accessed on May 25, 2017 at
http://www.cultureontheoffensive.com/non-binary-gender-where-the-mood-may-take-you/
[3] **Reprogenetics** is the use of reproductive and genetic technologies to select and genetically modify embryos for the purpose of human 'enhancement' (i.e. modification).
[4] **Implied consent** is consent that is *not expressly granted by a patient*, but is interpreted by others as implicitly granted based on the facts and circumstances of a particular situation, on the grounds that the patient would wish to give consent if he or she were able to do so.
[5] Ditum, Sarah, 'What is Gender, Anyway?', *New Statesman*, 16 May, 2016.

CHAPTER ELEVEN

IDEOLOGY AND IDEALISM: LESSONS FROM THE PAST

Theories of reality are implicit in everyday aspects of our culture. They provide the interpretative frame through which events are ordered into good and bad, right and wrong. In order for a theory of reality to actually work it must appear natural and conceal its construction and artificiality. An ideology's structuring principle needs to be unspoken, invisible, and apparently inevitable. While it has no material form, ideology has very tangible and measurable outcomes and effects. These may be discerned in political policies, public offices, laws, gender relations, modes of dress and customary behaviours.

Ideology is also the language (verbal, visual, and symbolic) through which social relationships take place and by means of which social and political structures come to be perceived as "natural". Ideology also obscures the processes of history, making all events seem inevitable or beyond the reach of human agency, while obscuring the competing interests that produce specific outcomes and influence the course of events.

Because it is a key source of both meaning and idealism in politics, ideology looks unlikely to disappear any time soon. People situate their personal stories and identities within broader historical narratives in order to make sense of their lives. We must bear in mind that political ideologies mould culture and influence action, but they also arise from *within* a set of historical circumstances and political ambitions. Ideologies provide a unifying set of ideas and values. Italian Marxist philosopher Antonio Gramsci (1860 – 1937) argued that the dominant ideas become embedded at every level of society, from art and literature to education and mass media. Ideology works its way so deeply into the mundane fabric of society that it becomes the "common sense" language and the popular culture.

According to German-American political theorist Hannah Arendt, ideology differs from a simple opinion. It offers or claims to possess ... "intimate knowledge of the hidden universal laws that are supposed to rule nature and man."[1] Arendt used the term "ideology" with great specificity. Because of its "totalizing" character, she thought it was best exemplified in communism and fascism. Ideologies, for her, were closed systems of thought that claimed a monopoly of truth and refused to tolerate dissenting ideas. Not all political creeds are ideologies by this definition. Liberalism, because of its definitive commitment to freedom, tolerance and diversity, is an "open" system of thought.[2]

All ideologies, despite their differences, have the following common features: (1) They give an account of the existing state of affairs or situation, identifying certain aspects of the current situation as "problematic", (2) They offer a blueprint for a desired future, including some model of the "good society", and (3) they suggest the necessary actions or solutions that will lead to the proposed change, and to achievement of the envisioned "good society".

Ideologies straddle the line between descriptive and prescriptive thought. Descriptions provide a kind of "intellectual map" of how the society works in relation to a more general worldview.[3] The descriptive accounts are entrenched within normative beliefs about the relative inadequacy of the present situation versus an alternative past, future or ideal society.

One implication of this blending of descriptive accounts of what "is" with normative accounts of what "ought" to be is that ideology and science become entwined such that a set of background theories or doctrines taints the very *process* of intellectual enquiry. The search for political knowledge takes place within a political framework and in the language of political discourse.[4] Ideology is the conceptual scheme that structures our world and imposes meaning on what we see. Ideology functions at the theoretical level as well as the practical level, where broad political mobilisation happens. The practical side of ideology is expressed in the struggle for power and its overt slogans, rhetoric and actual policies.

Hannah Arendt drew from both her life experiences and her work to analyse the events of her mid-twentieth century European milieu. For her, totalitarian ideology succeeds precisely because it destroys the process of *thinking*. Thinking is not the preserve of the elite few. Both Arendt and French analyst of propaganda Jacques Ellul observed that intellectuals are often the group *most* vulnerable to propaganda. Every human being is a thinking creature possessing a potential for reflection and independent judgment. Arendt was the living embodiment of her belief that to think always means to think in a critical manner. Thought undermines intellectual orthodoxies and generalisations. It questions "common sense". Arendt had perceived a sort of thought-suspending banality in Martin Heidegger's infamous 1933 speech when he became rector of Freiburg University. Arendt perceived a vacuum of critical dissent forming around her. Even within her intellectual milieu, the fashionable ideals of Germany's National Socialism had become an unspoken orthodoxy.

Arendt believed that all thinking can be scrutinised, and this is a kind of built-in safety mechanism because the biggest threat to flawed thinking is *more* critical thinking. Thus, there are no dangerous thoughts since all dangerous ideas can be undermined by new thinking. Non-thinking, by contrast, poses a real danger.

> "Caution in handling generally accepted opinions that claim to explain whole trends of history is especially important for the historian of modern times, because the last century has produced an abundance of ideologies that pretend to be keys to history but are actually nothing but desperate efforts to escape responsibility."

> — Hannah Arendt, *The Origins of Totalitarianism*

Arendt's contributions have enduring relevance, especially in light of Europe's migration "crisis", the barbarism of Islamic State and the growing gap between what Europeans are told by the political and media class and what they observe with their own eyes.

Arendt herself never found a home in any of the classic political ideologies. Her existential experience of being a Jewish exile was followed in her later life by more experience of being the consummate 'outsider'. Much of her writing is imbued with a dread of ideology. Arendt never became a classic liberal or conservative, nor a revolutionary Marxist or Zionist.

The displacement and political homelessness of the Jews made Arendt very sympathetic to the Zionist movement in the 1930's. However, in the 40's, she began to discern with growing dread the familiar direction the movement was taking. In *Zionism Reconsidered* (1944), Arendt expressed disappointment at how the revisionist program, so long eschewed by Leftist Socialist Zionism, was emerging victorious. Arendt saw how

Socialism's once inspirational, revolutionary and progressive ideals had fallen under the spell of simplistic victimhood narratives until its followers were willing to accept almost any inhuman situation. What had started as a socialist, revolutionary Jewish national movement with its lofty ideals had been transformed into a nationalistic chauvinism directed against even would-be allies and harmless neighbours.

If her critique of the Zionist movement's chauvinism made her a scandal, no less did she make Jewish enemies upon publication of *Eichmann in Jerusalem (1963)*, in which she refused to gloss the complexities of the Holocaust, and implicated the Jewish leadership. The whole truth, she remarked, was that the Jewish councils had cooperated in one way or another with the Nazis. Despite the fact that this was a relatively small part of the book, her critics seized on it and denounced her, accusing her of being a "self-hating Jew".

The publication of *Eichmann in Jerusalem* (1963) cost Arendt excommunication from the Jewish communities in America, Europe and Israel. She has suffered much notoriety, precisely because she was an independent, anti-mythological thinker, who eschewed the idea of Eichmann's 'Satanic greatness'. As someone who thought Nazism had been an organised attempt to eradicate the reality of the human individual, Arendt could not abide the cliché of Eichmann as monster, as sadistic anti-Semite.

In forming her response to Eichmann's trial, Arendt came to the conclusion that he was an individual with free will, who had become a functionary cog in the machine of terror. Arendt's ideas threatened national myths. As such, they also elevated her to the level of a quintessential public philosopher, the gadfly or stinging insect on the body politic. Such people are as irritating to the powerful elites as they are a stimulus to critical reflection on the dominant culture's propaganda. Arendt regarded the Eichmann trial as political theatre, with false history and cheap rhetoric. Eichmann had become an effigy that symbolically represented anti-Semitism throughout history. To view Eichmann's crime primarily as a crime against Jews *as such* was not false so much as it was trivial. The supreme crime with which the court was confronted was a crime against humanity.

Arendt concluded, after reading the 3600-page transcript of Eichmann's police hearing, that the man was intelligent but had an obtuse shallowness that isn't demonic. The banality of evil is to be found precisely in the superficial acceptance of clichés and conventional wisdom. We resist evil, she claimed, by resisting the seductive force of surface appearances and conventional things. In a letter to her mentor and friend Karl Jaspers, Arendt once said, "Any oversimplification, whether it is that of the Zionists, the assimilationists, or the anti-Semites, only serves to obscure the true problem."[5]

Eichmann had had a Jewish mistress. He didn't hate Jews *per se*. Rather, he was a conforming idealist; someone who believes in his idea and lives for it in a way that shelters him from the realities around him. Arendt's notes reveal that she was convinced that evil was closely intertwined with idealism. In saying that evil is "banal", she did not mean that there was nothing horrific in Nazi crimes. Rather, when ideology eradicates thinking to the extent that an inversion of reality becomes generally acceptable – under these conditions, the most deplorable acts appear as normal to the perpetrator. By contrast, thinking is when you inhabit an alienated space apart from the herd. The thinker is distinguished by her ability to experience dissonance amidst the "common sense" of the collective. This was what precisely what Eichmann did not do.

Jacques Ellul's analysis of propaganda and ideology concurs with Arendt's. First, to be effective propaganda must short-circuit all thought and independent decision. But in so doing it must operate at an unconscious level. Propaganda creates a division between thought and action, so that he who thinks can act only through the mediating agency of others. Conversely, he who acts cannot first think through or reflect upon his action. Propaganda needs to animate a kind of reflex response, so that the critical process is stunted.

Arendt observed that evil is both sentimental and conscientious. Eichmann's fatal flaw was that he wanted to cooperate. He wanted to say "we". Arendt uniquely perceived that evil's penetration into the real world does not come in obvious ways, riding on the clouds with fire and brimstone (or donning a wig and an orange spray tan while spewing obviously ignorant abuse at all good things). Our most hellish fantasies creep into reality not with the sensationalism of jackboots marching in step but with the banality of "common sense" and the apparent necessity of "common decency."

Twenty-First Century Idealism

To understand what it means to fall prey to "idealism", we must understand that the sympathetic left-wing *Guardian* reader is every bit as susceptible to this sentimentality and conscientiousness, this giddy intoxication for his ideals, as any right wing nationalist. In *Propaganda: the Formation of Men's Attitudes*, Jacques Ellul, a member of the French Resistance and professor of law and social history, explains the conditions that render propaganda effective. He describes "average culture" as one in which citizens are perfectly adapted to propaganda. This is where a large majority of people know how to read but do not exercise their intelligence beyond this. They attribute authority and eminent value to the written word or else reject it altogether. These people, says Ellul, believe or disbelieve, *in toto*, what they read. As such, they tend to select the easiest reading material and remain on a level at which "the printed word can seize and convince them without opposition."[6]

Ellul's complex analysis of propaganda provided a new template for understanding how mass manipulation works as a total system. He uniquely studied propaganda not only from a political but also from a sociological perspective. Ellul observed that most people are easy prey for propaganda precisely because they suppose themselves immune to it, based on the erroneous belief that propaganda is composed primarily of huge lies and that, by contrast, what is true cannot be propaganda.

However, Ellul disclosed the ways in which propaganda deploys many different kinds of truths – half-truths, limited truth, and truth out of context. The propagandist uses (often partial) truths *instrumentally* within an overall framework that is false, and towards adapting the individual's will towards "solutions" that are misleadingly narrow or apparently "necessary". It is precisely because *we* can be so enthralled with sanctimonious participation in the obviously "good" ideology, that we cease to think. And this is a danger that can be exploited.

During his 2017 *Voltaire Lecture*, British journalist and political commentator Nick Cohen admonished his listeners about cognitive bias and how it made the Anglo-American Left unable to conceive of the inconceivable, by which he meant a Trump election victory and a vote to leave the European Union. Ironically, Cohen's own cognitive bias had not dislodged his certainty that he, at least, had not been deceived. That much was inconceivable. His remarks were utterly banal insofar as they simply assumed, along with every other well-intentioned person, that unambiguous opposition to "Trump and Brexit" was a guarantee of political rectitude and that no further analysis of those two issues was required.

But this is to fail to see that political propaganda works not only on others, but on *us* (the good, educated people) too, because it short-circuits thinking, and replaces it with emotional appeals, demonisation and platitudes. Propaganda works with familiar ideas ("racism is bad") rather than introducing completely new ones. We might have to contemplate the truly inconceivable – which is not that the ignorant masses might actually succeed in screwing up our perfect world, but that we might be lured into doing so ourselves, under the assumption that we have a monopoly on the right ideas and cannot be deceived into embracing contradictory ones.

What liberals like Cohen apparently could not entertain was the possibility that Trump and "Islamophobia", rather than simply being deep sicknesses rotting the ferment in which our liberal roots are planted, were purposeful instruments of deception – the *means* by which our repulsion could be animated and then re-directed towards seemingly "necessary" alternatives.

We must ask whether liberals would otherwise have supported policies and leaders that, in the past, would have been deeply suspect to anyone with liberal sensibilities. In the past decade, liberals have supported unprecedented levels of repression in Europe, including the censorship of Western European journalists, the sacking of MP's for speaking out against child grooming by gangs of Pakistani males, murder of religious satirists, censorship and harassment of human rights and feminist lecturers, the purging of the internet and airwaves of even mild criticism of Islam or Islamism. Liberals have supported everything illiberal from female genital mutilation, religious/cultural gender-based dress codes, gender apartheid at universities, unlimited immigration from theocratic countries (a disproportion at odds with the very idea of "diversity"), Sharia law courts and the suppression of investigations, news stories and statistical data about rape.

If tolerance for religious fascism seems the only reasonable alternative to Trump's "Great" America or to European xenophobic nationalism, is this really an accident? There is the feeling of necessity in this "choice". In an atmosphere of ideological orthodoxy, Trump-bashing has become a synonym for common sense, a substitute for deep reflection, and an alternative to critical thinking about a complex set of new political circumstances. Expressing opposition to this spray-tanned embodiment of Evil has become the universal gambit to cement anyone's popularity and to quash any doubts about their basic human intelligence and/or liberal credentials.

This does not mean that Trump or his policies do not fully deserve criticism. It only means that in addition to his own ill-conceived policies, his power is exponentially magnified by the mythic quasi-Satanic status vested in him. For in this Manichean context, Trump's mere opposition to something or someone is sufficient to persuade liberals to defend it (or them) *unquestioningly*.

Jacques Ellul describes the two-phased process by which propaganda succeeds: first by creating pseudo-needs by means of **pre-propaganda**, then providing pseudo-satisfactions for them through **active propaganda**. Pre-propaganda serves to "soften up" the propagandee such that he can be mobilised by active propaganda later on, in moments of crisis. The essential objective of propaganda is to prepare man for action through conditioning so that he can be summonsed to action at the appropriate moment.

In the conditioning phase of pre-propaganda, false needs are created by two methods: (1) the conditioned reflex and (2) the myth. Building conditioned reflexes (whether individually or collectively) is a slow process and it may take months of patient work in order to elicit the desired reactions to certain words, signs or symbols. The explicit propaganda that is visible to us, says Ellul, is possible only because of the slow, imperceptible preparation that has already been done beforehand.

In addition, the propagandist tries to create myths that will compel peoples' entrenched loyalties and instil in them a sense of the sacred. Such an image propels action precisely because it evokes all-encompassing feelings about what is good, just and true. Race is one of the great myths that Ellul points to as exemplary. The propagandist cannot inject totally new values into an individual. Experience shows that in order to succeed, the propagandist must work with what is already there. It grafts itself onto an already existing psychological reality.

Douglas Murray has argued that the political heat unleashed by Enoch Powell's notorious speech of April 1968 allowed British politicians forever after to avoid having to defend their open immigration policies, even when they were deeply unpopular with a large majority of constituents, or when objections were different to those of Powell or the circumstances in which he spoke. The post 1960's taboo of racism is so firmly entrenched and ubiquitous in the modern West that many people would adopt incredibly simplistic (even racist) attitudes in order to avoid being seen as "racist". Londoners overlooked Sadiq Khan's past record of associating with radicals and extremists in a way that would be unimaginable if Khan had instead been a white bloke with past links to nationalists. It was as though "having a Muslim mayor" of *any stripe* was more important to voters than concerns about *which* Muslim individual would fulfil that noble ideal.

As Daniel Johnson pointed out in a *Standpoint* magazine article of July 2017, Khan is hugely popular amongst Brits despite the fact that he was the chief legal adviser to the Muslim Council of Britain, an Islamist organisation closely linked to the Muslim Brotherhood. He has been closely associated with groups such as CAGE, which notoriously defended Mohammed Emwazi, known as "Jihadi John", and other terrorists. It is true that Khan has now distanced himself from such organisations and *now* claims to support moderate Muslims, but it is worth asking whether this is a sudden change in his ideological bent or just in his political tactics. Khan's supporters conveniently forget that he used to call moderate Muslims "Uncle Toms" in the days when he appeared on the Iranian-backed Press TV and the extremist Islam Channel. As Mayor, he has failed to speak out strongly against the extremist Salafist preachers who promote anti-Semitism and homophobia, oppression of women and contempt for infidels. Khan's record on Muslim integration does not impress, and no serious effort has gone towards campaigns against forced marriage, honour killings and female genital mutilation. Instead his office has been used to both solicit and collect data on "Islamophobia" and to promote the idea (beloved of Islamists) that Muslims are perpetual victims of an irrational phobia. Khan also used his office to ban so-called "body shaming" billboard ads featuring scantily clad (i.e. immodest?) women in the London Underground.

Where there's a villain there's a victim

In the 80's, American conservative political pundits and talk-radio personalities sneeringly referred to liberals as "bleeding hearts" because of their constant attempts to remedy perceived social injustices that leave various minority groups socially or politically disenfranchised. Westbrook Pegler, an American syndicated newspaper columnist who opposed the labour movement, had coined the term "bleeding hearts" in 1938 in response to a bill before Congress that was intended to restrict lynching. In the mid-fifties the term was revived by Senator Joe McCarthy who called Edward R. Murrow one of the "extreme Left Wing bleeding-heart elements of television and radio."

In the 1960s "bleeding heart" came into common use in political contexts to denigrate "peaceniks" and "peace nuts" protesting the U.S. war in Vietnam. Ronald Reagan used it with reference to himself when he told *Newsweek* in 1967 "I was quite a bleeding-heart liberal once."

Christian conservatives dominated talk radio in the late 1980's and 90's, taking to the airwaves to excoriate feminists, atheists, abortionists, welfare moms, liberals, queers and the American Civil Liberties Union (ACLU). All of this vitriol only helped diverse minority groups to find common cause against the Christian right, who have consistently supported conservative Republicans in eroding social welfare programs, workers' rights, environmental protections and public education, while emphasising law and order and tougher sentencing. Real (not just rhetorical) victimhood became the glue that bound liberal groups together in opposition to religious and social conservatives.

If there is one thing American religious conservatives have always loathed about liberals, it is their compassion for the underdog. American Christian conservatives have championed a prosperity theology closely associated with social Darwinism. If someone has become rich or powerful, it is because of divine providence or because of his 'natural superiority' (which amounts to the same thing). Conversely, if someone fails to attain great success, his natural inferiority (often racialised) can explain why this is so. This kind of reasoning abounds among religious elements of the Republican party.

Moral Majority leader Jerry Falwell and political commentator Pat Buchanan (who ran for the Republican presidential nomination) opined that AIDS is God's punishment for sodomy. If someone gets AIDS...well, that is just God's way of "weeding his garden". According to this logic, bad things only happen to bad people, and vice-versa. This outlook de-politicises the world and assigns all causality to the workings of God's invisible hand. In response to the January 2010 Haiti earthquake, Christian broadcaster Pat Robertson claimed that Haiti's founders had been "cursed" for having sworn a pact with the devil in order to liberate themselves from French slave owners.[7] Even Ariel Sharon's ill health and hurricane Katrina were God's punishments. In response to the September 11, 2001 attacks on the World Trade Center, Jerry Falwell said that in addition to the American Civil Liberties Union, "the pagans, the abortionists, and the feminists and the gays (and the lesbians)" all helped that to happen.

We shouldn't be too surprised by any of this victim-bashing because even Christian scriptures see Jesus's crucifixion as a proxy punishment for the sins of all mankind. The idea that an innocent person might suffer is unimaginable. It was because humans so richly deserved God's punishment that he decided to sacrifice his own son to atone for their sins. Effectively God made undeserving humans a very generous loan, which they would be expected to pay back with interest (in the form of eternal obedience).

Religious conservatives' 'organicist' view of social relations, according to which social inequalities are perfectly natural, goes some way to explaining their historical distaste for supporting socially disenfranchised minorities. According to their religiously-infused social Darwinism, the socio-political status quo is the outcome of natural selection, and should not be interfered with by human reason or innovation. The world has evolved according to God's plans, and the only problem with this perfect world is *human* interference. For this reason, conservatives generally favour experience and tradition over principles and abstract ideas. Some people are natural leaders and others are born to follow. The poor are not politically disenfranchised, they are losers in the competitive real-world game of natural selection. The best man literally wins.

Liberals might be guilty of nothing worse than naïve underestimation of the extent to which Christian conservatives (and the Neocons with whom they have cooperated) have learned from their past political losses. If religious conservatives want to defeat progressive liberal policies and laws, they would be foolish to make underdogs of their *enemies*, as this only serves to cement liberal support for the victim. Strategically, it is far more effective to make underdogs of their *allies*.

Liberals understand that a when people suffer it is not always or only the sufferer who is to blame. Political circumstances are such that peoples' suffering is not necessarily completely their own fault. Liberals have always eschewed theories that negate the social conditions that mould individuals and the world. They see the individual's circumstances as the outcome of a dynamic interplay between external social forces and individual responsibility.

Conservatives, however, tend to see the suffering of individuals primarily (if not solely) as a failing in the victim. He alone is responsible for his misery, insofar as he was incapable of defending himself or protecting himself from the cause(s) of suffering. He is weak and/or "unfit" for survival. Moreover, God did not protect him, which also suggests a moral failing. In a sense, then, everyone deserves the suffering he gets. This outlook depoliticises social inequities.

Today we do not have a Führer uniting us into one grand ideal. Now our ideal is not to worship a demi-God but to oppose the Evil One. But the effect is the same. The individual is abolished, and so too is critical reflection. Trump's notoriety as an evil bully is the instrument through which support is mobilised for his apparent victims. A good political strategist knows that emotional appeals to sympathy for the oppressed minority will persuade liberals to champion the cause. So long as it can be perceived as a victim of powerful elitists, racists, or right-wing neo-Nazis, even the most illiberal ideology can be transformed into a liberal cause célèbre.

Even the best and brightest among us can be prevented from experiencing cognitive dissonance when we are swept up in the collective "common sense" of our milieu. This is why Hannah Arendt's writing serves both as a warning about present-day European and Israeli nationalism and, less obviously, gives us reason to pause and take stock of the mythological peddling of ubiquitous "Islamophobia" or blinkered demonisation of all critics of the authoritarian Islamist religious right as unambiguous racists or xenophobes.

Arendt maintained that history's worst crimes have been committed in the name of some kind of necessity. Arendt had perceived something like this thought-disrupting banality of evil in Martin Heidegger's famous 1933 speech when he became rector of Freiburg University. His rhetoric of "German reality" united individuals into one common ideal, thus abolishing the individual. In those grand ideas about Hitler, Arendt perceived something gruesome, and at the same time she felt a conspicuous absence of critical dissent closing in. This realisation made her exceptionally wary of the spheres in which intellectual experts operate.

We must contemplate that even we – the intellectual class – can fall prey to the common sense view that seems so rational, and so logical, that doubting it becomes a kind of thought crime, a precursor to violence or a psychological perversion. Perhaps we should revisit our own assumptions with some hesitation, for we too seem to have ceased to actively question whether multiculturalism *simpliciter* is always and everywhere a good thing; we *know* it is and we would sacrifice almost anything (even tolerance and free expression) for this grand ideal. Even with all the good intentions in the world, indiscriminate openness to the "other" can take the form of moral relativism – a refusal to judge – that can easily be exploited in ways that we did not foresee.

It is against the backdrop of harsh political realities and tactics that we must assess politically divisive mega-events such as The Women's March and Trump's "Muslim ban". Instead of looking at them in isolation, we should see these culturally divisive "moments" in terms of the wider political ends they serve, regardless of emotional rhetoric.

Liberals' identities are closely bound up with the anti-racist movements of its political forbears. They would do almost anything (even embrace an ultra-conservative religious ideology) to avoid being "racist". Trump is a symbol of everything liberals hate. When *he* suggested an immigration ban directed specifically at "Muslims", liberals were instantly mobilised as activists for Islam. Overnight, the quintessential opponents of the religious right were transformed into a welcome party for "immigrants" *simpliciter,* a disproportionate number of whom were packing conservative religious ideology in their suitcases. Muslims as an entire group became unambiguous "victims" of Trump-styled bigotry. They had to be defended as one big innocent bloc of "black" victims, the new minorities that liberals could champion (never mind that Islam is not a race).

Yet Donald Trump was obviously disingenuous about a ban on Muslims *per se*. Like all groups, "Muslims" are complex and heterogeneous, and many individuals and sub-groups live under the Islamic umbrella. A generalised "Muslim people" is a political fiction that works as well for Islamist extremists intent on monopolizing the definition of "Islam" just as well as it works for xenophobic nationalists bent on curbing immigration. Trump's executive order was not a blanket "Muslim ban" and the word "Muslim" appears nowhere in its text. Nor did the ban include any of the five most populous Muslim countries (Indonesia, India, Pakistan, Bangladesh, or Nigeria). The seven countries it *did list* (Syria, Libya, Sudan, Iran, Yemen and Somalia) are all heavily implicated in sectarian violence.

There were also conspicuous omissions on the list. The "ban" did not block immigration from the most conservative religious Wahhabi-Salafist country (Saudi Arabia) or from Turkey, which under the control of Tayyip Erdogan has become repressive and a host of ISIS militant training.[8] One cannot see these exceptions in ideological terms alone. America's economic allegiances are also relevant. Moreover the ban was not permanent, except in the case of Syrian refugees, who are banned indefinitely. The executive order was only valid for 90 days on immigrants from the seven named countries.

All of the above suggests that an analysis of the ideological purpose of the Muslim ban itself or of the earth-shaking mass media Trump-bashing frenzy it spawned cannot be simple.

It is tempting to imagine oneself treading in the footsteps of Arendt by transposing the situations she described in her works to the current European milieu. After all, part of Arendt's genius was to perceive important ideological similarities between discrete historical events. We would be foolish not to remain vigilant and active in seeking to apply lessons learned from the past. However, while it might be gratifying to draw reductive parallels between post-WWI migrants and the current European migrant situation, or between past and current nationalist movements, to fall prey to unreflective, facile assumptions would be a travesty of Hannah Arendt's legacy.

Notes

[1] Arendt, Hannah, *The Origins of Totalitarianism*, Penguin RandomHouse UK, 1951, p. 207.
[2] See for example, Popper, Karl, *The Open Society and Its Enemies*, University of Klagenfurt, 1994.
[3] Heywood, Andrew, *Political Ideologies*, 4th Edition, Palgrave MacMillan, 1992, p. 12.
[4] Ibid., p. 13.
[5] See *Vita Activa: The Spirit of Hannah Arendt*, a documentary by Ada Ushpiz.
[6] Ellul, Jacques, *Propaganda: the Formation of Men's Attitudes,* (New York: Vintage Books, 1973), pp. 108-9.
[7] 'Pat Robertson says Haiti paying for Pact with the Devil', *CNN News Online*, January 13, 2010, accessed on 25 June, 2017 at
http://edition.cnn.com/2010/US/01/13/haiti.pat.robertson/index.html
[8] Klein, Aaron, WorldNetDaily.com, 'Turkey Accused of Training ISIS Soldiers', 10 October, 2014, Read more at http://www.wnd.com/2014/10/turkey-accused-of-training-isis-soldiers/#IMBFdVCGBOuMgwAl.99. See also: Sengupta, Kim,

'Turkey and Saudi Arabia Alarm the West by Backing Islamist Extremists the Americans had Bombed in Syria', *The Independent,* 12 May, 2015.

CHAPTER TWELVE

GUILT TRANSFERENCE:
FROM ANCIENT TIMES TO THE PRESENT

Individual responsibility is one of the key foundations of modern ethics, and it too is crumbling. Having rights is about being respected as a human individual who shapes his life through choices. Whether with respect to honour-based violence, the burqa, "incitement" to violence/hatred, white guilt or original sin – the transference of moral responsibility from individual moral agents to others, or from others to the individual, makes a mockery of justice.

Either we are responsible for our own behaviour or we are not. Imagine how wonderful it would be if we could all take credit for other peoples' good deeds. Conversely, it would be awful if we could be blamed for other peoples' crimes.

Ironically, no one seems to have any trouble understanding what is wrong with the transference of blame from individuals to other people innocent of his crime when it comes to jihadist terrorists and "Muslims". Transference of guilt from the individual terrorist to Muslims as a group is, in this case at least, the most egregious error. In the context of generalisations about Muslims, guilt-by-association is seized upon and bewailed as a horrific error following every jihadist terror attack. Often, stigmatizing Muslims is treated as far more problematic than blowing apart innocent peoples' bodies and limbs. But in other contexts, such as when religions *themselves* promote the logic of guilt transference from individuals to groups, there is resounding silence on the matter.

The Doctrine of Original Sin

Transference of guilt has an ancient religious precedent in St. Paul's Christian doctrine of original sin, according to which the entire human species is tarnished by the sins of their disobedient progenitors, Adam and Eve. Transferring guilt across generations from ancient ancestors to their heirs was highly convenient for religious authorities. It created a very sizable market for their product. Since we're all born with a moral sickness, we *need* the medicine they're peddling – salvation. To get this remedy for our hereditary disease we need only assent to our guilt and then give eternal gratitude to God for providing his son Jesus – the sacrificial lamb who remedied the situation by enduring the punishment that *we* so richly deserved.

Honour Based Violence and Collective Morality

Muslims, Sikhs, and Hindus view honour and morality as a collective family matter. In the normative paradigms of these cultures, rights are primarily collective, not individual. Family, clan, and tribal rights supplant individual human rights[1].

The United Nations Population Fund estimates that 5,000 women are killed each year for dishonouring their families. The underlying belief of those who commit honour violence is that their victim's illicit action somehow stigmatises other family members. The individual is responsible not just for her own moral reputation, but for that of her entire family, who are also responsible for how she conducts herself.

Honour based violence (HBV) is defined by the UK's Crown Prosecution Service and the Association of Chief Police Officers as "a crime or incident which has or may have been committed to protect or defend the honour of the family and/or community."

While not all honour killings in the West are perpetrated by Muslims, the overwhelming majority are. In two studies of press-reported successful or attempted honour killings in North America between 1989–2008 and in Europe between 1998 – 2008, ninety percent of the honour killers were Muslim. In every case studied, perpetrators viewed their victims as violating rules of religious conduct and acted without remorse. Honour killings reported in the press in the United States, Canada, and Europe show the killings to be primarily a Muslim-on-Muslim crime.[2]

Religious Modesty Dress

Religious-based gender uniforms such as the burqa follow a similar logic. The immodestly dressed female is deemed to be responsible for the indecent behaviour of males, whose predatory sexual behaviour cannot be controlled absent a strict "modesty" dress code.

The rationale is that a man's biological sexual urges "naturally" overpower his will to the extent that he cannot really be expected to control them. Again, this idea is not far removed from Pauline Christianity, as we can see in St. Paul's letter to the Romans:

> 14 For we know that the law is spiritual; but I am of the flesh, sold into slavery under sin. 15 I do not understand my own actions. For I do not do what I want, but I do the very thing I hate. 16 Now if I do what I do not want, I agree that the law is good. 17 But in fact it is no longer I that do it, but sin that dwells within me. 18 For I know that nothing good dwells within me, that is, in my flesh. I can will what is right, but I cannot do it. 19…For I delight in the law of God in my inmost self, 23 but I see in my members another law at war with the law of my mind, making me captive to the law of sin that dwells in my members. 24 Wretched man that I am!

In a similar vein to this antiquated belief, a Muslim male cannot be expected to exercise sexual self-control. It would seem to follow from this that Muslim males are not really free and responsible moral agents capable of exercising self-discipline and personal responsibility. This is an insult to Muslim males with which not all of them would agree. But many others do.

The expectation that Muslim men should not be required to curb their natural sexual urges explains why women must be "modest". If women were to uncover their irresistible bodies (especially their hair) or to give them any "opportunity", then men would be right to molest them. It would be tantamount to leaving fresh meat out and then expecting that the cat will not eat the meat, according to Australia's most senior Islamic cleric.3

Transference of guilt from male sexual predators to their female victims is the rape culture mentality that UK Labour MP Sarah Champion was sacked for suggesting correlates to Pakistani perpetrators' ethnic heritage.[4] As Trevor Phillips astutely pointed out following the debacle, "What the perpetrators have in common is their proclaimed faith." Justifying the call for Champion's resignation, a source close to Jeremy Corbyn said: "There can be no question of stigmatising entire communities on the basis of race, **religion** or country of origin." [my emphasis] Indeed. But challenging specific communities on deeply held *beliefs and ideas* is not the same as stigmatising an entire group of people, unless one believes that all Muslims agree on Islamic veiling, "honour" and gender conventions, which they patently do not. Moreover, by challenging religious ideas about "modesty" we could hope to prevent people from stigmatising entire *groups of people* (namely women) on the basis of their biological sex.

In Saudi Arabia where the ultra-conservative version of Islam (Salafi-Wahhabism) prevalent among UK-based Islamist extremists originates, the guilt-transference logic is accorded a central place.[5] In 2006 the Qatif General Court sentenced a 19 year-old woman who had been gang raped to six months in jail and 200 lashes after "getting herself raped", which was treated as the natural outcome to be expected for her related crime of being alone with a male non-relative.[6]

Irrespective of hair-splitting exegetical debates about whether the veil is genuinely Islamic, it has been interpreted as such by ultra-conservative clerics who exert powerful cultural influence in Muslim communities. The fact that there is no official Islamic religious mandate to wear it becomes immaterial where there is cultural or familial coercion to do so.

Colonialism and White Guilt

Which brings me to the most colossally popular genre of guilt-transference current today: instilling "white guilt" in victims or critics of Islamist terrorism or of the Islamic faith. Actually, where identity politics holds sway, you don't even have to criticise *anything* to be guilty; all you have to do is to *be* a straight white male, or… just being "Western" will do.

The story goes like this: Islam is ideology-free and Islamism has nothing to do with waging jihad in conquest for the advance of Islam and a universal caliphate. Islam's rare violence is grievance-based; a mere *response to maltreatment* and injustices suffered at the hands of Western colonialism. It might be revenge, but it is just reparation, not aggressive religious imperialism seeking to conquer the world until all nations are brought under Sharia law and Dar Al-Islam[7]. The victims of Islamist terrorism are the distant descendants of past perpetrators of colonial crimes. As with original sin, the guilt transfers across generations. The individuals attacked by today's jihadis did not commit the colonial crimes for which they are being punished; but they are guilty by association and therefore attacking them is just.

Now let us imagine for a moment that everyone punished heirs for the sins of their forefathers. (In the case of jihadist terrorism, the victims may have no blood relationship to past perpetrators at all. But never mind that, white people are all the same.) The world would be a constant theatre of bloodshed if all of us felt that we had the right to dish out punishment to the progeny of every nation or tribe that has ever committed atrocities. In Rwanda, the grown-up children of Tutsis would avenge their parents' deaths by taking machetes to the skulls of Hutus' offspring. Would we really applaud this and say that Hutus' descendants deserve this? If not, then our enthusiasm for making white people bear the guilt for crimes they did not commit seems a bit, well … racist.

But, of course, evil Belgian colonialists propelled Hutus to slaughter Tutsis, so they had no free will and no moral responsibility for their crimes … which brings me to the next topic.

Incitement to Violence

Obviously, speech and expression are influential, otherwise liberals like myself would not spill so much ink defending them. But the fact that we are influenced does not allow us to abdicate personal responsibility for our actions. Human beings have competing desires and choose between them all the time. When someone influences me, it is because *I value* what he says or writes. I select these opinions or perceived truths from among other views and opinions and invest them with importance. If I did not, then the potential causes of my actions would be endless. I could point backwards at any number of "influencers" to justify my actions – films, books, parents, teachers, preachers, television personalities...any combination of these "influences" could be held accountable and I could be let off the hook. But how would we ever know which of them to blame for my action? Was it *a Netflix* documentary I watched or a *Guardian* columnist's opinions, or both?

It is true that ideas can be as pernicious as they can be enlightening. But more dangerous than bad ideas is the atmosphere of fear in which they may not be challenged by better ones. In every instance in which dangerous ideas have precipitated actual harms, from Nazi Germany to Rwanda, there has been a chilling silence from fearful listeners who (had their freedom to protest been protected) should have put a halt to the rhetoric by speaking back. It is in a climate of censorship and coerced conformity that the beast of bad ideas takes root and grows into a monster.

The "incitement" argument against free speech, in its current (distorted) usage, presupposes a direct causal link between someone's expression of extreme views and other peoples' violent behaviours. This causal theory undermines the presupposition of individual moral agency at the core of the justice system. If someone commits a criminal act of terrorism, defence attorneys may attempt to diminish the defendant's responsibility in various ways. However, if the forensic evidence points to his responsibility, and if he is an adult of sound mind, we do not accept outside influences as somehow *causing* him to act. We assume he is guilty.

The fact that adult citizens are responsible moral agents entitles them to basic rights and protections on the one hand and obligates them to accept moral accountability for their actions on the other. Civil liberties come with concomitant responsibilities. Only children or the mentally disabled, because of their relative naïveté, inexperience or disability, are incapable of responsible moral agency. To say that Hutu individuals were not responsible for the acts they committed in the Rwandan genocide only infantilises them and treats them with the kind of patronising contempt for which Western colonialists are roundly condemned.

Lessons from History

When World War II finally ended and the scale of Nazi atrocities came to light, some of those involved faced criminal charges. The defendants argued that only states and not individuals could be held responsible for the types of war crimes of which they stood accused. The court's rejection of this argument set a landmark precedent, establishing that state authority could not be used to shield individuals from criminal accountability.

Existentialists argued that excuses ("I was just following orders") were attempts to deny individual responsibility and to behave as though we have no choice. This is bad faith. Each of us knows, with agonizing certainty, that we have inescapable choices to make. No amount of duress, regardless how severe, can really force us to choose against our will. But taking on responsibility for other people's choices is just as weak as pretending that we have none for our own.

Notes

[1] See Chesler, Phyllis, 'Are Honour Killings Simply Domestic Violence?' in *Middle East Quarterly*, Spring 2009, pp. 61 – 69. Accessed on 23 Aug. 2017 at http://www.meforum.org/2067/are-honor-killings-simply-domestic-violence#_ftn1 See also Chesler, Phyllis, 'Worldwide Trends in Honor Killings' in *Middle East Quarterly*, Spring 2010, pp. 3 – 11, accessed on 23 Aug. 2017 at http://www.meforum.org/2646/worldwide-trends-in-honor-killings#_ftn5
[2] Ibid.
[3] Muslim Cleric: Women Without Scarf are 'uncovered meat', *Religion News Blog*, Oct. 26, 2006, accessed on 23 August, 2017 at http://www.religionnewsblog.com/16378/muslim-cleric-women-without-scarf-are-uncovered-meat
[4] https://www.politicshome.com/news/uk/home-affairs/policing/news/88302/sarah-champion-was-sacked-jeremy-corbyn-over-sun-article
[5] A 2007 report by a team of researchers over a two-year project, written by Dr Denis MacEoin, an Islamic studies expert at Newcastle who previously taught at the University of Fez, uncovered a hoard of malignant literature inside as many as a quarter of Britain's mosques. All of it had been published and distributed by agencies linked to the Saudi government of King Abdullah. Among the more choice recommendations in leaflets, DVDs and journals were statements that homosexuals should be burnt, stoned or thrown from mountains or tall buildings (and then stoned where they fell just to be on the safe side). Those who changed their religion or committed adultery should experience a similar fate. The 7/7 suicide bombers Mohammed Siddique Khan and Shehzad Tanweer were salafis. See, 'Wahhabism: A Deadly Scripture' at *The Independent* online edition, Nov. 2007. Accessed on 23 Aug., 2017 at http://www.independent.co.uk/news/uk/home-news/wahhabism-a-deadly-scripture-398516.html
[6] Rasheed Abou-Alsamh, 'Ruling Jolts Even Saudis, *New York Times*, Nov. 16, 2007, accessed on 23 August 2017 at http://www.nytimes.com/2007/11/16/world/middleeast/16saudi.html
[7] **Dār al-Islam,** in Islamic political ideology, the region in which Islam has ascendance; traditionally it has been matched/contrasted with the Dār al-●arb (abode of war), the region into which Islam could and should expand. This mental division of the world into two regions persisted even after Muslim political expansion had ended. *See* jihad. [Source: Encyclopaedia Britannica, online edition, accessed on 22 Aug. 2017

CHAPTER THIRTEEN

WHAT IS TO BE DONE?

"It was intended that when Newspeak had been adopted once and for all and Oldspeak forgotten, a heretical thought...should be literally unthinkable, at least so far as thought is dependent on words."

– George Orwell, 1984

Today, a socio-cultural movement that misleadingly self-identifies as the liberal or left wing of the political spectrum is leading a full-scale counter-Enlightenment. This separates it from liberal-left social justice movements of the past. The regressive left, as I shall call it, makes very effective use of deceptive rhetoric, new semantics and logical fallacies. Essentially, its advocates do what propagandists have always done best; they use kernels of truth to weave overarching lies.

If *authentic* progressive liberals are to have any hope of defeating this movement, they will first need to identify and dismantle the discursive tactics that give this movement its "liberal" sheen. They will also have to avoid falling into its rhetorical traps. This chapter offers a few "red flags" or fallacies that appear frequently in the regressive left's discourse.

To begin with, we must understand that the regressive left are liberalism's impersonators. Even the fact that I have to describe the movement and the set of ideas that I am presently referring to as the regressive "**left**" speaks volumes about how successful this movement has been in controlling and distorting the discourse, because the ideas and policies it promotes and defends are socially conservative/ right-wing policies and values.

The regressive left's pundits win not by opposing liberalism with an*other* (better) set of ideas, but by misrepresenting *their* illiberal, regressive values as though they *were* the ideas of liberalism. This is because the ultra-conservative ideas they peddle and defend are bankrupt and unpopular. Their arguments have no persuasive currency. They have neither better ideas nor more energy than progressive liberals; so they simply use liberal ideas and semantics to undermine and subvert genuinely liberal politics. The result has been to insidiously destroy liberalism *from within*.[1]

The immense success of liberalism's impersonators is owing in large part to semantics and symbols. The language and images of liberal politics, as well as the positive connotations and moral prestige associated with them, are routinely transferred to new and *seemingly* similar ideas or policies. Everywhere this regressive ship stops, it flies the liberal flags. Liberalism's political opponents have effectively re-branded conservative ideology in a manner very similar to how *Coca-Cola* added a leafy green image and the word "life" to their packaging – to give it new appeal. But like *Coke*, their socially conservative politics have the same old content, so the task ahead for *real* liberals will be to force an inspection of the contents and to get audiences to see past the labelling, or to change the labelling back to "OldSpeak". When people taste the actual contents of this product, it will become clear that what is being sold under new marketing is just the same old noxious stuff.

If liberal politics is to be restored, then real liberals will have to start by dissecting the regressives' creative use of semantics and tokenism. The pseudo-left now routinely uses misleading language to frame the issues advantageously for their (illiberal) agenda. Their propaganda has resulted in a re-branding of illiberal and socially conservative ideas and policies as "left wing" and of the ideas and policies that have always been liberal as "right-wing". This means that the well is already poisoned. Liberals will have to show courage and fortitude in standing up and arguing for a closer inspection of content because it has become dangerous and lonely to do so. Liberals today–including minorities and defenders of minorities – regularly find themselves misrepresented as speaking on behalf of "the right" or deceptively labelled as "racists" before they have been given an opportunity to utter a single word.

The regressive left has understood how to pander to the masses, blinding their audience to the distinction between good feelings and good reasons. Good sentiments have supplanted good substance and principled ethics just as short-term gratification can undermine long-term health.

Words matter. Words frame the debate. They force a particular interpretation on events and persons. When I teach my students about how documentaries frame the issues they represent, I sometimes show them a clip of archival footage from an historical event, perhaps taken from WWII. I turn down the volume and ask one of my students to make up some narration for the visual footage. Effectively my student plays the role of the voice-of-God narrator, explaining to us what we are seeing and helping us to link one sequence with the next, giving us a filter through which we unify the various images we see into a meaningful whole. Of course, the narration provided is complete balderdash. My student is no expert on WWII and has never even seen the footage he is narrating. He is improvising because I asked him to "make it up". Yet his voiceover shows the class how easy it is to force a particular "reading" onto the material and how easy it is for viewers to "read" the flow of images through the interpretative framing provided by his words.

So, what *are* liberal values?

Perhaps before we begin to dissect the methods of deception used by the regressive left, we should remind ourselves of the substance of our own liberal political philosophy. This is an important prophylactic against propaganda because of the way that catchwords have been used as magic incantations to arouse public concern and to propel us into action or mobilise our energies towards certain behaviours and outcomes. Jacques Ellul, the French academic who undertook a trenchant analysis of both political and sociological dimensions of propaganda in the nineteen sixties, observed that the propagandist can become an ardent defender of a religion or political ideology without believing its doctrines. A Communist propagandist, for example, can disseminate democratic ideology (even if he himself is anti-democratic) because it is both useful and effective insofar as democracy already forms part of public opinion. The fact that he works to consolidate public support for an ideology to which he himself does not subscribe is of no importance. By utilizing the democratic ideology instrumentally, the Communist party obtains the consent of the masses to its action, which then puts the Communist organisation in control. The transition is simple, because:

> "Public opinion is so uncertain and unclear as to the content of its ideologies that it follows the one that says the magic words, not realizing the contradictions between the proclamation of a catchword and the action that follows it. Once the 'Machine' is in control, there can be no objection to it by those who adhered to the previously prevailing ideology, which is always officially adopted and proclaimed by the new organization in power. People live therefore in the mental confusion that propaganda seeks to create."[2]

So we do well to remind ourselves of the substance and sinew of post-Enlightenment liberal values. Here I need to add a caveat. Liberalism has both social and economic dimensions. These two "halves" of liberalism are not always compatible. Therefore, liberal political philosophy has internal contradictions. But so too does conservatism.

Broadly speaking, modern liberals like myself have tended to affirm a quasi-socialist economic policy that allows some state interference into private wealth. We support progressive taxation and the redistribution of private wealth. At the same time, we have supported the widest possible individual liberty in what might be considered private, self-regarding behaviours, and have rejected state interference into the individual's (non-economic) private affairs.

On the other hand, social conservatives have tended to embrace economic *neo-liberalism*, which means that the state may *not* interfere with the individual's private wealth, while it may interfere with many areas of life that social liberals deem private.

The reason modern liberals like myself espouse a large state apparatus vis-à-vis taxation and personal wealth is that we believe that too wide a gap between rich and poor does become genuinely harmful to others. Hence, in order to prevent harm to others, and to level the playing field so that all have the opportunity to participate in civic life, the state is justified in interfering with both the means by which corporate entities and decision makers earn their profits and the impact of their businesses on market competitors as well as on private citizens and consumers. For the present purposes, I am defining liberalism in the *social* sense, as the maximisation of individual liberty (but not as in neo-liberal economics). Broadly speaking, liberal values can be summarised as follows:

- **secularism**, and anti-clericalism (secularism is not atheism), the neutral state
- free speech & **tolerance** (tolerance is not relativism)
- **freedom** – **individual liberty** over "community values" or "cultural values"
- the **primacy of the individual** over a "tyranny of the majority"
- the primacy of **reason** over superstition, custom and tradition
- civil rights, feminism, gay rights
- the widest possible **personal liberty** consistent with equal liberty for others (emphasis on the widest possible **private sphere**)

- **justice** – equal distribution of political goods, equal access to the law, equal application of the law, one law for all

Liberals should take back the language, shift the burden of proof and force real arguments with those who are denigrating genuine liberal values. Real liberals should not be on the ropes, fighting defensively. We have better arguments. If we force our impersonators to argue against us, rather than just posture *as* us, we will win. They know this, which is why they are doing everything in their power to prevent actual debate taking place.

Bad Analogies

Part of the purpose of this chapter is to show how the positive connotations and moral prestige associated with political and social liberalism are today routinely transferred to new and *seemingly* similar ideas or policies. This is accomplished in large part by means of **bad analogies**. Bad analogies invite a comparison between two ideas or situations that are not actually similar and may even be quite dissimilar in important respects.

One example of a bad analogy is the word "Islamophobia" which implies a similarity between irrational fear or prejudice of homosexuals ("homophobia") and irrational fear or prejudice against Muslims ("Islamophobia"). The word "Islamophobia" trades on the morally acceptable liberal idea that individuals or minority groups sometimes need protection from a tyranny of the majority in society. For this reason, states uphold the fundamental rights of minorities and protect them by means of laws. This protection extends to minorities no matter how unpopular or despised its members may be. However, in the case of "Islamophobia" legal protection from verbal criticism is being transferred to a group that is not actually similar to other minorities at all. First, Islam is the fastest growing religion and the second largest religion on earth, representing 24% of the world's population. Islam does not represent a beleaguered minority with no social standing and no voice in the public square. Its voice is dominant on the world stage and on the local level. It is the *only* religion or ideology that Europeans have privileged with special protection from ridicule, even suspending their own secular traditions and values to do so. The Muslim population size will have increased by a whopping 70% by 2060 with babies born to Muslims outnumbering Christian births by 2035.[3]

But more importantly, religion is a set of ideas. People can "opt in" or "opt out" of religion in a way that they cannot do with their biological sex, sexual orientation, skin colour, or other heritable conditions. Beliefs are not innate.

Moreover, religious beliefs are very seldom private or self-regarding matters. More often, religious institutions and religious spokespersons make huge claims about human nature (in general), the relationship of humans (*all* humans) to divine governors, and what constitutes the morally good life (for everyone, not just for believers). Religions often criticise and even proscribe *other* people's behaviour, including in matters that liberals view as private, such as what people can do with their own bodies. Religions have told people what they may eat or drink and when or how they may do so, whether, when, how and with whom they may have sexual relations, whether they may use contraception or terminate a pregnancy, what they may say, how they may dress, etc.

This kind of ideology has nothing in common with merely being "different" to others because of your biological inheritance. The kinds of sweeping claims that religious institutions and spokespeople make do not warrant immunity from criticism or ridicule in the way that *involuntary* aspects of a person's biological constitution should. Religious ideas are chosen. They imply moral content and consequences for others. This makes them fair game for public scrutiny and criticism.

As Benjamin Jones has perceptively noted, the result of using the word "Islamophobia" has been to confuse criticism with bigotry.

> "At present, Islamists and their apologists use this single term to shut down reform of Islam by labelling critics of (and within) the faith with the same neologism used to describe bigoted thugs. The word is repeatedly used to try and taint people by association;..."[4]

The consequence of such misleading terms, as Jones says, has been to constrict debate and thought.

Transference of "victimhood" to the de facto dominant group has worked in spades, and has allowed *bullies* to shut down marginal groups by claiming that *they* (the bullies) are the real "victims" who deserve our sympathies (inverting the actual situation). The Iraq War was an overt exercise in this inverted logic. In recent years, **race** has been used cynically for political gain. Again, a good sentiment (anti-racism) is applied to ideologies that have nothing to do with race, but are made to appear as though they do. This absurd inversion of victims and perpetrators has resulted in the absurdity of Ayaan Hirsi Ali being labelled an "Islamophobe". This is like saying that Angela Davies (in 1970) had an irrational phobia of white American cops. In context, these claims are absurd. Salman Rushdie, Raif Badawi and Hamed Abdel-Samad have all faced serious threats merely for "blaspheming" against the religious beliefs of other Muslims. If these Muslims are "phobic" then it is for very good reason – because Islamist fascists have threatened them with murder, torture or both. "Phobia" implies that you have an *irrational* fear, based on prejudice, not on very real threats to your safety and civil rights.

Other examples of **bad analogy** can be gleaned from the use of "hate speech" and "defamation" as applied to religious beliefs. "Hate speech" as it was originally conceived, implied hatred of biologically defined groups based on their inherent difference, as is the case with racial or homophobic speech. This move was already illiberal, since speech should be unfettered whatever the content. But in addition to censoring merely offensive words, the laws against "hate speech" have also changed to encompass protection of groups that are *not* biologically defined.

As I mentioned in chapter 5, the OIC's 1999 introduction of their draft resolution on "Defamation of Islam" contained the all-important conflation of religion and race. Since the United Nations' 2001 adoption of the "Combating defamation of religion as a means to promote human rights, social harmony and religious and cultural diversity" resolution, references to the concept of defamation of religion have increased considerably in UN fora as well as in member states' legislation. This is despite the absence of any definition of "defamation" in any of the UN resolutions.[5]

"Defamation" implies an analogy between **(a.)** false allegations about individuals and **(b.)** criticisms or satire of religious claims, which should be open to debate. To pretend that any statement or depiction that offends religious believers or hurts the "reputation" of the religion is equivalent to a false allegation about the religion or a smear against the reputation of those who follow it begs the question, or assumes what it needs to prove, which is that the religion's beliefs or claims are infallible, or that the religion *already* enjoys only a *positive* reputation. The infallibility premise itself deserves ridicule, but defamation forecloses the ability to poke fun at such an absurd conceit before any argument as to the merits of the vaunted infallibility has been had. To accuse his critics of "defamation" is a proclamation by the religious person by fiat that his religion is True…. or that his credibility in teaching it is irreproachable, not just for believing adherents but for everyone.

Muslims are not like homosexuals or racial minorities, they are more like a political party. No one would accept "Liberalismophobia" as a real word, and nor should we accept the misleading neologism "Islamophobia". Furthermore, if people *are* afraid of "Muslims" [as a group] then this is unfortunate, but not completely surprising given the demonstrable intolerance of some Muslims towards those who disagree with their religious claims or sacred cows. Criticism of Islam is misleadingly described as a "phobia" to imply that it is pathologically irrational.

Fear of Muslims does trade on a falsehood though. People might look around and see that nowadays Muslims perpetrate the majority of terrorist acts, sometimes even shouting Islamic slogans during or after their crimes. However, while today it may be true that most terrorists *are* Muslims, it would be a mistake to think the converse: i.e. that most Muslims are terrorists. The reasoning would be valid only if terrorism were entailed in being Muslim. It isn't. Being Muslim is neither a necessary nor a sufficient condition for being a terrorist. Many factors, such as culture, indoctrination or poor education can account for radicalisation and violent intimidation, and there is no evidence of any one-to-one correlation between terrorism and being a Muslim *per se.*

Question Begging, circular reasoning

Those who want to preserve Enlightenment values and liberties need to be wary of adopting new words; they should interrogate neologisms and scrutinise new semantics before deploying them. In saying this, I am not recommending the same kind of petty policing of language that I critiqued in Chapter 8. Unlike the word-police, I am not suggesting that we outlaw certain terms or confine ourselves to "accepted speech". I am asking that we subject language to analysis, which means that we will have to think about how words are used and to unpack their tacit implications. This is an acknowledgement of discursive power and a call to engage with assumptions, not an attempt to seal off certain terms from critical inspection, or to remove them from the language. We will have to talk about the way(s) in which we talk.

When we accept new words uncritically, by using them as though they are meaningful, we have often been duped into granting too much ground to the regressive left. Before deploying neologisms, we should ask whether the new term frames (or re-frames) a contested issue in a particular way. The regressive left uses loaded terms that contain unstated assumptions or conclusions. These need to be argued for! Unpack the assumptions *before* adopting them and deploying them in your own speech or writing. Be selective about what you say and how you say it. Just as with rhetorical questions ("How should we punish blasphemy?", "How should we judge Ayaan Hirsi Ali?"), words too can contain hidden assumptions.

We have already looked at the example of the term "non-binary" (the noun). If I say that I am "non-binary" is this really a meaningful statement? It would be a useful category only if some other sub-set of people were binary, which is questionable. Yet "non-binary" takes for granted this "binary" group's existence, or else there would be no point in claiming to be "non-binary" in the first place.

The fallacy here is in using terminology that **begs the question** or assumes what needs to be proved. For example, I once asked a student whether a particular film could be considered a documentary. Her answer was that it was indeed a documentary because it had been labelled one by critic x. But this still does not answer the question, which is whether critic x is correct in labelling that film a documentary. Similarly, if I ask you how you know that the Bible is True and you answer, "because it is the infallible word of God", then you are reasoning in circles, or begging the question, because your answer assumes, rather than offers reasons to believe, the conclusion. This fallacy happens when someone explains how he reached a conclusion with reference to the conclusion itself.

Other examples of misleading neologisms that have duped the left are: Trans kids, TERFs, the "Alt-Right", "Antifa" and "intersectionality". Circular reasoning is rife in the regressive left's semantics. Progressives must stop allowing regressive pseudo-liberals to beg the question. This tactic defeats genuine liberals' arguments *before* any debate takes place. This is crucial, because preventing actual debate is what their rhetoric is all about, since liberals have better arguments.

Misdirection – This includes: genetic fallacy, *ad hominem*, poisoning the well

The *genetic fallacy* is when a claim is evaluated only on the basis of its source instead of on its merit. If Adolph Hitler says that $2 + 2 = 4$ and

Ghandi says that $2 + 2 = 7$, then we do not allow that Ghandi must be correct just because he is a nicer person or has a far better reputation. This fallacy hinges on the idea that reason *itself* ought to be rejected depending upon where or with whom it happens to have originated. One version of the argument goes something like this:

- Reason is a Western notion deployed to delegitimise non-Western lived experience
- Therefore
- Reason ought to be rejected.

Ideas know no physical location or time. They cannot be eternally fixed to particular nations, people or eras. Ideas have no race or gender. Ideas form part of a rich collective reserve that we, as human beings, share. This is one of the most amazing aspects of humanity. Someone at the opposite end of the earth may share your idea of what constitutes the good life, while your next-door neighbour or brother might have a completely opposite one.

Reason is the universal faculty by means of which humans sift through good and bad ideas. Logical arguments form a common apparatus through which ideas can be rigorously tested for their soundness and validity. This marvellous exercise plays an important role in allowing progress to be made and individuals to flourish. As an example, imagine if someone living in America today rejected an idea solely because it was not part of his "lived experience". We would rightly condemn his attitude as narrow-minded and parochial. Don't let appeals to "lived experience" end arguments. Arguing on the basis of one's "lived experience" is tantamount to accepting total relativism. It is an ideal go-to phrase for anyone who hasn't got a good argument, because it is completely subjective. No one can refute your internal experiences; if you claim to be bored right now, or to have a headache, there isn't really anything I can do or say to persuade you that you're wrong. You know your own experiences better than anyone else.

However, in the context of debating important social issues, people often make claims *about* their experiences. An experience is always an experience *of* <u>something</u>. So, for example, the Yorkshire Ripper had an experience *of* "God" speaking to him and telling him that he must kill prostitutes. Hundreds of Americans have had "lived experiences" *of* seeing UFOs. We can then ask whether it is likely that beliefs *about the experience* are mistaken, or whether the claim about what caused the experience is really the best possible explanation. Merely reporting your experiences to others is rather trivial from a political perspective. It is like talking about your feelings. You don't reject, say, a policy legalising abortion on the basis that it makes you feel angry or offended.

Ad hominem – this fallacy is a kind of *personal* attack on a speaker in order to discredit his argument, instead of evaluating his/her argument itself. As an example, we might be tempted to dismiss the importance or truth of what Julian Assange has leaked about U.S. government's illegal surveillance of its citizens on the grounds that Assange has been smeared as a "dirty old man" or an "egomaniac". But this is classic misdirection.

Poisoning the well – this is when an audience is primed with adverse information about a speaker in order to discredit anything he says or does. Merely presenting unfavourable information about a person (even if it is true) hardly counts as evidence against the claims he/she might make. This tactic misdirects attention away from the argument and towards the person making it. An example would be to dismiss anything that Gatestone Institute reports by saying, "Ahh, yeah, but that is a right-wing organisation." The implication is that, because it is a "right-wing" organisation (hardly a meaningful classification these days), anything they may say is necessarily false. This does not follow. Right-wing organisations are no more likely to report only false information than left-wing organisations are to be absolutely infallible.

Misleading Statistics – One way to slant statistical reporting is to present an audience with an unrepresentative sample. One way in which this could be done is to ask the question "Do Muslim women *choose* to wear the hijab?" and then to interview only hijabis and not liberal Muslim women (who are mainly not hijabis) to seek the answer. Since the question is whether *Muslim women* (not whether Muslim religious conservatives) wish to wear the hijab, it would be misleading to draw exclusively from the hijabi section of the group "Muslim women" for an answer.

On 26 March, 2017, in the wake of the Westminster Bridge terrorist attack, London's *Guardian* newspaper ran a photo of "Muslim women" on the Westminster bridge accompanied by the headline: "Women Link Hands on Westminster Bridge to Remember Victims". This publicity stunt was organised by the same faux-feminist Women's March organiser – Linda Sarsour – who conjoined the American flag and the hijab as a new symbol of American "feminism". The subtext of this juxtaposition (of photo and headline) was that most of the women who wanted to "remember the victims" were Muslims, **and** that Muslim women are hijabis. Neither is true. If you look at the framing, you see that the photo is cropped to exclude many other people on the bridge that day, and to single out the hijabis for inclusion.

Douglas Murray cites another example. In his book *The Strange Death of Europe*, he explains how Tony Blair's government "analysed" the public costs of mass migration. Government units staffed with pro-immigration people re-framed the impact of immigration as an economic gain by presenting recent immigrants from the European Economic Area (the EU, plus Norway, Iceland and Lichtenstein) as the "average" immigrants. While they constantly stressed the approximately £22 billion that "recent migrants" had brought to the UK economy between 2001 and 2011, the truth was that non-EEA migrants had taken out about £95 billion more in services than they had paid in taxes. This was spin masquerading as research. A final report, produced later, estimated that the £95 billion cost of immigration was probably mistaken and that the actual figure was between £114 – £159 billion, but that didn't make the news.

Misleading statistics pervade all fields, including science and medicine. Alternative cancer therapies, such as Laetrile, have been discredited through mis-reporting clinical studies. In 1973, after months of extensive Laetrile tests on mice, the Southern Research Institute in Birmingham, Alabama released its findings to the National Cancer Institute (NCI). The NCI then spread the word that Laetrile had proven ineffective in the treatment of cancer. The reality was somewhat different. Dr. Dean Burk[6] assessed the data and discovered that there were three groups of mice in the experiment: (1) a large group that received too little Laetrile, (2) another large group that received too much, and (3) a small group that received an optimum dose. Those that received too little died just as quickly as those in the control group that received none at all. Those that received too much died sooner than those in the control group. But those who received the correct dosage survived significantly longer than those that received none at all. Yet the NCI conflated the statistics from all three groups to create the overall impression that these mice, *as a total group*, did not survive significantly longer than the control group that had received no Laetrile at all. Though it was not false to say that these mice, as a total group, did not survive longer when treated with Laetrile, the liars used the statistics to create a false impression.

No Principles – Double Standards When you ask whether the regressive left are really, in principle, committed to protecting minorities from the tyranny of the majority, we see that the protection of minorities evaporates as soon as the "minority" is a minority *within a minority group*. The same "Muslims" that demand protection from Britain's allegedly state-sponsored Islamophobia, apparently *because they are a victimised minority*, offer zero protection to Muslim minorities who dissent from **their** conservative Salafi-Wahhabism.

We need to ask *which* Muslim minorities are stripped of protection when the regressive left insist we protect an entire ideological group from critical scrutiny. If Islam's powerful spokespersons (who claim a representative status on behalf of "Muslims" in general) really believed in minority rights **in principle** they would support, not attack, Ayaan Hirsi Ali, Salman Rushdie, Maajid Nawaz, Raif Badawi, etc. The fact that the regressive left is not supporting *these individuals* – the most marginalised and *genuinely* victimised minorities – casts serious doubt on their commitment to the liberal principle of defending minorities.

Double standards seem to be perfectly acceptable where Islam is concerned. Generalisations about "all Muslims" are rightly deemed ignorant. Meanwhile, anyone who criticises Islamic ideology is automatically tarred with the "right wing" brush. Generalisations about *all* Europeans have become the norm: they are assumed to be a monolithic bloc of privileged, unconsciously racist, and probably biased white people. Anything they say about Islam is therefore illegitimate (see "Poisoning the Well" above).

Tu Quoque (a variant of false dilemma) – appeal to hypocrisy, "that's rich coming from you!" or "you too!". This fallacy assumes that people who are inconsistent or whose actions are inconsistent with principles they advocate for must therefore be wrong. While consistency is certainly preferable, the merits of the speaker's argument are irrelevant to whether the person making the argument has acted inconsistently with it. An example is when western feminists venture to oppose Islamic patriarchy and are reminded that Western culture sexualises women and objectifies them too. This is supposed to end the argument and silence the Western feminist. But, whether or not Western women are also subjected to patriarchal forms of sexism has no bearing on their ability to critique non-Western sexism. They would be more consistent to critique both, as most of them actually **do**, but this is not a necessary condition for them to make valid claims against non-Western forms of sexism.

False Dilemma – Here liberal values or causes are pitted against one another as though we had to choose EITHER/OR when in fact we can and should have both. As an example, liberals are told that **either** they can defend free speech (which is content-neutral) **OR** they can defend racial equality. The argument goes something like this: "If you defend (content-neutral) freedom of speech you cannot also be opposed to racism, since racists use free speech to express their beliefs." But free speech does not require that you like the content of speech that you would protect. To tolerate racist speech is not to approve of it. Liberals have always drawn a line between repugnant speech (which they tolerate) and repugnant acts, like assault, which they do not. Free speech is nothing if it is not for the unpopular voices. Liberals tolerate all manner of expression, whether polite or not, because they believe there is a greater public interest in the free flow of ideas than in protecting people from "unpleasant" offense. We can combat racism *with our free speech*, not by throwing it overboard. A good example of this is what happened when Nick Griffin went on the BBC's *Question Time* in 2009. He aired his views and his opponents easily punctured them generous helpings of better arguments.

"No True Scotsman" – this fallacy protects a universal generalisation (e.g. "Islam is a religion of peace.") from counterexamples by changing the definition in an *ad hoc* fashion to exclude counterexamples. Islam makes an excellent example because its meanings constantly shift depending upon the context and the speaker(s). Whenever a critic of Islamic religious doctrines or practices attempts to single out for criticism some aspect of Islam that *is*, intolerant, authoritarian, sexist, homophobic or violent, the response is invariably that the behaviour in question isn't *really* Islamic, or is somehow not representative of Islam. Any Islamic practice that would be open to critical scrutiny (e.g. jihad, honour-based violence) is immediately relegated to the "misrepresentation of Islam" category.

What can be done? Some tips

So, to summarise, here is some advice on what can be done to combat regressive politics and its supporting discourse:

1. **If liberal principles are used rhetorically, demand that the speaker holds to the principle(s)** and expose them when they do not. Adhere to those principles rather than compromising them to suit your own bias or agenda, even if your agenda is morally good. Defend *their* right to "hate speech" *and* our reciprocal right to so-

called "hate speech". Don't be tempted to abandon liberalism's core principles for short-term victories or advantages. This means that you will have to put up with people saying things that you regard as repugnant. But it also means that speech that intolerant or fascist religious elements deem "hateful" will also receive equal protection. Having principles means adhering to the same rule for all; not making special exceptions when it suits your agenda.

2. **Don't fall for false dilemmas.** Liberals **can and should be** both anti-racists **and** defenders of absolute freedom of expression. We can and should defend both, and we must use our freedom of speech to expose Islamism and oppose racist discrimination (when it really exists). Feminists, stop in-fighting. Patriarchal institutions and policies, not internal differences, ought to be your overriding concern. Be aware that stooges and "plants" will attempt to stir up controversy among you and to pit you against one another, often along racial or ethnic lines. When you fight among yourselves your adversaries delight in how this distracts you from tearing them down instead. Don't allow divide-and-rule tactics to undermine female solidarity and feminism by fracturing women into competing identity grouplets. All patriarchal religions oppress women, not just Islam. Unite the many to isolate the regressive few (i.e. the infiltrators who use "intersectionality" as a weapon to divide-and-conquer).

3. **Force relativists to accept the logical consequences of their relativism:** The idea that sexism is only "wrong" because of Western liberal culture's assumptions, but not wrong in any universal way that could make a religion's discriminatory practices objectively unethical, applies equally to the West's taboo of racism. The liberal values of egalitarianism and civil rights that make racism a cultural taboo are, according to the relativist's outlook, just a cultural "construct" with no independent validity and no objective moral claim on anyone else. This being the case, relativists really need to stop being so "culturally insensitive" towards racists or xenophobes. According to the logic of moral relativism, the caste system in India or systemic racism in the LAPD are valid cultural norms. Relativists should be made to respect them as such, since they respect cultural norms *per se*. It is almost as though Western pseudo-liberals want to colonise the whole world with anti-racist ideas, God forbid!

4. **Point out *their cultural imperialism*:** "Relativism is the only Truth that is absolutely true. Heretics be damned!" Show that this

orthodoxy is itself a sacrosanct outlook that is foisted upon all and sundry as though it were an infallible objective truth. By the relativists' logic, if a majority of British citizens vote for something then it is both valuable and morally correct, simply because a culture's values have been expressed. The relativist has no grounds to complain about anything so long as it is customary and culturally validated. So long as a majority in a particular society value a certain custom or have practiced it for a long time – then it is valid. The same logic holds whether a majority thinks British people deserve priority in employment at home or whether it thinks wives should be obedient to husbands.

5. **De-conflate the conflated concepts** of determinism and free will (biology and agency): this goes back to my point about whether Islam is a choice or a race. It is treated as both, depending upon the context. It is always whatever will best defend Islam and shame its critics. If Islam is a set of ideas, then stop treating its followers as victims of racism. Object to this absurdity. Go on the offensive.

In the post-Brexit and post-Trump discourse, the word "democracy" has been bent and twisted as badly as "liberalism". Re-described as "populism", democracy has been represented as a danger, even a fascist form of danger. In context, this is a complete inversion of what is actually happening. As Mick Hume has explained, the Brexit vote didn't lead to a discussion of Brexit, which was the issue at stake. Instead it led to a discussion of the value of democratic decision-making. The issue shifted away from what the electorate thought of the European Union, says Hume, and towards what the pro-EU elites thought of the revolting electorate.[7]

Meanwhile tyrants like Turkish leader Tayyip Erdogan write panegyrics about "democracy" as though they were its valiant protectors, and London's *Guardian* prints it. Only days before his audacious homage to the form of government he detests, Erdogan's Turkey was besieged by thousands of protestors from Turkey's main secular opposition CHP (Republican People's Party), who had dared to lead thousands in a 450-kilometre march from Ankara to Istanbul in protest at Erdogan's authoritarian styled government.[8]

Advertisers and political strategists alike subscribe to the behaviourist view of human nature that pictures human beings primarily as creatures who seek pleasure and avoid pain, reacting to external stimuli in predictable ways. To escape from this all-encompassing global political culture, citizens need only to have the time and resilience to think for themselves, to access wider and more independent sources of information than those provided by multinational corporations, and to speak to one another and organise in the real world and not just in the virtual one.

The increasing bureaucratisation of life saps much of our time and energy. The sheer scale and economic power exerted by multinational corporations makes all liberating action and thinking *feel* impotent. Real resistance requires acting in spite of this feeling. The "culture industry", as T.W. Adorno called our absorption in the false consciousness of consumer culture, is powered by us: our labour, our spending, our time, our attention, our children. Its dependency upon *our* gullibility and *our* energy shifts the power to the people.

Notes

[1] According to a captured internal document, the Shura Council of the Muslim Brotherhood referred to a long-term plan, first "approved and adopted" in 1987. The memo, intended as a supplement to that plan, talks about striving (in America) for "a kind of grand Jihad in eliminating and destroying the Western civilization *from within* and 'sabotaging' its miserable house by their hands." [my emphasis] Full article here:
https://www.investigativeproject.org/document/20-an-explanatory-memorandum-on-the-general
[2] Ellul, Jacques, *Propaganda: The Formation of Men's Attitudes*, (New York, Vintage Books, 1965), p. 198.
[3] Source: Pew Research Organisation, 2015.
[4] Jones, Benjamin, 'Why we Should Stop Saying "Islamophobia" ', at *National Secular Society* Website, 2 April, 2015.
[5] See 'Religious Freedom and Blasphemy Law in a Global Context: the Concept of Religious Defamation' by Mirjam van Schaik in Cliteur, Paul and Herrenberg, Tom, Eds., *The Fall and Rise of Blasphemy Law*, (Leiden University Press, 2016), pp. 177 – 207.
[6] See *Private Papers Relating to Laetrile*, edited by G. Edward Griffin, (Westlake Village, California: American Media, 1977) and Griffin, G. Edward, *World Without Cancer: the Story of Vitamin B17*, (Westlake Village, California: American Media, 2011), p. 38.
[7] in his book *Revolting: How the Establishment are Undermining Democracy and What They're Afraid Of*, (London: William Collins, 2017), p. 8, 9, 11, 12-13.
[8] Kemal Kılıçdaroğlu, 'We Are Marching to Halt Turkey's Slide Into Authoritarianism', Thursday 6 July, 2017. *The Guardian*, online edition.

INDEX